International Law in
the Russian Legal System

ELEMENTS OF INTERNATIONAL LAW

Series Editors

Mark Janis is William F. Starr Professor of Law at the University of Connecticut.

Douglas Guilfoyle is Associate Professor of International and Security Law at UNSW Canberra.

Stephan Schill is Professor of International and Economic Law and Governance at the University of Amsterdam.

Bruno Simma is Professor of Law at the University of Michigan and a Judge at the Iran-US Claims Tribunal in The Hague.

Kimberley Trapp is Professor of Public International Law at University College London.

Elements of International Law represents a fresh approach in the literature of international law. It is a long series of short books. *Elements* adopts an objective, non-argumentative approach to its subject matter, focusing on narrowly-defined core topics in international law. Eventually, the series will offer a comprehensive treatment of the whole of the field. At the same time, each individual title will be a reliable go-to source for practicing international lawyers, judges and arbitrators, government and military officers, scholars, teachers, and students engaged in the discipline of international law.

International Law in the Russian Legal System

William E Butler

OXFORD
UNIVERSITY PRESS

OXFORD
UNIVERSITY PRESS

Great Clarendon Street, Oxford, OX2 6DP,
United Kingdom

Oxford University Press is a department of the University of Oxford.
It furthers the University's objective of excellence in research, scholarship,
and education by publishing worldwide. Oxford is a registered trade mark of
Oxford University Press in the UK and in certain other countries

Published in the United States of America by Oxford University Press
198 Madison Avenue, New York, NY 10016, United States of America

British Library Cataloguing in Publication Data
Data available

Library of Congress Control Number: 2020936738

ISBN 978-0-19-884294-1 (hbk.)
ISBN 978-0-19-884295-8 (pbk.)

Printed and bound by
CPI Group (UK) Ltd, Croydon, CR0 4YY

Series Editor's Preface

Elements of International Law is a new Oxford University Press series focusing on concise and accessible doctrinal treatments of core international law topics. We, the editors, hope that over time *Elements* will grow to treat in a series of short books on subjects which, while foundational, are often the subject of only a chapter-length treatment in standard monographs. One such topic, inevitably, is the role of international law in national legal systems. Most standard texts can only gloss the topic briefly, usually in terms of a division between monist and dualist systems (typically accompanied by a disclaimer that every national system is different in practice).

We are very fortunate, then, to have as one of our first volumes in the series Bill Butler's *International Law in the Russian Legal System*. We are particularly fortunate in the author. Butler, currently the John Edward Fowler Distinguished Professor of Law at Pennsylvania State University, has had a long career as comparative legal scholar and arbitrator. The depth of his knowledge of the Russian legal system is indicated not only by his numerous publications—including multiple books in multiple editions on Russian law and legal institutions—but also his honorary doctorate from the Independent Ecological-Politological University of Moscow.

The historic range of this book is enormously helpful to the novice. While it certainly emphasises, the present position of treaty law within the Russian legal system as stemming from the significant changes introduced in the 1993 Russian Constitution, the author traces these developments back not only into the Soviet regime but the Tsarist period. All of this is done with an eye to the primary materials of legal history, often presented in helpfully annotated translation. Chapter 5 thus commences with The 1977 USSR Constitution and takes us through the developments in the Russian Federation between 1990 and 1993 with close reference to the drafting history and legal sources which led up to Article 15 of the 1993 Russian Constitution and its interpretation in the 2003 Decree of the Supreme Court. The result gives us not only historical context, but unique insight into the interactions with international law of various branches of the Russian state and the types of agreement which they may conclude.

This volume is also timely, in so far as Russia is once again asserting itself as an international actor of geostrategic significance with a distinctly
non-liberal outlook. As Butler observes, "Russian perceptions of the law of
treaties are an indicator of Russian perceptions of the international system
at large, including its legal dimensions, and Russian comfort with that
system." The fall of the Berlin Wall perhaps gave rise to the brief-lived impression that this was not a subject which we need to turn our attention any
longer, as progressively the Russian view of international law would surely
come to align more closely with that of western states. Increasingly, that is
self-evidently not the case. Labelling Russia a "revisionist power" obscures
the extent to which Russia seeks less to revise international law than re-
balance it. To understand that project, we must once again reacquaint
ourselves with distinctly Russian approaches to our subject. We are very
fortunate, then, to have such an expert treatment of such a consequential
topic as one of the first volumes in this new series.

Douglas Guilfoyle
Associate Professor of International and Security Law
University of New South Wales Canberra at
the Australian Defence Force Academy

Contents

List of Abbreviations

CIS	Commonwealth of Independent States
EAEU	Eurasian Economic Union
ECtHR	European Court of Human Rights
LNTS	*League of Nations Treaty Series*
MAK	Maritime Arbitration Commission
MKAC	International Commercial Arbitration Court
RSFSR	Russian Soviet Federated Socialist Republic
UNTS	*United Nations Treaty Series*
USSR	Union of Soviet Socialist Republics

Introduction

For more than most countries, treaties play a central role in the legal history of the antecedents of modern Russia, modern Ukraine, and modern Belarus—territories traditionally inhabited since at least the fourth century and perhaps earlier by peoples identified as Slavs. Treaties—international treaties in the Russian language[1]—constitute the earliest surviving documents by at least a century and perhaps more in not only the legal history, but also the general history, of these peoples. The dates generally accepted are 907 (860), 911 (874), 944, and 971. There are indications that such documents may have existed as early as 860 in connection with a military campaign of Kievan Rus against Byzantium, but this is conjecture and no conclusive surviving evidence confirms this.

Many issues addressed in the present study were embedded, whether perceived at the time or not, in the treaties of the ninth and tenth centuries: form and legal nature of the document, ratification procedures, relationship between the treaty and domestic legal rules of the parties, languages of the documents, obligatory quality of the agreement, measures deemed to be legitimate in the event of violation, and the implementation of the substantive provisions themselves. They are eternal or perpetual issues of the existence of an international legal system and a domestic, or municipal, legal system: how, if at all, do they interact; which one is to be preferred in the event of a conflict, or overlap; what principles or rules operate to determine which is to be preferred, and are they rules of international law or of municipal law, or both?

Or are these questions wrongly formulated? One should rather be asking whether one system operates within another, and if so, which within which? During the past nearly three decades, post-Soviet Russia has

---

[1] The word in Russian for treaty—договор—dates back to the tenth century and is still used to this day for "contract." In Russian the term "international treaty" is widely used to distinguish the domestic or private law contract from the public international legal agreement between States or other subjects of international law. To many in English the term "international treaty" sounds repetitive because, in modern parlance, a "treaty" is by definition almost always an international legal agreement, although in the past the term treaty was used more generally.

developed differing responses to these questions. In this study we examine the responses and the possible reasons for them.

Although doctrinal writings precede what happened, the legislative consolidation of the position in Russia[2] was formulated in Article 15 of the 1993 Russian Constitution. We shall concentrate mostly on Article 15(4), but the provision reads as follows in its entirety:

1. The Constitution of the Russian Federation shall have the highest legal force, direct effect, and be applied throughout the entire territory of the Russian Federation. Laws and other legal acts applicable in the Russian Federation must not be contrary to the Constitution of the Russian Federation.

2. Agencies of State power, agencies of local self-government, officials, citizens, and their associations shall be obliged to comply with the Constitution of the Russian Federation and laws.

3. Laws shall be subject to official publication. Unpublished laws shall not be applied. Any normative legal acts affecting the rights, freedoms, and duties of man and citizen may not be applied if they have not been published officially for general information.

4. Generally-recognized principles and norms of international law and international treaties of the Russian Federation shall be an integral part of its legal system. If other rules have been established by an international treaty of the Russian Federation than provided for by a law, the rules of the international treaty shall apply.[3]

The constitutional provisions in turn formed the basis for the Federal Law of the Russian Federation on International Treaties of the Russian Federation, of July 15, 1995, as amended three times, on December 1, 2007, December 25, 2012, and March 12, 2014 (hereinafter: 1995 Law on

---

[2] The Russian Empire was generally known as "Russia"; from the October 1917 Soviet revolution "Russia" became the Russian Soviet Federated Socialist Republic (RSFSR); the 1993 Russian Constitution provides in Article 1(1) that the country may now be known officially as "Russia" or as the "Russian Federation." The Union of Soviet Socialist Republics (USSR) was formed by Treaty on October 30, 1922 and dissolved on December 25, 1991; the two should not be confused. The RSFSR became a member of the USSR.

[3] My translation has appeared in numerous sources. See W E Butler, *Russian Law and Legal Institutions* (2nd edn.; 2018) 420–63; W E Butler, *Russian Public Law* (3rd edn.; 2013) 4–32; Butler, *Russia and the Republics: Legal Materials* (loose-leaf service; 2006–). I am, however, credited with another version which (a) is not my translation; and (b) in my view the translation is incorrect. See J Crawford, *Brownlie's International Law* (8th edn.; 2016) 91. The differences in the translations are material, and the issues raised will be explored below.

treaties).[4] There are several presidential edicts and governmental decrees of relevance to this subject, but of special importance are decrees of the Plenum of the Supreme Court of the Russian Federation and decisions or rulings of the Constitutional Court of the Russian Federation.

These and others will be discussed below as sources of the law of treaties in the Russian Federation. The discussion will be informed by reference to internal administrative materials which collectively constitute the actual law of treaties in the Russian Federation. They are of a nature not believed to be found in other legal systems, if not in their existence then in the level of detail they offer with respect to actually developing the texts of treaties. These materials have not been identified or discussed previously in English-language studies on the subject.

The importance of these issues and materials can hardly be overstated. The present author wrote back in the late Soviet period: "Few questions of law have engendered wider differences of opinion and approach in Soviet legal doctrine than the relationship between international treaties and Soviet legislation. In recent years the subject has engaged not merely international lawyers, but also constitutional lawyers, comparatists, and specialists in the theory of law."[5]

The relationship between the international legal system and the Russian legal system underwent cardinal changes with the adoption of the 1993 Russian Constitution, the roots of which dated back to the late Soviet era. The positions taken in 1993 are being re-evaluated in Russia and have been significantly modified, reflecting a fundamental reassessment of the position of Russia in the international order and her relationship to the international community. If the formulation of Article 15 of the 1993 Russian Constitution can be said to represent a "liberal" position in comparison with the position of other States vis-à-vis international law, then the "liberal" position is being revised in favor of a more cautious, flexible, casuistic, and selective approach that expresses a greater measure of skepticism or apprehension toward international law, including human rights.

To put the matter another way, Russian perceptions of the law of treaties are an indicator of Russian perceptions of the international system at large, including its legal dimensions, and Russian comfort with that system.

---

[4] See Butler (n. 3) (loose-leaf service), for the most recent version.
[5] W E Butler, *Soviet Law* (2nd edn.; 1988) 397.

The temporal scope of this volume is a reminder that treaties from the Imperial and Soviet periods of Russian history remain in force for Russia as the legal continuer of the Russian Empire and former Soviet Union, and the treaty legislation in force at the time often remains in force precisely because that body of law underpins the treaties. By way of example, the 1978 USSR law on treaties has not been repealed by the Russian Federation, although it has been superseded for treaties concluded after 1995. Similarly, the materials in the present volume which address the internal procedures for treaty-making and the legislative history of Article 15(4) of the 1993 Russian Constitution, to the best of my belief, have not been considered in either Russian- or English-language studies on the Russian law of treaties.

The present study builds upon my earlier studies of the Soviet and Russian law of treaties cited in the Further Reading suggestions at the end of this volume. I am indebted to Professor Mark Janis for inviting me to undertake this study; to Dickinson Law, Pennsylvania State University, for sabbatical leave during spring 2019 to initiate and a summer grant to complete the research; to Dr William Pomeranz, Deputy Director at the Kennan Institute in Washington D C for providing research facilities; to Peter Rudek at the Library of Congress for facilitating access to the research collections; to Elena Shelepchikova for locating indispensable materials, and to Consultant Plus for making their database available to assist with this study.

1
Historical Background

Precisely when those who inhabited Kievan Rus encountered the "treaty" as an instrument has not been identified. Irrespective of which date is accepted as correct (860 or 907), that treaty was not necessarily the first in Kievan experience. Whether treaty-making was learned from the Byzantines, had roots in earlier Kievan practices with other entities,[1] originated in Kievan experience, was a natural extension of inter-princely Kievan practices, or has another explanation are all questions that await their definitive answer. Byzantine and Ottoman archives, for example, seem not to have been thoroughly searched for survivals of texts or other mentions. In any event, what evidence survives indicates that Kievan Rus practiced one of the early features of treaty-making: "confirmation" [утверженная грамота; later утв ерждение; or подтверженная грамота][2]—what later came to be called on the territory of Kievan Rus and Muscovy "ratification" [ратификация].

---

[1] See V G Butkevich, "The International Legal Ideology of the Pre-Slavic Chiefdoms of the Ukrainian Ethnos," *Jus Gentium: Journal of International Legal History*, I (2016) 345–90; II (2017) 7–66, 389–442; III (2018) 7–62. Treaties are considered to be inherent in the very logic of inter-State relations: "Being the sole means for the peaceful resolution of questions by independent political formations, international agreements have their own history from the moment of the emergence of inter-State relations. Before that, the form of agreement was used to regulate links between tribes." I I Lukashuk, in Lukashuk (ed.), Курс международного права в семи томах [*Course of International Law in Seven Volumes*] (1990) IV, 11. Also see A Iu Sem'ianova, История дипломатического права России до конца XIX века [History of Diplomatic Law of Russia to the End of the XIX Century] (Kazan, 2001) 91 (diss kand iurid nauk). The learned literature contains references to the Armistice of Amastris, possibly concluded in the Roman Province of Paphlagonia, that may date as far back as the year 838. See A N Sakharov, Дипломатия древней Руси [*Diplomacy of Medieval Rus*] (1980) 11. The treaty was believed to have contained provisions on the freeing of prisoners, cessation of plundering of Orthodox churches and monasteries, and cessation of violence and insults by the Rus' against the population of captured territories.

[2] These two terms were treated as synonyms or variants of the same institution. See F P Sergeev, Русская терминология международного права XI–XVII вв. [*Russian Terminology of International Law of the XI–XVII Centuries*] (Kishinev, 1972) 214–17. Neither term, although widely used in diplomatic correspondence and treaties, appears in S G Pushkarev (comp), *Dictionary of Russian Historical Terms from the Eleventh Century to 1917* (1970), or in: M A Isaev, Толковый словарь древнерусских юридических терминов. От договоров с Византией до Соборного Уложения царя Алексея Михайловича (XI–XVII вв.) [*Interpretative Dictionary of Legal Terms from the Treaties with Byzantium to the Sobornoe Ulozhenie of Tsar Aleksei Mikhailovich (XI–XVII Centuries)*] (2nd edn.; 2017).

Ratification is a word whose origins are traced to the medieval Latin (*rat-ificātio*) of the fourteenth century and therefore an imported term first observed in Petrine times in the Russian language.[3] The word is widely but not exclusively used with reference to treaties.

The first original work in the Russian language on public international law[4] used—and defined—the term: ратификация. Shafirov explained the term by using words of Russian origin rather than foreign calques: подтверженные грамоты. In fact, often the respective terms were understood as synonyms,[5] and it was a matter of taste whether one resorted to the original Russian term or preferred international usage. The point was that a treaty required or was commonly accompanied, once negotiated and agreed, by a procedure of con-firmation or ratification. In modern practice, however, the two terms began to be differentiated in Russian legislation and State practice: the term ratification described the most formal procedure by the highest State agencies or officials, and "confirmation" occurred for treaties not requiring formal ratification.

Insofar as the terms were synonyms, one may say that the concept and practice of "confirmation" is evident in the earliest treaties of Kievan Rus.

Who may ratify and under what circumstances became a matter of State practice in Russia from Kievan Rus onward to 1917. Russian legislation did not address the subject. The Treaty of 907 provided:

> ... and both sides swore [to uphold the treaty]: [the Greeks] themselves kissed the cross, and having led Oleg and his men to the oath according

---

[3] "In Russia the term 'ratification' was not used until the era of Peter I." O E Polents, Ратификация международных договоров [Ratification of International Treaties] (1950) 7–8. This monograph originated as a dissertation for the degree of кандидат юридических наук and was seen through press by the supervisor, V N Durdenevskii, with a print run of 10,000 copies. A product of its time, it is nevertheless a rich source for Soviet treaty practice and the mechanics of treaty ratification. Sergeev found the word used in Russian diplomatic materials as early as 1698. See Sergeev (n. 2) 218.

[4] P P Shafirov, *A Discourse Concerning the Just Causes of the War between Sweden and Russia: 1700–1721*, intro W E Butler (1973) 17–18. First published in 1717, the work appeared again in 1719 and 1722 in Russia and was translated into German and English. The 1722 anonymous English translation was reprinted in the work above. The terms "ratification" and "instruments of ratification" appeared in the Treaty of 10 June 1710 concluded in St Petersburg between the Russian ministers and envoys of Courland concerning the marriage between the "Tsarevna Anna Ioannovna and Duke of Courland, Frederic Wilhelm." Cited in Polents (n. 3) 8.

[5] Polents defined "ratification" as "confirmation" [утверждение]. Polents (n. 3) 7–8. The same view is shared by R L Khachaturov, Международные договоры Руси с Византией, заключенные в X веке [*International Treaties of Rus' with Byzantium Concluded in the Tenth Century*] (2015). On Rus' foreign policy generally, including with Byzantium, see V T Pashuto, Внешняя политика древней Руси [*Foreign Policy of Medieval Rus'*] (2nd edn.; 2019).

to Rus' law, they swore by their weapons and by their god Perun and by Volos [Veles], god of cattle. And so they confirmed peace.[6]

The Treaty of 911 contained a similar clause:

For confirmation and inviolability, we have compiled in vermillion the present peace treaty between you [Byzantine] Christians and us Rus' men in two parchment copies: one, which was signed by your Emperor and ratified by oath to the true cross and the holy indivisible trinity of the one true god of yours, they gave to our emissaries. To your Emperor, who was placed on the throne by the mercy of God, we swear according to the law and regulation of our people, that neither we nor anyone from our land will violate these agreed-upon points of the peace treaty. And this written copy we have given to your Emperors for safekeeping, so that by this treaty will be confirmed and strengthened the peace which exists between us.[7]

Taking the four treaties together, the parties negotiated the provisions of the treaty, swore an oath to their respective deities, symbolically laid down their weapons, and, in at least the last three treaties, reduced the agreement to written form. In each case, whoever negotiated the provisions of the treaty, the respective ruler signed or otherwise gave assent to the treaty.

To the North, in what later became Muscovy, the principalities of Novgorod and Tver entered into treaties. The first of these, dated *c.* 1264–65, began with a confirmation of prior agreements concluded by the father of Grand Prince Iaroslav Iaroslavovich and other treaties negotiated between

---

[6] D H Kaiser (trans. and ed.), *The Laws of Rus'—Tenth to Fifteenth Centuries* (1992) 3. Views differ as to whether this treaty, dated 907, should in fact be dated *c.* 860 or whether there was an earlier treaty whose text has not survived. The presumption of most scholars is that these treaties followed the long-established practices of Byzantium in form. There is a substantial literature, but for Russian views, see S M Kashtanov, "О процедуре заключения договоров между Византией и Русью в X в." ["On the Procedure for the Conclusion of Treaties between Byzantium and Rus' in the Tenth Century"], in V T Pashuto (ed.), Феодальная Россия во всемирно-историческом процессе: Сборник статей, посвященный Льву Владимировичс Черепнину [*Feudal Russia in the World Historical Process: Collection of Articles Dedicated to Lev Vladimirovich Cherepnin*] (1972) 209–24.

[7] Kaiser (n. 6) 7. The translator's use of the term "ratification" reflects a modern perception of what transpired; the word itself was not used, but "confirmation" was, as was appropriate at the time. Similar sentiments and procedures were recounted in the treaties of 944 and 971. See ibid, 12–13.

Novgorod and its princes. Confirmation of the treaty by swearing an oath (kissing the cross) was duly provided.[8] The next generation, concluding a treaty in 1304–05, followed similar practices.[9]

As these examples suggest and Grabar reinforced, the principalities of Rus and later Muscovy had a "definite and clear concept" of the law of treaties. A treaty was concluded in writing, "confirmed" (or, in modern parlance, ratified), and the instruments of the treaty were sealed and exchanged. The confirmation or ratification of a treaty was consummated by the kissing of the cross (after Christianity was accepted in Kievan Rus ca 988). As Grabar noted, the sovereign kissed the cross in the presence of the envoys who brought the instrument, and the envoys, the other instrument on behalf of their sovereign. This instrument was sent with a special embassy to the contracting sovereign, who also kissed the cross or the instrument.[10] This policy and practice was emphasized from time to time in Muscovite foreign policy. In relations with King Johann III (1537–92) of Sweden, Russian diplomats declared: "In no States is it done that ambassadors negotiate and affirm by kissing the cross, and then violate."[11] On another occasion, "among our Great Lords, save for kissing the cross, how is it to be confirmed? To what will ambassadors and envoys refer if the ambassadorial kissing of the cross is not strong and is not insisted on?"[12]

Treaty-making was personal to the sovereign. The principalities of Rus and Muscovy took the view (widely shared elsewhere in the world at the time) in a pre-State international society that a treaty, once concluded, lasted so long as the respective sovereigns were alive. The treaty terminated upon the death of the sovereign. The Russian position was explained to Swedish diplomats in 1561 as follows:

> We marvel at your understanding that you, people of the same maturity, speak so unproductively, which is not done between States. For the position of the sovereign in any territory is the same as the position of the

[8] Ibid, 67–8.

[9] For the text, see ibid, 69–71. Similar practices were observed in the treaty between Novgorod and Tver in 1326–27, and again in 1371.

[10] V E Grabar, *The History of International Law in Russia: 1647–1917: A Bio-Bibliographical Survey*, trans W E Butler (1990) 10.

[11] Ibid, 11.

[12] A I Zaozerskii, "К характеристике Московской дипломатии XVII века" ["On the Characteristics of Muscovite Diplomacy of the XVII Century"], in Сборник статей, посвященных С. Ф. Платонову [*Collected Articles Dedicated to S F Platonov*] (1911) 349.

armistice instruments, but when the sovereign no longer lives and another sovereign comes to power in a State, new armistices are made, and matters are no longer governed by the old armistices.[13]

As for the relationship between treaties and municipal law, the Muscovy view was that in the event of a conflict between the two, the treaty should prevail. The domestic legal order could not serve as a pretext for the failure to perform a treaty obligation. Tsar Ivan III (1440–1505), also known as Ivan the Great, entered into a treaty with the Grand Prince of Lithuania, Alexander Jagiellon (1461–1506), under which a Russian Orthodox church would be built in catholic Lithuania so that Ivan's daughter, Elena, might worship in the traditional way as a condition of her marriage to the Grand Prince. Once the marriage was concluded, the Grand Prince recalled a long-standing prohibition in his realm against increasing the number of Orthodox churches. Ivan III vigorously objected: "He has the same right as his ancestors; our brother the Grand Prince made [an agreement] with us that our daughter will maintain her Greek faith."[14] The implication was evident that the treaty should override any prior domestic legislation to the contrary.

Another refusal to "ratify" a treaty signed in 1577 in Moscow between the envoys of Stefan Báthory (1533–86) and Tsar Ivan the Terrible (1530–84) by the Polish side provoked a strong reaction from the Muscovy side.[15]

A thorough study of Russian policies and attitudes toward ratification and the meaning of ratification for municipal legal systems remains to be undertaken. Fragmentary episodes exist, however, from the prerevolutionary period. One Decembrist, Nikita Mikhailovich Murav'ev (1796–1844), prepared a draft constitution in the event that revolutionary change should come to Russia during the 1820s. Based on a constitutional monarchy, it

---

[13] This reply was given to the statement of the Swedish ambassadors that the King of Sweden would "uphold the armistice according to the ancient armistice instrument of his father" and the King would not take up arms before a new agreement. By then in Europe this view had been renounced and treaties were considered to be concluded by a sovereign on his own behalf and his heirs; that is, "in the name of the State." Grabar (n. 10) 10.

[14] Ibid.

[15] See L Iuzefovich, Путь посла. Русский посольский обычай. Обиход. Этикет. Церемониал. Конец XV—первая половина XVII в. [*Path of an Ambassador: Russian Ambassadorial Custom. Practice. Etiquette. Ceremonial. End of Fifteenth—First Half of Seventeenth Centuries*] (2007) 282–3. Iuzefovich wrote: "Ratification was considered to be obligatory" (282), although this would appear to be a premature use of the word "ratification." In the sixteenth century examples are reported of the ruler kissing not the cross, but one or both papers on which the text of the treaty was written. Ibid, 291.

contemplated a federated system in Russia analogous in certain respects to experience in the United States. A bicameral legislature would be formed, but supreme executive power would remain with the Emperor, who would conduct "negotiations with foreign powers" and conclude "peace treaties with the advice and consent of the Supreme Duma" (§101, point 7). The conclusion of treaties would "become numbered among the supreme laws." The Decembrist movement was viewed by the Emperor as treasonous and seditious; the leading figures were executed or exiled.

The texts of Russian treaties were included in the principal official collections of Russian legislation. When in 1825 under Tsar Nicholas I (1796–1855) the Russian Government undertook the most far-reaching systematization of domestic legislation in human history, international treaties appeared in the Полное собрание законов Российской империи [Complete Collection of Laws of the Russian Empire]. The Collection itself extended from 1649 to 1917; there were gaps, of course—treaties overlooked or not found—but the Collection "published annually from 1830 incorporated in chronological order normative acts adopted, including international agreements."[16] Whether the inclusion of treaties in the official collection of laws of the Russian Empire was tantamount to deeming such treaties to be incorporated into Russian law, however, was seen as a separate issue.

When Russia ultimately secured a Constitution in the form of a "Code of Fundamental State Law" (1906), treaty-making powers were reserved to the Emperor: "13. Our Sovereign the Emperor declares war, concludes peace, and makes treaties with foreign States."[17] The foreign relations of Russia were consequently the exclusive prerogative of the Emperor. Given that the 1906 Constitution established a Russian parliament, the question is whether it had any role, informal or formal, in treaty-making or ratification. As for ratification, the answer was clearly negative; the State Duma was in effect excluded from all involvement in Russian foreign relations (an exclusion similar to that under the 1889 Constitution of Japan). However, insofar as the entry of a treaty into force required adjustments to Russian legislation, the State Duma would

---

[16] E S Tret'iakova, Организационно-правовая институционализация внешнеполитической деятельности Российского государства в XIX—начале XX в. [*Organizational-Legal Institutionalization of Foreign Policy Activity of the Russian State in the XIX—Early XX Centuries*] (2019) 46.

[17] Marc Szeftel (1902–85), *The Russian Constitution of April 23, 1906: Political Institutions of the Duma Monarchy* (1976) 86.

have been involved (unless such adjustments could be made by Edict of the Emperor alone).[18]

So-Called "Internal Treaties"

The view is dominant in Russian historiography since at least the nineteenth century, and largely accepted by foreign historians, that treaties concluded between grand princes, or between grand princes and appanage princes, on what today is Russian, Belorussian, and Ukrainian territory should be distinguished from treaties concluded between these parties and "real" foreigners—Lithuania, Poland, Hanseatic League, Scandinavia, and the like. The inclination is to distinguish, therefore, between real "international treaties" and what often are called "constitutional treaties."

One outcome of this distinction is to regard the "constitutional treaties" as domestic public law documents rather than international legal documents, subject to a different legal regime and not subject to the rules of the law of nations or to analysis under the principles of the law of nations. Early Russian treaty collections were structured on this basis.[19]

Certain propositions follow from the distinction between "international" and "constitutional" or "internal" treaties. First, it is agreed that many more treaties must have existed between these polities, or formations, than have survived. Many, perhaps most, of the texts perished over time or remain unlocated (or were concluded in oral form without a written text).[20] This follows from the references in existing treaties to prior treaties whose texts we have never seen and from events, such as armistices, or ransoming of captives, or other eventualities of war, which we would expect to

---

[18] Ibid, 127.

[19] A leading example was the collection initiated and financed by Count N P Rumiantsev, Собрание государственных грамот, хранящихся в Государственной коллегии иностранных дел [*Collection of State Instruments and Treaties Kept in the State College of Foreign Affairs*] (1813–28, 1894) 5 vols. The issue plagued compilers of treaty collections in the West and East. For an inventory of Russian treaty collections containing pre-1917 materials, see P Macalister-Smith and J Schwietzke, "Treaty Collections Relating to Russia: A Baseline Historical Survey in Comparative Perspective," *Jus Gentium: Journal of International Legal History*, III (2018) 307–72. On the history of Russian treaty collections, see W E Butler, "Treaty Collections in Eighteenth-Century Russia: Encounters with European Experience," in Butler, *Russia and the Law of Nations in Historical Perspective: Collected Essays* (2009) 259–67.

[20] S M Kashtanov, Русская дипломатика [*Russian Diplomatic*] (1988) 229: "Medieval Russian agreements of Rus', for example of the ninth century, were concluded rather in oral form, and inter-princely treaties of Kievan Rus' often were of the character of an oral 'distribution of possessions' [ряд]."

produce an agreement. Second, the category of "internal" treaty operates to deprive the polities concerned of international legal status or autonomy, to treat them as something less than a subject of the law of nations at the time. These polities are effectively excluded from the dialogue surrounding the history and development of international law.

There would appear to be no justification for this other than to reinforce the perception of a fragmented but united Muscovy—the formation of a Russian State—much earlier than may have happened. This proves to be a self-fulfilling prophecy, where the outcome is read back into the process and assumed to have been inevitable. That is unlikely. But in any event, there seems to be no reason to treat the polities on the territories of modern Belarus, Russia, and Ukraine differently in this respect from other polities throughout Europe (Italy, Prussia, for example) which were subdivided into dozens if not hundreds of entities of various kinds, strengths, capacities, lineage, fates, and so on. Some unifications were achieved, some festered over a considerable period of time, some remain unresolved to this day. But the instrument which bound them together in various loose forms of alliance or union was the international treaty, usually bilateral but often multilateral. The same analytical perspective might be applied, for example, to China, southeast Asia, Asia, and Latin America. The subject-matter of treaties may be whatever the polities choose, but there would seem to be no reason to subtract them from the domain of international relations purely for this reason.

In the case of Russia, Feldbrugge is in the mainstream of historical scholarship when he distinguishes between so-called "foreign" treaties and "internal" treaties. Most "internal" treaties are presumed to have emanated from the breakup of the Kievan State (empire?) and were "replaced by an amalgam of principalities ruled by the numerous descendants of the Rurikid dynasty."[21] Because these are perceived as appanage principalities, based chiefly on kinship relations, and the princes of Muscovy ultimately succeeded over centuries in imposing their supremacy upon these principalities and absorbing them into the Muscovite State, these treaty relationships are placed in a different legal category. But principalities they were, and they entered into treaty relations with their near and their far neighbors—all of which were "foreign" to them.[22] The operation of dynastic succession,

---

[21]   See F J M Feldbrugge, *A History of Russian Law: From Ancient Times to the Council Code (Ulozhenie) of Tsar Aleksei Mikhailovich of 1649* (2018) 164.

[22]   For what the present writer considers to be a contrary perception, see V A Kuchkin, Договорные грамоты московских князей XIV века: внешнеполитические договоры

whether formalized or not within treaty relations, has nothing to do with the classification of the documents themselves. The parties believed they were exercising their legal capacity when entering into the treaties, that the treaties should be observed, and that the treaties were binding on them.

This area of Belarus, Russia, and Ukraine was a micro international legal system in which, as Feldbrugge aptly described, "the legal relations between the Russian principalities were shaped ... by treaties between ruling princes, and, occasionally, city-states, especially Novgorod and Pskov)." In modern parlance, it would be appropriate to speak of the "international-legal status" of these polities—although that is rarely done. The subjugation of most of these territories to the Tatar khanates from about 1240 onward for nearly three centuries will, of course, have limited the treaty-making capacity of the polities concerned, subject to the variations in strength of the Mongol presence. Indeed, the precise international-legal parameters of suzerainty in this part of the world under Tatar dominance deserve further exploration. One suspects that the polities concerned were more active at the level of treaty-making and in foreign relations generally than is often assumed.

Nonetheless, Feldbrugge follows the general line when he suggests:

Russian treaties from this period can therefore be divided into two major groups: internal Russian treaties, *i.e.* treaties between Russian princes themselves (including the city-states of Novgorod and Pskov), and treaties with genuine foreign powers, which are more like traditional international law treaties. A secondary division can be made on the basis of content. In that respect the most important category would be general treaties, which were aimed at creating a comprehensive framework for the relations between the two treaty partners, treaties concerning peace or an armistice, treaties regulating commercial relations and treaties concerning taxation, although fiscal questions turned up in most other treaties as well.[23]

[*Treaty Instruments of the Moscovite Princes of the XIV Century: Foreign Policy Treaties*] (2003). Kuchkin refers to the lost Peace Treaty of 1026 between Iaroslav the Wise and Prince Mstislav of Chernihov, and treats in detail the treaty of 1318 between Iurii Daniloskii of Moscow and Novgorod and Mikhail Iaroslavich of Tver; the Moscow-Novgorod treaty of 1371; the Moscow-Lithuanian treaty of 1372, the treaty of Moscow and Novgorod the Great with Tver of 1375, the Moscow-Riazan treaty of 1381, and the Moscow-Tver treaty of 1399. In each case the cross was kissed by the parties and the formalities of confirmation observed.

[23] Ibid, 165.

If classifications of this nature are made purely for analytical purposes, there is no harm. International legal doctrine is replete with various classifications of treaties, including alleged distinctions between "treaty-law" and "treaty-contract" developed in later centuries. But in the Russian example, the classifications are used for quite a different purpose: to exclude the "internal" treaties from the operation of international law and make only the "foreign" category subject to the international law of treaties. Although Feldbrugge and others do not articulate the proposition in precisely this manner, they do acknowledge the implications:

> The internal Russian treaties of the Moscow grand prince generally reflected Moscow's long-term strategy of imposing its supremacy on other Russian principalities. This sub-group may further be divided into treaties between the Moscow grand prince and his immediate male relatives (brothers, cousins, nephews) and treaties between the same prince and his more distant Rurikid relatives.[24]

An analytical classification, supported by a refined terminology, has been elaborated by diplomatic historians:

(1) international treaty (международный договор), from at least the tenth century;
(2) princely treaty (докончание), from at least the thirteenth century, often an armistice or peace treaty;
(3) treaties between princes and Novgorod;
(4) treaties between grand princes;
(5) treaties between grand princes and appanage princes;
(6) treaties between grand princes and the church.[25]

The alternative view was well expressed by Baron Mikhail Aleksandrovich von Taube (1869–1961) on several occasions during the interwar period, but notably in his lectures at the Hague Academy of International Law in 1926. While acknowledging the elements of separation and isolation of the Slavic lands from western Europe, Taube also criticized the view widely shared by Russian historians that a continuous Russian State existed from

---

[24] Ibid, 166.
[25] Kashtanov (n. 20) 151. These classifications were not necessarily significant from the standpoint of the law of nations.

Kievan Rus onward; this view, he said, was a "later, and politically inspired, fantasy." Relations between Russian principalities were international relations, governed by local perceptions of the law of nations, and similar to inter-princely relations in western Europe. For Taube, regionalism was a key element in the history of international relations, including international legal relations.[26]

Although the subject-matter of treaties varied from one to another and some addressed hegemonial matters whereas other were engaged with issues of war and peace, or trade relations, or the legal status of foreigners, or other matters of municipal law, nothing in the materials suggests that the procedure for the conclusion of treaties, their procedure of confirmation (ratification), their binding force, response in the event of violation, or their expectation that the treaty provisions would be respected and complied with varied from one treaty to another. In these respects, the law of treaties operated, and the polities concerned were assumed to have treaty capacity.

The fact that treaties in this period were assumed to be personal commitments of the prince does not alter the equation; the same was true throughout Europe at the time, although the transition to a State-conceived international system was gathering impetus.

Russian international legal doctrine up to 1917 rarely discussed the interface between Russian law and international law or the details of treaty ratification, other than the provisions in the 1906 Basic Law discussed above. These matters were left for the revolutionary Soviet Government. Some were content merely to suggest that international law and municipal law "influenced" or "interacted" with one another in their capacities as entirely separate and autonomous legal systems. Martens fell into this group:

National laws and governmental measures, insofar as they have their own subject-matter of relations transcending the limits of State territory also can and should be deemed to be a source familiar with the principles of international law … Rather often international relations provided

---

[26] M A Taube, "Études sur le développement du droit international dans l'Europe orientale," *Recueil des cours*, XI (1926) 341–535. See also Lauri Mälksoo, *"Insula deserta?* Thoughts on the History of International Law Scholarship in Central Eastern and Eastern Europe," *Baltic Yearbook of International Law*, VII (2007) 5–24. Taube was influenced by Sir Paul Vinogradoff (1854–1925) and his views on "historical types of international law." Taube identified what he considered to be the "international law of Eastern Europe/Russia of the Middle Ages," together with seventeen other types of civilization. On Vinogradoff, see W E Butler (ed.), *On the History of International Law and International Organization: Collected Papers of Sir Paul Vinogradoff* (2009).

the initial impetus to well-known legislative works in the State or to a change in legislation inconsistent with treaties, the content of which, in turn, depended on orientations and views dominant in the administration of the country. In a word, interaction between the domestic life of a State and its international relations is an undoubted fact.[27]

One exception was Petr Evgen'evich Kazanskii (1868–1947), who may perhaps be credited with being among the pioneers of Russian doctrine on this point: "For the provisions of a treaty to replace or repeal a law in force, it is necessary that the treaty insofar it affects legislation in force take the form of a law."[28] Elsewhere Kazanskii took the view that international law "replaces the municipal law of States ... in those instances when under some circumstances municipal law proves to be unconstituted."[29] However, he was categorical that "municipal law may not be contrary to international."[30] A later Russian jurist commented that Kazanskii's view, as quoted, "reflects as a whole the conceptual attitude of the Russian State to this question in the nineteenth century."[31]

But a "gap" remained between the generalization that treaties might, under certain circumstances, become part of national law and precisely how any such transformation might occur. The institution of ratification played a role in this dialogue. Various international lawyers have expressed different notions as to how international legal norms might become part of national law: (1) by *renvoi*, or reference: when a State incorporates norms of international law into domestic law by referring to them, as a result of which reference the norms of international law may operate directly in municipal law; (2) by *incorporation*, which assumes the need to enact a special law in order to include international-legal norms in domestic law; or (3) *legitimation*, the enactment of a municipal normative legal act which ensures that the State will perform its respective treaty obligations—the State choosing in this example precisely how it will perform such obligations.

---

[27] F F Martens, Современное международное право цивилизованных народов [*Contemporary International Law of Civilized Peoples*] (5th edn.; 1904; reprint edn., 2008) I, 166–7.

[28] P E Kazanskii, Очерки международных и государственных отношений России [*Survey of the International and State Relations of Russia*] (1913) 80.

[29] Kazanskii, Учебник международного права публичного и гражданского [*Textbook of International Public and Civil Law*] (2nd edn.; 1904) lvi.

[30] Kazanskii, Введение в курс международного права [*Introduction to the Course of International Law*] (1901) 264.

[31] Tret'iakova (n. 16) 42.

Under this approach, "ratification" of a treaty is part of the process of assuming and performing obligations. Some trace "ratification" to the ancient Romans or further back into human history. As noted above, the requirement of ratification gave rulers the opportunity to ensure that their envoys had negotiated properly with the opposite party and not exceeded their instructions, but this was also buying time and leaving open the possibility that the treaty would not be "ratified." Others see "ratification" as a medieval instrument but serving essentially the same purposes.[32]

Some Russian jurists suggested that ratification was an essential attribute of treaty-making. Martens wrote: "authorities of international law are agreed that ratification is necessary for the binding force and operation of a treaty."[33] Vsevolod Pievich Danevskii (1852–98) believed that "only ratification transforms a draft treaty into a treaty, and therefore it absolutely is necessary, or it may be *de jure* rejected."[34]

We dwell on these historical considerations because they do not disappear from view; they will arise once more in the twentieth and twenty-first centuries with respect to the Russian Federation and its neighbors. One example of recent historical scholarship seeks in the Martens spirit to synthesize the overall course of Russian developments into a periodization of the interface between international law and Russian law. The correlation, it is suggested, must be seen from multiple perspectives: historical origin, doctrinal, and normative/practical.[35] The periodization is so broad as to be meaningless: nineteenth century to the early twentieth century (in effect, 1800 to 1917). During these years, it is suggested, "Russian legal doctrine on the whole adhered to a dualist conception and regarded international law as a system of norms in direct interconnection with national law."[36] The development of the nation-State system, in turn, exerted a certain influence on the "intensity of the development of international law," although precisely how such intensity is to be measured and demonstrated remains a mystery. A "catalyst" in this respect is seen to be the Russian judicial reforms of 1864, "when national legislation" of Russia was "brought into conformity with European standards."

---

[32] See D I Kudriavtsev, in Основы международного права [*Fundamental Principles of International Law*] (1978) 166.

[33] Martens (n. 27) (4th edn.; 1900) I, 399.

[34] V P Danevskii, Пособие к изучению истории и системы международного права [*Manual for the Study of the History and System of International Law*] (Kharkov, 1892) I, 221.

[35] Tret'iakova (n. 16) 52.

[36] Ibid, 53.

But the role of treaties in this process, if accurately described, is not identified.

The mutual "interaction" or "influence" of international law on municipal law and *vice versa*, is now broadly accepted as a reality historically and in modern times:

> Norms of national law consolidate at the municipal level the principles of foreign policy of a State, regulate the foreign policy activity of the State (questions connected with the legal status of foreign diplomatic and consular missions, and others); regulate relations between subjects of national law of different States, municipal relations which may give rise to international relations; establish and ensure the internal coordination of legal systems. International law to a great extent determines the position of a State in inter-State relations.

Many principles of international law were formed under a certain fluence of national legal systems (principle of sovereignty, principle of nationality, and others). The developing symmetry of legislation of different States also, it seems, facilitates the elaboration of a uniform international practice and the legal formalization thereof.[37]

All of which, at a general level of abstraction is so, but this level of interaction begs the question of the priority of one system with respect to the other. Soviet experience well illustrates the dilemmas.

The Soviet Period: 1917–91

The periodization of Soviet treaty policy follows in broad outlines a combination of constitutional developments and specific legislation and other developments that addressed or reflected the policies of the RSFSR and then the USSR with respect to treaties. It should be noted at the outset, however, that the ratification of treaties is sometimes regarded as resting on the principle of separation of powers and "checks-and-balances." Although this may be true in some constitutional systems, it does not necessarily follow from the nature of the institution of ratification itself. The rulers of Russia seem to have conceived confirmation, as the institution was known in Russia until

---

[37] Ibid, 53–4.

the Petrine period, as a "check" on whether their plenipotentiaries followed instructions in negotiating a treaty with another polity and as an expression of the ruler's right to ultimately determine what arrangements would be negotiated with another ruler. The ultimate say as to whether there would be a treaty and what it would contain was perceived as the rulers' prerogative.

As for written expression and crystallization of the right and/or power to ratify treaties, the Soviet Government inherited only prior Russian practice and the provisions in the 1906 Constitution which reserved the powers of ratification to the Emperor. There was no time to reflect on how ratification might be conceived and structured in a Soviet State. The prerevolutionary writings of Karl Marx (1818–83), Friedrich Engels (1820–95), Vladimir Lenin (1870–1924), and other philosophers and ideologues of revolution had nothing to say about approaches to ratification. But the revolutionaries were forced by circumstances to respond to the urgent need for conceptualizing ratification at once upon seizing power. There was the fate of Imperial Russian treaties to be considered (which would affect attitudes toward continuing to participate in World War I and negotiate arrangements with the Central Powers) and the immediate prospect of negotiating arrangements to terminate Russian involvement in the War—which would require treaties with whomsoever. In fact, the Central Powers insisted upon ratification of the Peace Treaties negotiated with the Bolsheviks, which meant that ratification procedures had to be considered. The earliest treaties were controversial, and when submitted for ratification, encountered significant opposition.

It therefore was not possible to eliminate the institution of ratification any more than it was possible to discard "bourgeois" international law. The instinct was to emulate prior Russian practices by reserving ratification, in those instances where it was required, to the highest State agencies: the Congress of Soviets, the Central Executive Committee, or the Presidium thereof. The RSFSR and Soviet Union up to 1925 entered into approximately 325 international treaties, agreements, and contracts,[38] relatively few of which were ratified,[39] but may have been "confirmed" by relevant

---

[38] The contract [договор, контракт] poses some conundrums in this instance. The word is the same as treaty, and on the Soviet side, after the introduction of the monopoly of foreign trade in April 1918, these were entered into by ministries. On the foreign side, there was often State involvement, but usually the ultimate party was a private juridical person. See, for example, such documents entered into with the Swedish Chamber of Commerce for what were purchases and sales of agricultural equipment.

[39] J F Triska and R M Slusser, *The Theory, Law, and Policy of Soviet Treaties* (1962) 65.

authorities in Russia. The general practice seems to have been that peace treaties were ratified, as were treaties which one of the parties insisted be ratified either because its domestic law so provided, or treaties which the parties believed should be subject to ratification.

The RSFSR: 1917–1922. The Soviet authorities were required to deal with issues of international treaties immediately upon coming to power. Dekret No. I on Peace, adopted November 8, 1917—the day following the so-called October Revolution (old style, October 26)—provided as follows with respect to treaties:

> The Government abolishes secret diplomacy and, on its part, expresses its firm intention to carry on all negotiations completely only before all the people, and is acting immediately to publish in full the secret treaties confirmed or concluded by the Government of landowners and capitalists from February to 25 October 1917. The Government announces the unconditional and immediate abrogation of the entire content of these secret treaties, inasmuch as they were directed, in the majority of instances, to giving advantages and privileges to Russian landowners and capitalists, and to retaining and increasing annexations of Great Russians.[40]

The precise contours of the clause quoted above generated controversy for decades. A careful reading, however, establishes that the Russian Soviet Federated Socialist Republic (RSFSR) did not disengage from the entire international legal system. It has been suggested that the treaties abrogated fell into three groups:

(1)   the secret treaties concluded by the Imperial Russian Government prior to October 25, 1917 (that is, prior to the October Revolution), disclosure and publication of which embarrassed the western governments for some years;[41]

---

[40] W E Butler (trans.), *Soviet Statutes and Decisions*, III, no. 4 (1967) 49. The term "Dekret" is a calque from the French, perhaps a legacy of the French Revolution or the Paris Commune; it was used in the early days following the Russian Revolution, and also in Ukraine, where the term "Universal," likewise borrowed from the French, was deployed by the early provisional governments established on Ukrainian territory. Not for long, however, and the Russian term which the present writer translates as "decree" [постановление] was the replacement.

[41] Renunciation of secret diplomacy notwithstanding, reports persist that the RSFSR entered into secret treaties as early as December 22, 1917—a Convention concerning Poland concluded between "representatives of the Russian Government" and the German High Command. Under this Convention, it was agreed that Polish policy was to be conducted by

(2) so-called "unequal treaties" which violated the rights of other peoples. These were addressed generally in the Declaration of the Rights of Peoples of Russia of November 2 (15), 1917, which recognized the right of every people to self-determination. These sentiments were elaborated in the Appeal to All Toiling Muslims of Russia and the East, of November 20 (December 3) 1917;

(3) the third group did not comprise treaties so much as private-law loans with foreign parties, including foreign States. The Dekret on the Annulment of State Loans of January 28 (February 10) 1918 provided: "all foreign loans shall be annulled unconditionally and without any exceptions" (Article 3).[42]

The above are categories of treaties. Precisely which treaties fell into which category was unclear, and which treaties were considered to be outside all categories was likewise uncertain.[43] Some construed the categories as directed to the subject-matter of treaties; others to what countries were parties. And what of treaties that contained some objectionable clauses but were otherwise useful or even essential.[44] The Government of the USSR

---

the German Government and the Russian Government agreed not to interfere in any way regarding the organization of Poland or to protest or demand explanations. Seven allegedly secret treaties are reproduced in translation or summarized in L Shapiro (ed.), *Soviet Treaty Series: A Collection of Bilateral Treaties, Agreements and Conventions, Etc., Concluded between the Soviet Union and Foreign Powers* (1950) I, 381–3.

[42] V S Khizhniak, Конституционно-правовой механизм взаимодействия внутригосударственного права Российской Федерации и международное право [*Constitutional-Legal Mechanism of International of Municipal Law of the Russian Federation and International Law*] (Saratov, 2004) 148–9 (diss. doktor iurid. nauk).

[43] On May 30, 1918, a "Recourse" signed by Lenin on behalf of the Council of People's Commissars to the International Red Cross that the Geneva Convention [of 1864] in the original and all later versions and "all other international conventions and agreements concerning the Red Cross recognized by Russia before October 1917 are recognized and will be complied with by the Russian Soviet Government, which preserves all rights and prerogatives based on these conventions and agreements" (n. 41) I, 333–4.

[44] On August 29, 1918 a Dekret of the Council of People's Commissars specifically renounced treaties of the Government of the former Russian Empire with German, Austria-Hungary, Prussia, Bavaria, the Duchy of Hessen, Oldenburg, and Saxe-Meiningen and the City of Lubeck. Thirteen treaties with Germany, three with Prussia, two with Bavaria, two with Hessen, one with Oldenberg, one with Saxe-Meiningen, and two with the City of Lubeck were enumerated, together with fifteen concluded with Austria-Hungary. The secret treaties concluded with Austria-Hungary, Germany, and "states within the last" were confirmed as abrogated pursuant to the Dekret on Peace. See n. 41, I, 459–60. Among the Conventions abrogated was the Russian-German agreement on inheritance of 1874; this was later partially reinstated by the Russo-German Financial Agreement of August 27, 1918.

sought to clarify matters in a Letter to the Institute of International Law on April 2, 1924, as follows:

> Dekret I, adopted by the Second Congress of Soviets on 26 October (8 November) 1918, announced the invalidity of all secret political treaties concluded by the former government "for the benefit of landowners and capitalists." The attitude of the Soviet Government toward other treaties and agreements depends on a number of conditions. The unusually prolonged break of political relations with all countries of the world, which followed the Revolution of 1917, and changes which occurred in the whole totality of international circumstances, do not permit all treaties of the old Russian Government to be simply and unreservedly re-established. It is doubtful if any of these actually might be carried out without contradicting the most recent regulation of these questions which has ensued since 1917 without the participation of one of the parties to such treaty.
>
> Therefore, in its Note of 8 February 1924 to the British Government, the Government of the Soviet Union expressed readiness to conclude an agreement "concerning the question of replacement of treaties which lost force as a result of events of the war and postwar period." This question must be resolved in each individual instance at the discretion of the respective governments. It is clear from the Note of 8 February 1924 that no category of treaties may be placed in another position, except those which were mentioned in the Decret of 26 October 1917.
>
> The Soviet Government has never declared a general renunciation of all treaties concluded by Russia under the Tsarist regime or under the Provisional Government. But it does not follow from this that all treaties obligatorily must be re-concluded. The present question must be considered from the viewpoint of the reservation *rebus sic stantibus* for each State and each treaty individually.
>
> All that has been said relates to treaties and agreements in the literal sense of the word and does not affect financial obligations of the former Russian Government.[45]

The first treaty concluded by the RSFSR was an Armistice negotiated at Brest-Litovsk on December 5, 1917, the summary of which did not name

---

[45] Translated in Butler, *Soviet Statutes and Decisions*, III, no. 4 (1967) 62–3.

the parties or make provision for any formalities of confirmation or ratification. This Armistice was replaced by another dated December 15, 1917; although there is a reference in the text to a "Russian Government," no mention is made of who is the other Party (presumed to be the Central Powers). A separate "Supplement to the Armistice" was concluded on the same date, but with similar non-identification of the parties.

On March 1, 1918 the RSFSR concluded a Treaty of Friendship with the Independent Finnish Socialist Republic of Working People, which in the English text was butchered to read: "The Soviet of the Commissioners of the People of the Russian Federal Republic of Soviets."[46]

Two days later Germany, Austria-Hungary, Bulgaria, and Turkey, on one side, and "Russia" on the other concluded at Treaty of Peace at Brest-Litovsk on March 3, 1918. In this case the document—the first in Soviet experience—made provision for ratification, the documents of ratification to be exchanged as soon as possible in Berlin, which occurred on March 29, 1918. There was no RSFSR Constitution or other legislation to guide the Soviet authorities on who should ratify the Peace of Brest-Litovsk. The treaty was submitted to the IV Extraordinary All-Russian Congress of Soviets, which on May 15 decreed: "The Congress confirms (ratifies) the Peace Treaty, concluded by our representatives at Brest-Litovsk on 3 March 1918."[47]

On March 5/9, 1918 Russia concluded an agreement with Romania on the evacuation of Bessarabia by Romania; the document contained no

[46] The text was published by Iu V Kliuchnikov and A V Sabanin (eds.), Международная политика новейшего времени в договорах, нотах и декларациях [*International Politics of the New Period in Treaties, Notes, and Declarations*] (1925–28) II, 120–1. An English version appears in Shapiro, n. 41, I, 2–4; and in an Annex to Alla Pozdnakova (ed.), *The Russian Revolutions: Scandinavian Perspectives* (2019) 155–9.

[47] Документы внешней политики СССР [Documents of Foreign Policy of the USSR] (1957) I, 213–14. The words "confirms (ratifies)" indicates the processes were at this time regarded as identical. The Decree made no mention of the Legal-Political Treaty Supplementary to the Treaty of Peace, also subject to ratification; apparently the Decree regarded the two documents as a package, for instruments of ratification for both were exchanged on March 29, 1918 at Berlin. The decision to submit the treaty to the Extraordinary Congress was taken by decision of the All-Russian Central Executive Committee on March 3 by a vote of 166 to 85, with 26 abstentions, which itself was unwilling to do so, given the harsh conditions of the treaty. On November 13, 1918 the ratification was annulled in the name of the All-Russian Central Executive Committee because of a "coup d'etat" in Germany; in effect, the ratification was undone by repealing the ratification Decree of March 3, 1918. See СУ РСФСР (1918) no 95, item 947. This is the only known example of such a practice in Soviet Russian or USSR experience; at the time there were no objections from Germany. See V N Durdenevskii, "Международные договоры в конституционном праве Союза ССР" ["International Treaties in the Constitutional Law of the USSR"], Советское право [Soviet Law], no. 4 (1925) 25, fn 1.

formalities regarding confirmation or ratification and was concluded at the local level on behalf of Russia by the Chairman of the Supreme Autonomous Collegium of the Council of People's Commissars for Russian-Romanian Affairs, Christian Rakovskii (1873–1941).[48]

Several agreements supplementary to the Peace Treaty entered into at Brest-Litovsk were concluded between the RSFSR and Germany during late August 1918; these were subject to and received ratification. On behalf of the RSFSR, ratification was completed by the Central Executive Committee.

It should be noted that the RSFSR Constitution, ultimately adopted on July 10, 1918, was consistent with early Russian practices. Article 49 provided that the All-Russian Congress of Soviets and the All-Russian Central Executive Committee had jurisdiction over "relations with foreign States, the declaration of war, and the conclusion of peace," as well as with "making loans, customs, and commercial treaties, and financial agreements." The ratification of peace treaties, however, was placed solely with the All-Russian Congress of Soviets (Article 51), no doubt reflecting the experience with the Brest-Litovsk Treaty of Peace.[49]

USSR Treaty Policy: 1923–78. The former Union of Soviet Socialist Republics (hereinafter: USSR; Soviet Union) was formed by treaty signed at Moscow on December 30, 1922 by four independent countries: the RSFSR; Ukrainian Soviet Socialist Republic; Belorussian Soviet Socialist Republic; and Transcaucasian Soviet Federated Soviet Republic (comprised of Armenia, Azerbaidzhan, and Georgia). The USSR was given the competence, in the person of its highest institutions, *inter alia*, to conclude treaties concerning the admission of new republics into the Union, declare war and conclude peace, and ratify foreign treaties (Article 1). The highest agencies of the Union were the Congress of Soviets of the SSR and, in the interval between sessions thereof, the Central Executive Committee of the USSR. In intervals between sessions of the Central Executive Committee, its Presidium operated. The treaty contained no provision for ratification or entry into force.

---

[48] See n. 41, I, 210–11.

[49] It should be noted, though, that the Brest-Litovsk Treaty of Peace was augmented by supplementary agreements in late August 1918; these were duly ratified, and the provisions of Article 51 of the 1918 RSFSR Constitution were in force and duly followed. Nothing was said about the right to annul a treaty. The Treaty of Brest-Litovsk was annulled on November 13, 1918 by the Central Executive Committee. Moreover, the said Committee ratified the treaties of peace between Russia and Turkey of March 16, 1921; Russia and Persia of February 26, 1921; and Russia and Bukhara of March 4, 1921.

On the basis of the treaty, the USSR in 1924 adopted a Constitution which, in Article 1, reiterated the jurisdiction of the Union with respect to the "ratification of international treaties."

The Central Executive Committee of the USSR began to enact procedural legislation with respect to the conclusion and ratification of treaties. Pursuant to Articles 17 and 29 of the 1924 USSR Constitution, the Central Executive Committee added to its own Statute, also of November 12, 1923, a clause which gave the Presidium of the Central Executive Committee the right to ratify treaties and agreements in intervals between sessions of the full Committee.[50] The Statute on the Council of People's Commissars, confirmed by Decree of the Central Executive Committee on November 12, 1923, gave the Council jurisdiction over the "consideration of treaties and agreements with governments of foreign States, as well as confirmation of those which do not require ratification" (Article 3(e)).[51] On the same day the People's Commissariat of Foreign Affairs was given the tasks of: (a) fulfillment of decrees concerning the conclusion of treaties and agreements with foreign States; (b) direction of putting into practice treaties and agreements concluded with foreign States and cooperation with appropriate institutions of the USSR and union republics in carrying out rights established by such treaties; and (c) observance over the fulfillment of treaties, agreements, and acts concluded with foreign States by appropriate agencies of authority (Article 2(b)(c) and (d)).[52]

In a separate Decree "On the Procedure for the Conclusion and Ratification of International Treaties of the USSR," dated May 21, 1925, the distinction was first drawn in legislation between inter-State and intergovernmental treaties, although those terms were not used. The Decree clarified for the first time which treaties must be ratified. There were three categories: (a) peace treaties; (b) treaties changing the border of the USSR; and (c) treaties with countries whose legislation required ratification of the respective treaty. Ratification in the USSR was in the name of and by the Congress of Soviets if that body adopted a decree concerning the conclusion of the treaty; otherwise, treaties were concluded in the name of the Council of People's Commissars if they did not require ratification.[53]

---

[50] The amendment was made on May 21, 1925. See Butler, *Soviet Statutes and Decisions*, III, no 4 (1967) 52.

[51] Translated by W. E. Butler, ibid, 51.

[52] Ibid, 51–2.

[53] Ibid, 53.

This left open the question of treaties concluded by the union republics prior to the formation of the USSR. On June 15, 1927 amendments were introduced into the Decree of May 21, 1925 to, first, amend the title of the Decree to "On the Procedure for the Conclusion, Ratification (Confirmation), and Denunciation (Declaration Concerning Termination of Effect) of International Treaties of the USSR." Second, those treaties confirmed by the Council of People's Commissars of the USSR or those concluded by union republic councils of people's commissars before the formation of the USSR were subject to being denounced by the Council of People's Commissars of the USSR.[54]

The procedure for submitting international treaties to the Government of the USSR had, so far as can be determined, never been provided for in legislation. This was addressed on October 2, 1925 in the Decree "On the Procedure for the Submission of International Treaties and Agreements Concluded in the Name of the USSR for Approval, Confirmation, and Ratification of the Government of the USSR."[55] Before being signed in the name of the USSR, the treaty was to be submitted by the People's Commissariat of Foreign Affairs for preliminary approval by the Council of People's Commissars. The procedure to be followed in seeking preliminary approval depended upon certain circumstances. If the plenipotentiary of the USSR intended to put forward his own draft treaty, the basic provisions were to be submitted for approval in advance of beginning negotiations. If negotiations had commenced and the USSR plenipotentiary did not intend to put forward his own draft, the draft submitted by the other Party, together with notations thereon by the plenipotentiary or a counter-draft, were to be submitted to the Council of People's Commissars. Once a draft had been agreed with the other Party, it was to be submitted to the People's Commissariat of Foreign Affairs, discussed therein, and submitted for ultimate approval by the Council of People's Commissars, whereupon either permission will be given to sign or further changes will be suggested.

The reasons for establishing this procedure were set out at some length: (a) to inform the Council of People's Commissars about treaties or other acts which entered into force upon signature; (b) to confirm treaties which were not subject to ratification; and (c) to consider treaties which were subject to ratification in advance of their submission to the Congress

---

[54] Ibid, 53–4.
[55] Ibid, 54–6.

of Soviets or to the Central Executive Committee, or the Presidium thereof. This procedure was not required when the individual concluding treaties in the name of the USSR had unlimited authority to do so from the Government of the USSR.

Given the distinctions being drawn between "ratification" and "confirmation," the question again arose: what is the difference between the two? Durdenevskii suggested, so far as international law was concerned, there was no difference whatsoever: "In the event of 'confirmation' a treaty goes back to the Council of People's Commissars, and in the event of 'ratification' it goes back to the same Council and with its opinion is submitted to the Presidium of the Central Executive Committee. In other words, ratification is two-stage confirmation under which the opinion of the Council of People's Commissars forming the first stage is in practice exceedingly important."[56]

On the example of ratification constituting a "two-stage" process, Durdenevskii asked, is not "confirmation" merely a precarious conditional act in the form of a decree which, just as any other decree of the Council of People's Commissars, might be repealed by the Central Executive Committee or its Presidium? In his view, the reply should be negative and he gave an example. On November 12, 1923 the Council of People's Commissars submitted twelve treaties, having confirmed them, to the Central Executive Committee, which in his view meant that the Central Executive Committee considered that the "confirmation" given made the treaties "final, concluded, firm." Any other view, Durdenevskii said, would be a contradiction with the word "confirm." Therefore, any reference to "repeal of a decree on confirmation" makes no sense because this cannot eliminate the "fact" that the treaty was concluded and was in force "even for a short time." This approach would be tantamount to dissolution of the treaty or suspension of its operation; to be sure, he added, constitutionally the Central Executive Committee might dissolve any treaty, even one ratified or which entered into force upon signature. Such an eventuality he regarded as unlikely for a number of reasons and did not believe the two-stage process was, in practice, a precarious one because: (1) the likelihood of dissolution at this stage was low given various practical inconveniences that would arise, and (2) the likelihood of dissolution was "purely academic" because if there were any doubts about the advisability of the treaty, these would have

---

[56] Durdenevskii (n. 47) 25.

been expressed by the Council of People's Commissars when referring its opinion on ratification to the Central Executive Committee.[57]

In the case of accession to a multilateral agreement, the draft decree of accession would be submitted by the People's Commissariat of Foreign Affairs to the Council of People's Commissars in the usual procedure; if the decree were confirmed, publication of the decree would occur in the usual manner.

Considering the above enactments in aggregate, the general picture of Soviet law as compared with western approaches at the time was to place greater emphasis upon the "confirmation" of treaties in preference to "ratification." Confirmation was regarded as an institution well-known to customary international law, but not often mentioned in western constitutions. The types of treaties specifically requiring "ratification" in the 1924 Constitution of the USSR was reduced to the bare minimum (peace, change of boundaries). But more important, perhaps, was the perception of Soviet international legal doctrine at the time that the concept of "Head of State" differed from western countries, and although there was a separation of powers (executive, legislative, judicial), the concept of checks and balances was absent and not intended to be a feature of Soviet-type constitutions. The prerogatives of the principal Soviet agencies of State power—Congress of Soviets, Central Executive Committee, and Presidium of the Central Executive Committee—were deemed to have more extensive powers, including especially legislative, than foreign monarchs or presidents. Soviet constitutional concepts were based on the principle of a "dictatorship of the proletariat," on a "concentration of power," rather than a limitation of State power. Durdenevskii expressed the position in 1925 as follows: "ratification of international treaties in the law of the Soviet Union is the constitutional prerogative of the sovereign representation of the toiling masses in its threefold appearance—Congress, Committee, Presidium. This is an entirely unique legal form connected with the principle of the concentration of power."[58]

It would follow that the great majority of international treaties of the Soviet Union would be concluded in the name of the Council of People's Commissars and confirmed by it. But under the Statute on the Council of People's Commissars, the role of the Council was not confined to the conclusion of treaties: the Council also to a significant degree drafted them or

---

[57] Ibid.
[58] Ibid, 26.

was involved in the drafting by way of "consideration" (point 3(3), Statute). This procedure the USSR inherited from the RSFSR, where there were a number of precedents, especially from 1921 when Soviet Russian contacts with the foreign world greatly expanded. One example cited in doctrinal writings related to the so-called "Small Council" [Малый совет] of the Council of People's Commissars, which on January 24, 1921 decreed that trade treaties must be agreed with the People's Commissariat of Foreign Trade; and another Decree of April 21, 1921 on the procedure for the movement of treaties with foreign States through the Government. Under the Decree of April 21, treaties and agreements of the RSFSR must be approved prior to signature by the Council of People's Commissars; the Council in effect wanted to keep a close eye on the negotiations, be advised of any editorial changes or changes which improved the position of Soviet Russia, and if urgent instructions or decisions were required, an emergency session of the Small Council would be convened. For all practical purposes, the entire treaty negotiating process was under prior governmental control. The role of the Council, in other words, was far more extensive that mere "confirmation" of the ultimate result of drafting treaties.[59]

These precedents of practice influenced subsequent USSR developments, but were not replicated exactly. The USSR had no "Small Council," so relegated the preliminary work on treaty preparation to the Legislative Proposals Commission, or with respect to financial aspects of treaties, to the Administrative-Financial Commission. The details were set out in the Decree of October 2, 1925, described above, on the procedure for submitting international treaties and agreements to be concluded in the name of the USSR for approval, confirmation, or ratification. In general, the Council of People's Commissars would take an interest in the preparation of all treaties, but for two instances when this procedure was considered to be superfluous: (1) when delegations are sent abroad to conclude treaties "with unlimited powers"—a rare occasion, or (2) more often, when the USSR acceded to an international convention whose text is already determined and known in advance.[60]

Given that the Union of Soviet Socialist Republics was itself formed by treaty, the question arose whether the union republics which were part of

---

[59] Ibid, 27. Durdenevskii cited unpublished materials on this aspect and undoubtedly was directly or indirectly involved in the deliberations.

[60] In this last instance the act of accession is published as a domestic law of the USSR. An example was the accession of the Soviet Union in 1925 to the international metric convention.

the USSR could, under the law of the USSR, themselves conclude international treaties with foreign States. The 1924 USSR Constitution formally did not contain a direct answer to this question. The sense of the Constitution, however, was believed to have left no doubt that the foreign policy of the Soviet Union was centralized and within the exclusive jurisdiction of the Union. One reason for forming the Soviet Union was to present a united front on foreign policy issues, and the Constitution reserved the conduct of diplomatic relations to the jurisdiction of the Union. There was a brief period during roughly from July to late autumn 1923 when the constituent republics of the USSR did conclude treaties directly with foreign States, but by autumn 1923 the republics confined themselves to assisting the Union in individual foreign policy matters. The RSFSR may have continued to conclude minor bilateral treaties with Central Asian entities until they became part of the USSR.

In 1936 the Soviet Union replaced the 1924 Constitution with a new version. This was more carefully drafted than its predecessor and contained several provisions relating to treaties. The competence of the Soviet Union extended to the "representation of the USSR in international relations, conclusion, ratification, and denunciation of treaties of the USSR with other States … " (Article 14(a)). Amendments in 1944 added the right of "each union republic to enter into direct relations with foreign States, to conclude agreements with them, and to exchange diplomatic and consular representatives" (Article 18a). The Supreme Soviet of the USSR exercised all rights vested in the Union of Soviet Socialist Republics insofar as the Constitution did not place these within the competence of agencies of the USSR accountable to the Supreme Soviet, such as the Presidium of the USSR Supreme Soviet, USSR Council of Ministers, and ministries of the USSR.

The Presidium of the USSR Supreme Soviet (the collective Head of State) ratified and denounced international treaties of the USSR (Article 49). The USSR Council of Ministers coordinated and directed the work of the all-union and union republic ministries and other institutions and exercised general direction with respect to relations with foreign States (Article 68).[61]

Further to Article 49(1) of the 1936 Constitution, the Supreme Soviet adopted the Law of August 20, 1938, "On the Procedure for the Ratification and Denunciation of International Treaties of the USSR." The Presidium of the Supreme Soviet was vested with the ratification (by an edict subject

---

[61] Butler, *Soviet Statutes and Decisions*, III, no. 4 (1967) 52. Translated by Butler, ibid, 50.

to confirmation by the plenary Supreme Soviet)[62] and denunciation (by an Edict) of international treaties. The List of treaties subject to ratification was changed by the 1938 Law: peace treaties, treaties concerning mutual defense against aggression, and treaties of mutual nonaggression, together with any treaties in which the parties have agreed to subsequent ratification.[63]

None of the enactments above addressed the relationship between an international treaty of the USSR and national legislation. That process commenced indirectly in 1957 when the 1936 USSR Constitution was amended to authorize the enactment of the all-union fundamental principles of legislation in individual branches of law, to be elaborated by union republic codes of law which would incorporate, usually verbatim, the provisions of all-union principles but add greater detail consistent with those principles. The 1961 Fundamental Principles of Civil Legislation took the first step with the following clause:

> If other rules have been established by an international treaty or international agreement in which the USSR participates than those which are contained in Soviet civil legislation, the rules of the international treaty or international agreement shall be applied.[64]

The full rationale for and legislative history of this change awaits its full explanation. In the post-Stalin Soviet Union the isolation of the "Cold War" was being reversed in favor of peaceful coexistence and cooperation with foreign States. The doctrine of the inevitability of war between capitalist and socialist States was, in the nuclear age, abandoned by the Soviet Union at the cost of disagreement with the Chinese leadership. Soviet foreign policy initiatives recognized the importance of foreign trade and foreign economic assistance; the "third world" was recognized by both the western and Soviet camps as an opportunity not to be squandered. Treaties

---

[62] This requirement of an edict being confirmed by the plenary Supreme Soviet, including the union republics, was either overlooked or not fully appreciated abroad. The ratifications by Edict of the United Nations Charter in 1945 by the Belorussian SSR and Ukrainian SSR were accepted by the depositary (Department of State of the United States) of the Charter as final, although it was formally not. See P P Kremnev, "On Ukrainian and Belorussian Membership in the United Nations and Entry of the United Nations Charter into Force," *Sudebnik*, IX (2004) 457–92.

[63] Butler, *Soviet Statutes and Decisions*, III, no. 4 (1967) 56–7. The Presidium of the Supreme Soviet on April 26, 1940 repealed the Decree of the Central Executive Committee of May 21, 1925 and subsequent additions and changes in connection with the adoption of the 1938 Law.

[64] Article 129; trans in Butler, *The Soviet Legal System: Selected Contemporary Legislation and Documents* (1978) 429.

would play a central role in the process of expanding foreign relations, and it may be that their sheer numbers persuaded the Soviet leadership the conundrum of the relationship between treaties and municipal law had to be resolved in a way that placed foreign relations in the forefront of Soviet policy-making.

Other factors were at work. In principle, the move in the direction of "decentralization" represented by eschewing all-union codes of law in key areas of legislation in favor of Fundamental Principles/union republic codes meant that policy-makers were concerned that the union republics might be inclined to adopt their own legislation contrary to treaties concluded at the all-Union level. The primacy of treaties expressed from 1960 onward in the majority of Fundamental Principles and many other laws would have forestalled excessive union republic liberality in this respect.

This formulation, although it did not represent a departure from dualism, no longer equated a treaty with a law or other normative legal act. It represented a change from the policy that the enactment or treaty latest in time governs. Under this formulation, the treaty always took precedence over an act of legislation inconsistent with the treaty, whether it preceded or followed the entry of the treaty into force. The question became whether this was a general rule of Soviet law or a provision applicable only to those branches of Soviet law in which the provision was contained. On this, the views of Soviet jurists differed.

The 1978 USSR Law on Treaties (Article 12) did not contain a provision concerning the primacy of treaties over inconsistent Soviet legislation but did provide that "treaties establishing rules other than those which are contained in legislative acts of the USSR shall be subject to ratification." This formulation extended to any type of treaty: inter-State, intergovernmental, or interdepartmental. Ratification under the 1977 USSR Constitution (Article 121(6)) was entrusted to the Presidium of the USSR Supreme Soviet in the form of an edict (Article 15, USSR 1978 Law on Treaties).

The 1978 USSR Law on Treaties used a dual approach to stipulating which treaties of the USSR were or were not subject to ratification. Those subject to ratification (Article 12) were enumerated as follows: (a) treaties on friendship, cooperation, and mutual assistance; (b) treaties on the mutual renunciation of the use or threat of force; (c) peace treaties; (d) treaties on the territorial delimitation of the USSR with other States; (e) treaties establish rules other than those contained in legislative acts of the USSR.

Those not subject to ratification but which were subject to confirmation (Article 17) because the treaties so provided were the following: (a) treaties concluded in the name of the USSR by the Presidium of the USSR Supreme Soviet: by the Presidium of the USSR Supreme Soviet; (b) with respect to treaties concluded in the name of the USSR relating to questions appertaining by the jurisdiction of the Government of the USSR: by the USSR Council of Ministers; (c) treaties concluded in the name of the Presidium of the USSR Supreme Soviet: by the Presidium of the USSR Supreme Soviet; (d) treaties concluded in the name of the Government of the USSR: by the USSR Council of Ministers.

The confirmation or adoption of international treaties of the USSR of an interdepartmental character which provided for their entry into force after confirmation or adoption was performed by the ministries, State committees, or departments of the USSR in whose name they were signed (point 7, Decree of August 28, 1980, No. 743).

Special procedures governed decisions of the Soviet Union to accede to international treaties (Article 18, 1978 Law on Treaties). Decisions were adopted as follows:

(1) treaties subject to ratification by the Presidium of the USSR Supreme Soviet: by the Presidium of the USSR Supreme Soviet;

(2) treaties not subject to ratification, accession to which was made in the name of the Union of Soviet Socialist Republics: by the Presidium of the USSR Supreme Soviet;

(3) treaties not subject to ratification, accession to which was made in the name of the USSR relating to questions appertaining to the jurisdiction of the Government of the USSR: by the USSR Council of Ministers;

(4) treaties not subject to ratification, accession to which was made in the name of the Presidium of the USSR Supreme Soviet: by the Presidium of the USSR Supreme Soviet;

(5) treaties not subject to ratification, accession to which was made in the name of the Government of the USSR: by the USSR Council of Ministers;

(6) treaties of an interdepartmental character: by the ministers of the USSR, chairmen of State committees of the USSR, and executives of departments of the USSR within whose competence are the questions regulated by such treaties, by agreement with the Ministry of Foreign Affairs of the USSR.

Soviet Doctrinal Perspectives

Ratification as an institution of treaty-making required explanation and rationalization on the part of Soviet international lawyers and ideologists. There could be no question of rejecting or dispensing with the institution. If Soviet Russia and later the USSR were to enter into treaties with foreign States, or form their own confederation on the basis of a treaty, the formalities had to be either observed as they existed prior to the Revolution or reshaped to accommodate post-revolutionary ideals, values, and interests. In this case, practice preceded theory, as noted above. Ratification as an element of international law was acknowledged to be bourgeois in origin. As a legal principle and practice it crossed the domains of international law and domestic (constitutional) law.

How, if at all, did treaty ratification by the Soviet Union differ from the pre-Soviet period. Various explanations were offered in Soviet international legal doctrine at various times. A primary point of departure was the difference in the identity of the "sovereign." In bourgeois times, the monarch was the ruler who personified the State and in whose name a treaty was made. The creation of Soviet-type governments based on the will of the working class changed the identity of the sovereign, it was pointed out, and in the context of Marxism-Leninism this was perceived as a qualitative change in social relations within the State.[65] To put it otherwise, the "Head of State" had changed, the duration of ratification was not the life span of a natural person/ruler, but in perpetuity so long as the State endured, the treaty did not provide otherwise, and the parties were content to maintain the treaty in force.

Who within a State should ratify treaties? Soviet doctrine held that this was a matter for each State in its sovereign capacity to determine internally. But in 1950 this position linked the discretion to choose whether ratification was necessary with the exercise of State sovereignty in making that choice. The State—and "only the State"—has the "right to determine the system of structuring State agencies and the competence of each of them."[66] This right inhered in each State and was not "conferred" or "delegated" by

---

[65] Polents wrote in 1950: "The main distinction between ratifying agencies in the USSR and ratifying agencies in a bourgeois State arises from their genuinely democratic essence as agencies of supreme power of a socialist State of workers and peasants … Thus, an act of ratification in the Soviet Union is effectuated by agencies expressing the will of the people and under the control of the popular masses" Polents (n. 3) 35–6.

[66] Ibid, 30.

international law; it was not a consequence, in other words, of the "primacy" of international law over municipal law.[67]

In the era of "perestroika" under M S Gorbachev, the "primacy" of international law was revived as a doctrine and enjoyed some currency between 1988 and 1991.

Which treaties should be subject to ratification or merely "confirmation"? International law, Soviet jurists acknowledged, was infinitely flexible on this and imposed no requirements. Soviet doctrine shared the universally accepted position that treaties were subject to ratification: (1) if the constitution or legislation of either or any party so required; or (2) the parties agreed that ratification was necessary in the text of the treaty and/or the powers issued to negotiate or conclude the treaty. In practice "ratification" as a term is commonly the prerogative of the "highest agencies of State power" or the highest (Head of State) official. But there is no rule that would prohibit a State, for example, from not using the term "ratification" and preferring instead "confirmation," if these procedures were considered to be synonymous.

What would be the outcome if an international treaty ratified or confirmed by the Soviet Union contained provisions that were contrary to Soviet normative legal acts? The general view, without asserting the primacy of the treaty, was that the Soviet State was obliged to make necessary changes in legislation or enact new legislation to implement the relevant treaty provisions. But the problem was, of course, more complex. In the interwar period only one doctrinal contribution addressed the problem, and that article was published abroad by the Soviet author and remains unknown, it would seem, to Soviet and post-Soviet legal science.

The author was none other than V N Durdenevskii, who according to the article, was based in Irkutsk at the time.[68] Dismissing foreign theory and practice on this question as inappropriate for the Soviet Union and considering himself (rightly it would appear) as the first to address the issue in Soviet international legal doctrine, Durdenevskii invoked the principle that the enactment later in time governed. Thus, if either the Central Executive Committee or the Council of People's Commissars enacted a Decree which

---

[67] Ibid, citing and rejecting H Kelsen, "La transformation du droit international en droit interne," *Revue générale de droit international public*, no. 1 (1936) 24–34.

[68] See V N Durdenevskii, "Der Vorrang des völkerrechtlichen Vertrages oder des inneren Gesetzes im Rätrecht," *Zeitschrift für Ostrecht*, IV, no. 8/9 (1930) 793–9. The article was submitted in the Russian language and translated by Dr. Axel Rambach. Fel'dman was unaware of it; see D I Fel'dman (ed.), Международное право. Библиография 1917–72 [*International Law. Bibliography 1917–72*] (1976). Triska and Slusser summarized it. See n. 39, 109–10. There is no record of the article having been published in the Soviet Union at the time.

was inconsistent or in conflict with a treaty previously ratified or confirmed, the Decree would prevail. Likewise, if either body ratified or confirmed a treaty which was in conflict with an earlier Decree, the treaty would prevail:

> To put it more precisely, a later Soviet law would supersede an earlier ratified treaty, as long as this treaty had not been published in the procedure prescribed for legislation or as long as the text of the treaty had not been made officially known to the appropriate organs for execution; the time element is here decisive. A treaty that had already been published or made official known acquires the force of law and replaces an earlier conflicting law, without any necessity of changing the text thereof (although it may be desirable to specify the meaning of the change). A later Soviet law can, however, supersede even a treaty already published [and made officially known] . . . [69]

Treaties, once ratified or confirmed and published, were part of the domestic legal system of the USSR and sat side by side with laws and other normative legal acts. The act latest in time operated in the event of a conflict. If, however, a union republic enactment proved to be in conflict with a treaty of the Soviet Union, the treaty would be regarded as a Union enactment and the inconsistency would therefore be between a Union enactment/treaty and the union republic enactment, in which event this would be a domestic matter: at the time the People's Commissariat for Foreign Affairs would at its own initiative or upon the protest of the Procurator General draw the attention of the Central Executive Committee to the existence of the conflict with either the 1924 Constitution of the USSR or other Union enactment. The Union authorities would then require that the union republic authorities either change or repeal their enactment.

Post-World War II legal doctrine initially emphasized, as noted above, the importance of a dualist approach to the interface between international and municipal law for the protection of State sovereignty and a reduction of foreign interference in Soviet internal affairs. A leading treatise by Vladimir Mikhailovich Shurshalov (1913–90) expressed the position as follows:

> Treaties, however, do not contain provisions confirming that municipal agencies or a court should directly be guided by the norms of an

---

[69] Triska and Slusser (n. 39) 110.

international treaty as legal grounds for the performance of certain actions.

From this the conclusion follows that international treaties establish only the obligation of the parties to publish State laws but themselves do not create legal norms of municipal law, for the publication of a State law—is within the sole competence of respective agencies of State power, the sovereign right of the State, purely its internal affair.

Thus, an international treaty does not replace a State law and does not directly create norms of municipal law. It merely gives an occasion and legal grounds for the publication of certain State legislative acts. Such State acts cannot fail to have the specific feature inherent in them arising from the specific features of the social and State system of each country.[70]

Having expressed that view, Shurshalov promptly denied the possibility of a conflict between the treaty and legislative practice of the Soviet State:

The treaty and legislative practice of the Soviet Union offers no examples of conflicts or inconsistencies between laws and international treaties. This is explained by the fact that the Soviet State system ensures the manifestation of a single and monolithic will in foreign and internal affairs which exclude any conflicts between the norms of a treaty and a law. In this connection the questions do not arise before Soviet courts and other State agencies of which norm (treaty or law) to apply. The experience of the treaty and legislative practice of the USSR shows that the very raising of the question of the primacy of an international treaty over a law or, vice versa, has no real grounds.[71]

Shurshalov's treatise was defended as a higher doctorate, submitted for press on September 8, 1959 (1,600 copies were printed) and was the product of an individual who had served in academic and in Communist Party positions. The 1958 Fundamental Principles of criminal law and procedure contained no provisions on treaty supremacy, but there was plainly a debate in progress within Soviet policy-making circles that within a short time after the appearance of Shurshalov's work proceeded to move in the opposite

---

[70] V M Shurshalov, Основные вопросы теории международного договора [*Basic Questions of the Theory of the International Treaty*] (1959) 354–5.
[71] Ibid, 357–8.

direction. A treaty supremacy clause was included in the Fundamental Principles of civil law and of civil procedure of December 8, 1961.[72] The drafts would have been in progress when Shurshalov defended his dissertation, although a final decision may not have been reached.

What Shurshalov counseled at the time was an approach which would not take any such conflict between a treaty and a law to an extreme. First, he observed that "instances of conflicts or inconsistency of norms of an international treaty and a law are episodic, are an exception which does not characterize the essence of the correlation of international treaties and State laws."[73] This "essence" to which Shurshalov referred was the mutual influence of State laws and international treaties on one another. Such influence, he said, occurred through the establishment or inclusion of norms or provisions of domestic legislation in treaty texts or, on the other hand, the adoption of domestic laws which contain or implement treaty provisions. However, he was insistent that the "norms of a treaty might be embodied in a norm of municipal law only by way of the publication of respective legislative acts." National courts, he observed, are always guided by laws, although some of these laws reproduce the respective provisions in international treaties.

Under this approach to interaction, Shurshalov said, the full autonomy of the international and municipal legal systems is preserved and the internal and external affairs of the State are sharply delineated. This is "exceedingly essential for the preservation of the sovereignty and independence of the participants of the international community." The replacement of norms of municipal law by norms of international law and *vice versa* is excluded, and the distinction in principle between international-legal regulation and legal regulation within individual States is retained.

In practice, Shurshalov noted, inconsistencies or conflicts between treaty norms and municipal legal norms arise in two instances: (a) when a State fails to enact legislation directly or indirectly flowing from international obligations, usually by making amendments in legislation to reflect the treaty provisions; or (b) when a State adopts laws that are incompatible with its international obligations. When these exceptional matters occur, the best approach is to resolve them by negotiation between the parties. A State which fails to comply with its treaty obligations is in violation of the treaty and accountable to the other parties to the treaty; but domestically, national

---

[72] For translations of all the Fundamental Principles up to 1978, see Butler (n. 64).
[73] Shurshalov (n. 70) 361.

courts, agencies, and officials have no alternative to complying with the national legislation of their State and will be expected to do so. In any event, concluded Shurshalov, in order to eliminate such conflicts there is no need to be guided by "theoretical postulates" concerning the primacy of national or international law. The application of either theory would, in practice, entail a "violation of the basic principles of international law," such as, for example, sovereign equality and non-interference.[74]

The introduction of a treaty supremacy clause in some Soviet legislative acts inaugurated a new period in Soviet legal doctrine. The essential disagreement was whether the treaty supremacy principle operated throughout the entire body of legislation or only in the branches of law and legislation. The Soviet Union took an active role in the Vienna Conference on the Law of Treaties and ultimately ratified the 1969 Vienna Convention on the Law of Treaties. The 1978 USSR Law on treaties represented the introduction of the 1969 Vienna Convention provisions into Soviet law. Soviet legal doctrine thereafter concentrated, with respect to the law of treaties, on the Vienna Convention, the 1978 USSR Law on treaties, and implementing subordinate normative legal acts. We turn to these in relevant part below.

---

[74] Ibid, 362–4.

2
Sources of the Russian Law of Treaties

It will be noted that the title of this chapter does not address the role of treaties as a source of international law. Article 38(1)(a) of the Statute of the International Court of Justice lists "international conventions, whether general or particular" first as the source of international law which the Court may apply to decide a dispute submitted to it. Russian,[1] Soviet,[2] and post-Soviet[3] legal doctrine have from the outset accepted treaties not only as a source of international law, but as a preferred source of international law. In the Soviet era treaties were regarded as the primary source of international law and customary rules secondarily as such a source. They were reinforced in this view by the fact that the Statute on the International Court of Justice enumerated "international conventions" ahead of "international custom."

The Russian Federation is, moreover, a party to the 1969 Vienna Convention on the Law of Treaties.[4]

---

[1] "International treaties are the principal source of international law." N M Korkunov, "Лекции по международному праву Профессора Н. М. Коркунова Читанные в Военно-Юридической Академии в 1883–1884 году" ["Lectures on International Law of Professor N. M. Korkunov Read at the Military Law Academy in 1883–1884"], reproduced in Золотой Фонд Российской науки международного права [*Golden Fund of the Russian Science of International Law*] (reprint edn.; 2007) I, 323.

[2] "In contemporary conditions the principal means of creating norms of international law is a treaty." See G I Tunkin, "Co-Existence and International Law," in W E Butler and V G Tunkin (eds.), *The Tunkin Diary and Lectures: The Diary and Collected Lectures of G. I. Tunkin at The Hague Academy of International Law* (2012) 153.

[3] Post-Soviet doctrinal views are various and more willing to acknowledge the important role of customary rules of international law: "There is no sense in continuing the dispute as to which type of source of international law is more important. Of major importance is the place which customary or treaty norms occupy in the international-legal system." I I Lukashuk, in V I Kuznetsov and B R Tuzkukhamedov (eds.), *International Law—A Russian Introduction*, ed. and trans. W E Butler (2009) 80.

[4] The Soviet Union acceded to the 1969 Vienna Convention on April 29, 1986; the Russian Federation is a party to the Convention in its capacity as the legal continuer of the former Soviet Union.

But that is not the issue addressed here. The question is: what Russian legislation, judicial practice, and doctrinal views regulate the conclusion, ratification, entry into force, or termination of treaties under Russian law or, to put the matter otherwise, how does Russian law interact with and/or implement the international law of treaties. We are not asking here whether and how international treaties operate in the Russian legal system, but what Russian legislation, judicial practice, and/or legal doctrine enable or explain whether and how treaties become part, if at all, of that system.

The sources of Russian law generally are also the sources of Russian foreign relations law, including the Russian law of treaties—that is, a body of legislation, judicial practice, and doctrinal literature which determines how treaties are to be concluded, ratified, confirmed, approved, or provisionally applied by relevant State agencies, terminated, denounced, or suspended if necessary, and otherwise procedurally dealt with under Russian law.

The sources of the Russian law of treaties are, in general, the same sources of other branches or rules of Russian law. We refer to "sources" in their technical sense: rules, or norms, created, sanctioned, or recognized by the State or its agencies in a duly established manner. Not all acts fall within this definition;[5] only those prescribing general rules of conduct, or so-called *normative legal acts*. Non-normative acts regulate individual, specific matters and are adopted on the basis of legal norms. Normative legal acts are binding on an indefinite group of persons, intended for repeated application, and operate irrespective of whether specific legal relations provided for by the act have arisen or ceased to operate.[6]

---

[5] Sources of law are treated extensively in W E Butler, *Russian Law and Legal System* (2nd edn.; 2018) 122–71.

[6] This formulation adapts a definition once given, but later repealed, by the Plenum of the Supreme Court of the Russian Federation in Decree No 19 (point 2), adopted May 25, 2000, but repealed on January 20, 2003; the same definition appeared in a Decree of the Plenum of the said Supreme Court "On Certain Questions Arising When Considering Cases upon the Applications of Procurators concerning the Deeming of Legal Acts Contrary to a Law," of April 27, 1993, No 5, as amended December 21, 1993. In a Recourse to the Constitutional Court of the Russian Federation by the State Duma of the Federal Assembly of the Russian Federation of November 11, 1996, the Duma noted that "there is no definition of the concept of 'normative legal act' in legislation in force. In legal doctrine one proceeds from the fact that a 'normative legal act—is a written official document adopted (or issued) in a certain form by a law-making agency within the limits of its competence and directed towards the establishment, change, or repeal of legal norms. In turn, by legal act it is accepted to understand a generally-binding State prescription of a permanent or temporary character intended for repeated application." СЗ РФ (1996), no 49, item 5506. This definition is recommended for use by the Ministry of Justice of the Russian Federation in an Order of May 4, 2007, No. 88, "On Confirmation of Explanations on the Application of Rules for the Preparation of Normative Legal Acts of Federal Agencies of Executive Power and Their State Registration." Available on Consultant Plus.

Natural Law

It follows from this approach that not all sources of law originate with the State itself. Natural lawyers, of whom there are many among Russian jurists, believe there is a law above the State; customs are recognized as a subsidiary source of law, and some jurists recognize judicial precedent and/or doctrinal writings in this capacity. Some State corporations in Russia are explicitly given the legal capacity to conclude international treaties of the Russian Federation—which are classified as interdepartmental treaties. Moreover, so-called "local" normative acts are adopted by or within non-State entities, such as commercial juridical persons. Russian law attaches importance to a formalistic hierarchy of the sources of law. The 1993 Russian Constitution has introduced an entirely new dimension to that hierarchy, whose implications continue to unfold and to affect, and be affected by, the Russian law of treaties. Indeed, the law of treaties could be said to challenge the classical hierarchy of Russian normative legal acts.

A natural law approach is widely shared in the modern Russian general theory of law: "law [*jus*, право] does not reduce itself to the aggregate of laws [*lex*, закон]. It is considered that law [*jus*, право] stands by virtue of its own laws [*lex*, закон]."[7] A former judge on the Constitutional Court of the Russian Federation expressed the position as follows:

Law cannot be reduced only to the written part thereof, to positive law ... Natural law includes the aggregate of rights and freedoms historically recognized by mankind as inalienably inherent in every person from birth. These rights and freedoms do not depend upon the will of the State and are not a gift on its part. On the contrary, the State is bound by these primary moral and reasonable imperatives and obliged to recognize, comply with, and guarantee them ... A truth must be contained in the flesh and blood of people's life: if a law [*lex*] is contrary to natural law [*jus*], it is void.[8]

[7] A A Rubanov, "Понятие источника права как проявление метафоричности юридического сознания" ["Concept of Source of Law as a Manifestation of a Metaphor of Legal Consciousness"], in Судебная практика как источник права [*Judicial Practice as a Source of Law*] (1997) 47.

[8] M V Baglai, Конституционное право Российской Федерации [*Constitutional Law of the Russian Federation*] (13th edn.; 2018) 31–3.

The rules to which Baglai refers originate to a considerable extent in, or are restated or codified by, treaties to which the Russian Federation is a party. Human rights treaties are an important example. Whether the rules of *jus* be of divine origin, or the natural order of the universe, or the laws of societal development, or the fabric of Russian (or Slavic, or Eurasian) socio-cultural values, or otherwise has for decades been the subject of an important lively debate relevant to the future of a Russian civil society.[9]

Soviet Law

Treaties, other international documents, and legislation of the former Soviet Union continue to have a significant, albeit declining, role in the Russian law of treaties. The locus of the Russian revolutions during 1917 and largest and principal moving force behind the formation of the Union of Soviet Socialist Republics in 1922 was what became the RSFSR. With the formation of the USSR, however, the RSFSR became a minor actor in foreign relations of all types (although not completely excluded). When a compromise was reached in 1944 regarding membership of the Soviet union republics in the United Nations, only Ukraine and the Belorussian SSR were chosen to be founders of the Organization and to have full membership in their own right; the interests of the RSFSR were represented by the USSR. With the withdrawal of the RSFSR from the 1922 Treaty of the Union and secession from the USSR on December 12, 1991, the Russian Federation as the "legal-continuer" of the former Soviet Union returned to the international community as a full-fledged member.

Prior to formal secession from the USSR by means of denouncing the Treaty of the Union, however, the RSFSR had taken a number of measures to disengage from USSR legislation, on one hand, and to remain a party to international treaties of the USSR. In its Declaration of State Sovereignty of June 12, 1990, the RSFSR had established the "supremacy of the RSFSR Constitution and laws of the RSFSR throughout the territory of the RSFSR; the operation of acts of the USSR which are contrary to the sovereign rights of the RSFSR shall be suspended by the Republic on its territory."[10]

---

[9] See W E Butler, "*Jus* and *Lex* in Russian Law: A Discussion Agenda," in D J Galligan and M Kurkchiyan (eds.), *Law and Informal Practices: The Post-Communist Experience* (2003) 47–60; R S Wortman, *The Power of Language and Rhetoric in Russian Political History: Charismatic Words from the 18th to the 21st Centuries* (2018) 133–58.

[10] Translated in W E Butler, *Russian Public Law* (3rd edn.; 2013) 1–2.

No attempt was made in this formulation to address the international legal obligations of the USSR and their relevance to the sovereignty of the RSFSR.

In pursuance of the Declaration, the RSFSR adopted on October 24, 1990 the Law on the Operation of Acts of Agencies of the USSR on the Territory of the RSFSR.[11] According to this enactment, recognition would be accorded to the operation of laws and other acts of the highest agencies of State power of the USSR, edicts and other acts of the President of the USSR, acts of the Council of Ministers and of ministries and departments of the USSR only insofar as they were adopted within the powers transferred by the Russian Federation to the USSR in accordance with the Declaration and certain other enactments. Provided that USSR enactments met this test, they were of direct application on the territory of the RSFSR; if they violated the sovereignty of the Russian Federation, they were subject to suspension by the RSFSR Supreme Soviet or by the RSFSR Council of Ministers. However, if USSR enactments did not meet the criteria set out above, they would enter into force in the Russian Federation only after having been "ratified" by the RSFSR Supreme Soviet, RSFSR Council of Ministers, or empowered State agencies of the RSFSR respectively. The acts of agencies of the USSR prior to October 24, 1990 operated on the territory of the RSFSR unless they were suspended by the RSFSR Supreme Soviet or the RSFSR Council of Ministers.

This legislation affected the Russian law of treaties in at least two respects. First, insofar as treaties of the USSR had been ratified, confirmed, adopted, accepted, or acceded to by federal laws, decrees, or other enactments, all those enactments remained in force on the territory of the RSFSR. To this day, the 1978 USSR Law on treaties has not been repealed, although superseded in many respects by the 1995 Law on International Treaties of the Russian Federation.

Second, although the Law of October 24, 1990 made no specific mention of international treaties or other international documents themselves, it could be argued that insofar as treaties and agreements were ratified by a law of the USSR or consented to by decrees of the Government, or in the case of interdepartmental treaties, by decisions of the relevant USSR agencies, they were covered by the Law of October 24. No evidence has been found to suggest that the Law of October 24, 1990 was invoked to disengage

---

[11]   Translated in W E Butler, *Basic Legal Documents of the Russian Federation* (1992) 49–50.

from international legal obligations of any kind whatsoever. Alternatively, the Law of October 24, 1990 may be regarded as not extending to international treaties of the Soviet Union.

The issue of Soviet legislation was addressed in the Decree of the RSFSR dated December 12, 1991 ratifying the Agreement on the Creation of the Commonwealth of Independent States (point 2):

> For the purposes of creating conditions necessary for the realization of Article 11 of the said Agreement, to establish that the norms of the former USSR shall apply on the territory of the RSFSR until the adoption of respective legislative acts of the RSFSR in that part which is not contrary to the Constitution of the RSFSR, legislation of the RSFSR, and the present Agreement.[12]

In sum the legislation of the former USSR may apply on the territory of the Russian Federation unless (i) it has been expressly repealed or suspended; or (ii) it is contrary to the Constitution of the Russian Federation and other Russian legislation adopted after June 12, 1990; or (iii) it has become obsolete. Special provision was made in individual instances for USSR legislation to continue to operate even though Russian enactments were in force. An example was the 1991 Fundamental Principles of Civil Legislation of the USSR and Republics, stipulated to enter into force on January 1, 1992. Because the USSR had been dissolved before the date of its entry into force, it did not become legally binding. However, the Russian Federation by a Decree of the Supreme Soviet adopted July 14, 1992 did introduce it into operation as from August 3, 1992. The provisions of the Fundamental Principles concerned, *inter alia*, treaties; Article 170 preserved the priority of treaties of the USSR over inconsistent provisions of USSR civil legislation, which then applied, *mutatis mutandis*, to Russian Federation civil legislation.[13]

Moreover, the Family Code of the Russian Federation recognizes legal relations established under prerevolutionary Russian and Soviet legislation, and also relations arising under international treaties of the Russian Empire, irrespective of whether those treaties remain in force.

---

[12] Translated in Butler (n. 10) 51. It should be noted that the very ratification of the Agreement of December 12, 1991 was pursuant to the 1978 USSR Law on treaties, as there was no other to be drawn upon.

[13] See W E Butler, *Basic Documents on the Soviet Legal System* (3rd edn.; 1992) 177.

In its Decree of October 10, 2003, the Supreme Court of the Russian Federation reminded lower courts that "International treaties of the USSR which are binding upon the Russian Federation as the State-continuer of the USSR have been published in official publications of the Supreme Soviet of the USSR and Council of Ministers (or Cabinet of Ministers) of the USSR. The texts of the said treaties also have been published in the collections of international treaties of the USSR, but this publication was not official."[14]

Legislation

Constitution of the Russian Federation

At the level of positive law, we turn first to the classical Russian perception. The 1993 Constitution of the Russian Federation is regarded, by reason of being adopted by an all-people's referendum and by reason of its substance, as the highest source of man-made, or positive, law in the Russian Federation. The Constitution has "the highest legal force, direct effect" (Article 15), and other legal acts must not be contrary to the Constitution.

It should be noted that the 1993 Russian Constitution contains two "qualities" of norms. The "highest" are those contained in Chapters 1, 2, and 9, which may not be revised by the Federal Assembly of the Russian Federation. Rather, any proposal to revise them must be supported by three-fifths of the total numbers of the lower and upper chambers of the Federal Assembly and then convoke a Constitutional Assembly, which in turn must either confirm the immutability of the Constitution or draft a new Constitution. If the latter course is followed, two-thirds of the members must approve the new Constitution or the Assembly must decide to submit the draft to a national referendum, which must be quorate (more than 50 percent of registered voters taking part) and must approve the Constitution by more than half of the voters. This deliberately complex procedure has never been undertaken or seriously proposed. The provisions on international treaties and human rights fall within Chapters 1 and 2 of the Constitution.[15] Article 16(2), for example, provides that no other provisions of the Constitution may be contrary to that chapter.

---

[14] Point 4, trans. in Butler (n. 10) 50.
[15] Article 135, 1993 Constitution; trans in ibid, 30.

The Constitution being the "highest law," all other enactments are subordinate [подзаконный, literally, sub-law]. Note that the term "delegated legislation" is avoided, for subordinate acts may be issued without delegation so long as they are "on the basis and in execution of" the acts of superior agencies or agencies at the same level as the issuing organ. Although legislation is the paramount source of positive law in Russia, hierarchical relationships among subordinate acts containing legal rules (normative) are confused and confusing—a situation aggravated by the existence of treaties of the Russian Federation.

Federal Assembly

Beneath the 1993 Russian Constitution in the hierarchy of normative legal acts are Federal Constitutional Laws and Federal Laws. The Russian Constitution confers on the bicameral Federal Assembly of the Russian Federation the right to adopt (a) constitutional laws specially enumerated in the Constitution; and (b) federal laws. A qualified majority is required to adopt a Federal Constitutional Law in the Federal Assembly of the Russian Federation, whereas a simple majority is sufficient for a Federal Law. A Federal Law may also be adopted by referendum. Treaties are ratified by an ordinary Federal Law. A Federal Constitutional Law is superior in the hierarchy of laws to a Federal Law but, in practice, they are not concerned with treaties. Nonetheless, their superiority in the hierarchy of legislation raises the question of whether the superiority of international treaties set out in Article 15(4) of the Constitution applies only to federal laws (and all other inferior normative legal acts) or includes federal constitutional laws.

In addition, the bicameral Federal Assembly (the State Duma is the lower chamber; the Soviet of the Federation is the senior chamber) may adopt decrees relegated specifically to their jurisdiction, including decrees relating to certain internal matters, for example, the decision to consider a treaty for potential ratification.

President of Russian Federation

The President of the Russian Federation adopts enactments in the form of an edict [указ] and regulation [распоряжение]. These must not be contrary to either the Constitution or to federal constitutional laws or federal laws. Both the edict and the regulation are a form of subordinate legislation, and the Constitution does not specify which type of enactment should be used for what purpose. In practice, both, but especially the edict, may deal with treaty matters.

Government of Russian Federation

Executive power in the Russian Federation is exercised by the Government, which "on the basis of and in execution of" the Constitution, federal constitutional laws, federal laws, and normative edicts of the President, adopts enactments in the form of a decree [постановление] or regulation [распоряжение]. The procedure for the submission, preparation, and consideration of draft enactments by the Government is enormously complex and regulated in detail by the Reglament of the Government of the Russian Federation, confirmed by Decree of the Government of June 1, 2004, as amended.[16] There are special provisions relating to proposals for the conclusion, confirmation, or ratification of treaties.

Decrees and regulations of the Government are binding throughout the Russian Federation without further confirmation by the Federal Assembly or President and without further action by subjects of the Russian Federation. Dozens each year relate to treaties.

Ministries and Departments

The various ministries and departments of the Russian Federation may enter into what are called "interdepartmental" treaties with analogous entities in foreign States. These in each instance require a set of internal enactments within the respective ministry or department and/or the Government at large. In practice the denominations of ministry and ministerial enactments are determined by statutes on the ministries or State committees, and the terminology of the past largely survives. Among the relevant denominations are decrees, instructions, instructive regulations, and orders [приказ].

---

[16] Trans in W E Butler, *Russia & The Republics: Legal Materials* (loose-leaf service; 2006–).

Russian Federation ministries and officials are empowered to issue, and frequently do, joint instructions and other joint normative acts. These acquire no greater force in the hierarchy of normative acts by reason of their joint issuance. Other State agencies or officials holding equivalent positions within the State system as ministries or federal services or ministers or heads of federal services promulgate enactments of various appellations. These may relate to the conclusion, confirmation, termination, or implementation of treaties.

State Corporations

Beginning in 2003, the Russian Federation began to create State corporations to undertake certain administrative, managerial, and production tasks. Eight have been created in all, of which one has been liquidated and one transformed into an open joint-stock society. Of the remaining six, two have been given powers and functions relating to international cooperation, including the conclusion and implementation of international treaties of the Russian Federation. Rosatom, formed by Federal Law of December 1, 2007, is empowered as follows:

Article 14. Powers and Functions of Corporation with Regard to Participation in International Cooperation in Domain of Use of Atomic Energy

1. The Corporation shall ensure within the limits of its competence the fulfillment of obligations of the Russian Federation under international treaties of the Russian Federation and effectuation of the rights of Russian Party arising from these treaties if such treaties regulate questions within the competence of the Corporation.

2. The Corporation shall be an empowered organization, submit to the President of the Russian Federation or Government of the Russian Federation proposals concerning the conclusion, fulfillment, and termination of international treaties of the Russian Federation in accordance with the Federal Law of 15 July 1995, No. 101-ФЗ, 'On International Treaties of the Russian Federation'. The Corporation shall conclude international treaties of an interdepartmental character with regard to questions within its competence in accordance with the said Federal Law.

The international treaties concluded by Rosatom are relegated to the category of treaties of an interdepartmental character.

The other State Corporation so empowered is Roskosmos, which works in the domain of outer space activity. The formulation of its treaty-making powers differs slightly from Rosatom, the relevant Federal Law providing:

Article 13. Powers and Functions of Corporation with Regard to Participation in International Activity for the Research and Use of Outer Space

1. The Corporation shall ensure within the limits of its competence the fulfillment of obligations of the Russian Federation under international treaties of the Russian Federation and the effectuation of the rights of the Russian Federation arising from these treaties.

2. The Corporation in accordance with the Federal Law of 15 July 1995, No. 101-ФЗ, 'On International Treaties of the Russian Federation', shall be an empowered organization and conclude within the limits of its competence international treaties of the Russian Federation of an interdepartmental character within the established sphere of activity in accordance with the said Federal Law....

Treaties concluded by Roskosmos likewise are classified as treaties of an interdepartmental character of the Russian Federation.

Subjects of the Russian Federation

The presently eighty-five subjects of the Russian Federation enter into treaties with foreign States or entities thereof, between themselves, and with the Russian Federation itself. Which, if any, of these treaties are deemed to be "international treaties of the Russian Federation" or are classified as constitutional treaties is a subject unto itself and treated in chapter six of the present work.

The Russian Federation is a treaty-based structure. On March 31, 1992 the Russian Federation concluded three treaties, collectively known in the singular as the "Treaty of the Federation" but in fact three separate documents, as a step toward drafting a new Constitution of the Russian Federation to replace the Soviet version adopted in 1978, as amended in

1989, 1990 (three times), 1991 (twice), and 1992 (three times). These "Treaty of the Federation" (a collective noun in this case) or "Treaties of the Federation" (there are three) are an integral part of the 1993 Russian Constitution.

Local Self-Government

Agencies of "local self-government" bear different names in various municipalities, although the term "soviet" continues to be widely used. They adopt decisions within the limits of their powers granted to them by legislation of the Russian Federation. Three cities of Russia (Moscow, St Petersburg, Sevastopol) are classified constitutionally as "subjects of the Federation" and therefore fall under the section above.

Agencies of local self-government could, for example, enter into treaties with municipalities in foreign States (assuming the foreign municipalities had treaty-making capacity). This is provided for by Article 17(1)(8) of the Federal Law "On General Principles of the Organization of Local Self-Government in the Russian Federation,"[17] which provides:

Article 17. Powers of Agencies of Local Self-Government with Regard to Deciding Questions of Local Significance

1. For the purposes of deciding questions of local significance, agencies of local self-government of settlements, municipal districts, municipal national areas, city national areas, city national areas with an intra-city division or intra-city areas shall possess the following powers [as amended May 27, 2014, No. 136-ФЗ, and May 1, 2019, No. 87-ФЗ]:

...

(8) effectuation of international and foreign economic ties in accordance with federal laws;

...

Russian agencies of local self-government have in fact adopted legislation enabling links with foreign municipalities to be established. Commonly

---

[17] СЗ РФ (2003) no 40, item 3822, as amended to July 3, 2019.

these encourage cultural, educational, or economic relations, twinned towns being a frequently encountered arrangement. Surgut, for example, has arrangements with municipalities in China, Greece, and Hungary.[18] There seem to be no formal requirements that the Ministry of Foreign Affairs of the Russian Federation approve or sanction such arrangements, although these ties must be in accordance with federal laws. Such authorization would imply that a treaty of his nature engaged the responsibility of the Russian Federation.

Binding Acts of International Organizations

Article 25 of the United Nations Charter provides that members of the United Nations "agree to accept and carry out the decisions of the Security Council in accordance with the present Charter." Decisions of the Security Council on other than procedural matters are made by an affirmative vote of nine members, including the concurring votes of the permanent members, provided that under certain conditions a party to a dispute shall abstain from voting (Article 27).

On May 1, 2019 the Russian Federation amended the Federal Law on Special Economic Measures as follows:[19]

---

[18] See N P Aleshkova, Конституционно-правовые основы муниципального правотворчества в Российской Федерации [*Constitutional Legal Foundations of Municipal Law-Making in the Russian Federation*] (Ekaterinburg, 2012).

[19] СЗ РФ (2007) no. 1(I), item 44; (2019) no. 18, item 2207. This change was in a sense foreshadowed in the 2013 Draft Federal Law on Normative Legal Acts in the Russian Federation, Article 19 of which was devoted to "Decisions of International Organizations Having a Binding Character for the Russian Federation in the Legal System of the Russian Federation." The draft provided that: "Decisions of international organizations having a binding character for the Russian Federation are an integral part of the legal system of the Russian Federation and subject to good-faith fulfillment" (Article 19(1)). The draft continued: "The binding character of decisions of international organizations shall be established in accordance with the constitutive international treaty determining the legal status and competence of the respective international organization" (Article 19(2)). The "provisions of officially published decisions of international organizations having a binding character for the Russian Federation not requiring the issuance of laws and subordinate normative legal acts for realization shall operate in the Russian Federation directly. Respective laws and subordinate normative legal acts shall be adopted for the effectuation of other provisions of the decisions of international organizations having a binding character for the Russian Federation" (Article 19(3)). See T Ia Khabrieva (ed.), Проект федерального закона о нормативных правовых актах в Российской Федерации (инициативный законопроект) [*Draft Federal Law on Normative Legal Acts in the Russian Federation (Initiative Draft Law)*] (2013) 23.

Article 6. Publication of Resolutions of United Nations Security Council Providing for Introduction, Change, Suspension, or Revocation of Enforcement Measures [added May 1, 2019]

1. Resolutions of the United Nations Security Council providing for the introduction, change, suspension, or revocation of enforcement measures shall be subject to official publication, which shall be considered to be the first publication of the full texts thereof in [Russian Newspaper] or first placement (or publication) on the "Official Internet-Portal of Legal Information" (www.pravo.gov.ru).

2. The texts of resolutions of the United Nations Security Council for official publication shall be provided by the empowered federal agency of executive power within two work days from the day following the day of their placement in the Russian language on the official internet-portal of the United Nations (www.un.org). The placement (or publication) of texts of United Nations Security Council resolutions of the "Official Internet-Portal of Legal Information" (www.pravo.gov.ru) shall be effectuated by the agency of executive power in the domain of State protection immediately after their provision by the empowered federal agency of executive power.

3. The empowered federal agency of executive power shall within two work days from the day following the day of adoption of the United Nations Security Council resolutions providing for the introduction, change, suspension, or revocation of enforcement measures in the procedure established by the empowered federal agency of executive power bring to the information of interested federal agency of executive power and other agencies and organizations additional information necessary for the fulfillment of the said resolutions, including the decisions of auxiliary organs of the United Nations Security Council concerning the inclusion of natural and juridical persons, and also organizations on the sanctions list of the United Nations Security Council and the exclusion thereof from this list.

Russian media understand the amendments of May 1, 2019 to mean that United Nations Security Council resolutions become "binding after the official publication" in either the newspaper so designated or the internet-portal of the Government of the Russian Federation. In effect, the Security Council resolution is viewed as an extension of an international treaty (United Nations Charter); these are not subject to ratification, of course, but inasmuch as the Charter requires members of the United Nations to implement them, they represent an application of the Treaty. Sergei Vershinin, Deputy Minister of Foreign Affairs of the Russian Federation, said at the time of amending the federal law, thirteen sanctions regimes introduced by the United Nations Security Council were in place and more than thirty Presidential edicts had been adopted to enforce them. The procedure for drafting the enforcement edicts had become so complicated in obtaining interdepartmental coordination and subsequent consideration in the Government and Presidential Administration, that the situation leading to the enforcement measure may have changed in the interim. Some draft edicts were obsolete before they were finally agreed.[20]

"Soft Law" Recommendatory International Acts

In Russian legal doctrine the term "soft law" has come to be used to designate municipal recommendatory documents of various types and, more commonly, acts adopted by international organs, agencies, organizations, conferences, or other bodies. The reference in Article 15(4) of the 1993 Russian Constitution to generally-recognized principles and norms of international law may be responsible, at least in part, for this:

> [T]he said constitutional principle is perceived by agencies of State power not only in the formal juridical sense. On the contrary, courts have elaborated its literal content and rely on virtually all elements of the international legal system—resolutions and recommendations of international organizations, decisions of international agencies, model acts, legal holdings and decisions of international judicial institutions.[21]

In many countries matters of approving "soft law" documents in some fashion would be left to the non-State sector insofar as these documents are adopted by non-State actors. These materials are by definition not

---

[20] Russian Information Agency "Novosti," May 1, 2019.
[21] S Marochkin, Действие и реализация норм международного права в правовой системе Российской Федерации [*Operation and Realization of Norms of International Law in the Legal System of the Russian Federation*] (2011) 280–1.

"international treaties"; nonetheless, they may have a role or impact in crystallizing "*opinio juris*" of the international community and influence State practice. In Russia the formalities of drafting and signing intergovernmental acts which are not treaties is regulated by the Statute on the Preparation and Signing of International Intergovernmental Acts Which are Not International Treaties of the Russian Federation, confirmed by Decree No. 79 of the Government of the Russian Federation on February 7, 2003.[22] The Statute regulates how decisions with Russia are to be prepared and adopted with regard to signing intergovernmental acts, irrespective of their names, with the governments of foreign States or with international organizations, or organs thereof, which do not fall into the category of international treaties. The Statute does not extend to international acts adopted by the international organizations acting autonomously. As a rule, the acts concerned are called declarations, memoranda, joint statements, plans, programs for cooperation, and the like. Such acts will not contain binding provisions, although they may refer to obligations assumed by the parties under treaties.

These materials represent a challenge to the hierarchy of normative acts, not least because they are not by definition normative acts. Nonetheless, they play a role in international life, and they are referred to with some frequency by Russian courts. It follows that such acts may not be in their content contrary to the 1993 Russian Constitution, international treaties of the Russian Federation, normative legal acts of the President or Government of the Russian Federation, or, most interestingly, "international acts previously signed by Russia which are not international treaties of the Russian Federation" (point 3).

The Constitutional Court of the Russian Federation has on a number of occasions made reference in its decisions to "international treaties and international legal acts," "international documents," and "international acts in the domain of human rights."[23] The Federal Law of the Russian Federation "On Communications" of July 7, 2003 requires the Government of Russia to determine procedures for the distribution and use of resources by taking into account the "recommendations of international organizations in which the Russian Federation is a participant" (Article 26).[24]

---

[22] СЗ РФ (2003) no. 7, item 647.
[23] See, among others, the Decree of the Constitutional Court of April 4, 1996, and the Ruling of the Constitutional Court of February 19, 2009. Available on Consultant Plus.
[24] СЗ РФ (2003) no. 28, item 2895, as amended.

Russian Judicial Practice

Whether and how Russian judicial practice may be a source of law in the Russian Federation is a comparatively new topic with its own history.[25] There was a certain amount of experience in the Soviet Union with international treaties and judicial decisions—more than has been traditionally imagined to be the case.[26] In the present study these matters are of sufficient import to justify a separate chapter (chapter seven, which appears below).

Customs of Business Turnover and Usages

These are species of customary law and may originate in international treaties and/or in Russian legislation. Usages are mentioned, for example, in the 1980 United Nations Convention on Contracts for the International Sale of Goods (Article 9)—to which the Russian Federation is a party—and customs of business turnover in the Civil Code of the Russian Federation (Article 5), 1999 Merchant Shipping Code of the Russian Federation, and 1993 Law on International Commercial Arbitration. They comprise rules of behavior formed and extensively applied in any domain of entrepreneurial activity and have not been created or provided for by legislation. Treaties may be or contain evidence of customs of business turnover or usages. Generally, they are fixed in commercial or entrepreneurial documents, including industry manuals or standards. They may not be applied if they are contrary either to legislation or to the provisions of a contract binding upon the parties; that is, they may not override legislation or contractual provisions agreed by the parties.

Customs of business turnover or usages may exist at any level: local, regional, national, or international, and they may appertain to branches of industry or to spheres of activity, or be inter-branch in character.

The term is broadly construed to encompass commercial customs, business customs, trade customs, and so on, and in the view of many jurists, also usages. That customs of business turnover or usages have not been provided for by "legislation" means any normative legal acts, including laws, of presidential, governmental, or departmental origin. Such customs or usages

---

[25] See A Vereshchagin, *Judicial Law-Making in Post-Soviet Russia* (2007).
[26] S Marochkin, *The Operation of International Law in the Russian Legal System: A Changing Approach* (2019) xiv.

must be stable and generally-recognized in the respective domain of entrepreneurial activity and may be oral or written. The existence of a custom or usage is a matter of proof. They are dispositive, and parties may therefore include them or incorporate contractual provisions which are contrary to them. Such customs or usages need not be of general application within their own sphere; that is, they could apply solely to foreigners and stateless persons.

Acts of the Union State

Another treaty-creation, mostly unknown in the western world, is the Union State, formed by a Treaty concluded on December 8, 1999 between the Russian Federation and Belarus. The Union State is precisely what it says—a newly formed supranational entity created by two independent States. The Union State has its own organs: the High State Council, the Parliament of the Union State, the Council of Ministers, the Court of the Union State, and the Counting Chamber (an auditing body intended primarily to oversee the proper expenditure of the budget of the Union). Within their competence, the agencies of the Union State adopt normative legal acts provided for by the Treaty of December 8, 1999: laws, fundamental principles of legislation, decrees, decrees, directives, and resolutions, recommendations, and opinions.

These normative legal acts are adopted in implementation of the Treaty of December 8, 1999. In this sense, they may be regarded as an extension of the treaty. On matters within the exclusive jurisdiction of the Union State as determined by the treaty, decrets and decrees are adopted. Agencies of the Union State adopt decrets and decrees pursuant to the laws of the Union State. With regard to questions within the joint jurisdiction of the Union States and the States-parties, fundamental principles of legislation, directives, and resolutions are enacted. The States-parties are then to implement these normative legal acts by adopting their respective normative legal acts. Although this terminology is not used, it would appear that enactments of the Union State serve as the foundation for "subordinate" legislation by Russia and Belarus respectively.

Enactments of the Union State ultimately have a "treaty origin" and face similar problems in being integrated into the national legal systems of Russia and Belarus. Laws and decrees intended for general application are binding in all respects and after their official publication are subject to direct application on the territory of Russia and Belarus. Should there be a conflict between a law or decret of the Union State and norms of municipal law of Russia or Belarus, the norm of the law or decret of the Union State has preferential force, except that this rule does not apply in the event of a conflict with norms contained in the constitutions and constitutional acts of Russia or Belarus.

In effect, the Treaty of December 8, 1999 is placed in an interesting situation. It is intended to create a new supranational entity, to accomplish a "merger" between Russia and Belarus. But its enactments—and presumably the treaty itself—remain subject to the Russian and Belarus constitutions; that is, occupy a lower place in the hierarchy of sources of law. By its nature and provisions, the Treaty of December 8, 1999 is a more ambitious integrative exercise than, for example, Eurasian economic integration, but in the end is subject to the constraints of the national legal system. With respect to Russia, the 1999 Treaty is governed by Article 15(4) of the 1993 Russian Constitution and therefore an integral part of the Russian legal system, but is conceptually designed to create a super-State above the Russian Constitution. Moreover, there has been no suggestion that the 1999 Treaty is a *sui generis* document not subject, for example, to the 1969 Vienna Convention on the Law of Treaties—to which both Russia and Belarus are parties.

Decrees of the Union State and its agencies are binding in all respects upon the States-parties and the natural and juridical persons to whom they are addressed. Directives are binding upon each State-party to whom they are addressed, but the agencies of the respective State retain freedom of choice as to the forms and methods of action. Resolutions are acts by means of which the current activities of agencies of the Union State are ensured. Decisions of the Court of the Union State are binding and subject to official publication; only Russia, Belarus, and agencies of the Union State may transfer questions for the Court to consider; these must be connected with the interpretation and application of the 1999 Treaty or with normative legal acts of the Union State.

Documents of the Commonwealth of Independent States

Since its formation in December 1991, the Commonwealth of Independent States (CIS) has generated more than 16,000 normative documents. The forms are various: international treaties and agreements, decisions of CIS organs, protocols, among others. Publication is irregular, although many matters addressed by these documents are of considerable legal importance. Insofar as these documents are in form and/or substance international treaties, they are under Article 15(4) of the 1993 Russian Constitution an integral part of the Russian legal system. The great majority of these documents would be classified as treaties of an interdepartmental character. Here there are minimal overtones of supranationality. The CIS documents would appear to readily fall into the category of classical international treaties adopted within an international organization.

Generally-Recognized and Customary Principles of International Law

Generally-recognized principles and norms of international law are, according to Article 15(4) of the 1993 Russian Constitution, an integral part of the legal system of the Russian Federation. This formulation, with slight adjustments, has been incorporated in the 1995 Law on treaties (Article 5). In the view of the present writer, the formal recognition of generally-recognized principles and norms of international law as part of the Russian legal system is among the significant changes of the twentieth century in the development of Russian law.

Russian international legal doctrine accepts that "generally-recognized" principles of international law, at a minimum, encompass *jus cogens* norms, although the Russian-language text of the 1969 Vienna Convention on the Law of Treaties translates "*jus cogens*" as "imperative" rules of international law—which is a lower standard than the English term used in the Vienna Convention: "peremptory." The Supreme Court of the Russian Federation paraphrased Article 53 of the 1969 Vienna Convention in the Plenum Decree of October 10, 2003, declaring that "by generally-recognized principles of international law should be understood the basic imperative norms of international law adopted and recognized by the international community of States as a whole, deviation from which is inadmissible."

The implications of translating *jus cogens* as merely imperative can lead to unusual doctrinal characterizations. For example: with respect to the legal regime of foreigners and stateless persons, "the discrimination against foreigners for indicia of race, sex, confession of faith, and so on is prohibited" even though "no rights and duties of foreigners have been consolidated expressly in norms of international law." The domestic legislation of a State concerning foreigners must "take into account" its international obligations, and to legislate or act outside the framework of those obligations would "signify a violation of generally-recognized principles of international law."[27]

Russian doctrinal writings have identified the 1948 Universal Declaration of Human Rights and the 1966 International Covenant on Civil and Political Rights as containing rules deemed to be generally-recognized even though the Declaration is a recommendatory United Nations General Assembly resolution and the 1966 Covenant is a treaty not universally ratified. These authors believe State practice of the international community has deemed these documents to contain generally-recognized principles.

The precise place of generally-recognized norms of international law within the Russian legal system is not determined by the 1993 Russian Constitution. The status of such norms appears to fall into two distinct categories, depending upon the subject-matter of the norms. Article 15(4), in providing that "generally-recognized principles and norms of international law ... are an integral part of the Russian legal system," (a) accepts generally-recognized principles and norms of international law as part of the Russian legal system, including Russian law, and (b) places such principles and norms side by side with norms of Russian municipal law. The formulation may imply that such norms and principles are incorporated into domestic Russian law and overridden by norms of Russian law later in time or *lex specialis*. That is, Article 15(4) does not give generally-recognized principles and norms of international law priority over inconsistent provisions of Russian municipal law.

The 1993 Russian Constitution placed human rights at the foundation of the legal system, providing that the basic rights and freedoms

---

[27] Iu A Dmitriev and K A Korsik, Правовое положение иностранцев в Российской Федерации [*Legal Status of Foreigners in the Russian Federation*] (1997) 30. This is not exactly so. Foreign citizens and stateless persons are human beings, and their rights originate in their status as such, as recognized in Article 1 of the 1966 human rights covenants, rather than in domestic legislation, although this provision is incorporated in Article 17(2) of the 1993 Russian Constitution.

contained in the 1993 Constitution must not be construed as a denial or impingement on other generally-recognized rights and freedoms of man and citizen, and that laws repealing or abridging the rights of man and citizen may not be adopted (Article 55). The 1993 Constitution (Article 17) further provides that "the rights and freedoms of man and citizen shall be recognized and guaranteed in the Russian Constitution according to generally-recognized principles and norms of international law and in accordance with the present Constitution." This formulation places international law ahead of the Constitution and, in so doing, imparts to international law a special status in the Russian legal system that is not accorded to other generally-recognized norms of international law. This formulation also would appear to extend to all generally-recognized principles and norms of international human rights law and not merely, in the language of the Plenum of the Russian Supreme Court, to the "principle of universal respect for human rights."

It arguably follows that the applicable law clauses in contracts which choose Russian law automatically incorporate the generally-recognized principles and norms of international law, customary rules of international law, and the provisions of international treaties of the Russian Federation.

Some Russian jurists equate "generally-recognized principles and norms" with "customary rules" of international law. Russian legal doctrine has in the post-Soviet era been more favorably disposed toward customary international law. In some instances Russian courts have recognized the existence of and applied generally-recognized rules of international law as an integral part of the Russian legal system. In one of the *Khodorovsky* cases, for example, The Body of Principles for the Protection of All Persons under any Form of Detention or Imprisonment, adopted by United Nations General Assembly Resolution 43/173 of December 9, 1988 was deemed to reflect generally-recognized principles of international law and applied as such by a Russian court.[28] Insofar as that Body of Principles (Principle 18) was inconsistent with the Rules of Internal Discipline in Penitentiary Institutions (point 83), confirmed November 3, 2005, point 83 of the Rules was unconstitutional.

---

[28] For the decision, see 133 *International Law Reports* 365–70.

International Treaties of Russian Federation

The Union of Soviet Socialist Republics acceded to the 1969 Vienna Convention on the Law of Treaties with effect from April 29, 1986.[29] The 1995 Federal Law on International Treaties of the Russian Federation was intended to fully reflect the provisions of the 1969 Vienna Convention and the new stature of international treaties within the Russian legal system pursuant to Article 15 of the 1993 Russian Constitution. Some account is taken in the 1995 Law on Treaties of the 1986 Vienna Convention on the Law of Treaties Between States and International Organizations or Between International Organizations, although Russia is not a signatory of that Convention, nor is Russia a signatory to the 1978 Vienna Convention on the Legal Succession of States with Respect to Treaties.

The definition of a treaty is incorporated and adapted to Russian circumstances in the 1995 Law on Treaties from the 1969 Vienna Convention. The distinction among inter-State, intergovernmental, and interdepartmental treaties—which owes its origins in Russia to Soviet doctrinal writings and the 1978 USSR Law on the Procedure for the Conclusion, Execution, and Denunciation of International Treaties, was carried over to the 1995 Law on Treaties.[30]

Inter-State treaties are those concluded in the name of the highest agencies of State power—the State in the person of the President, in the name of the Russian Federation. Intergovernmental treaties are those concluded in the name of the Government of the Russian Federation, whereas those concluded in the name of federal agencies of executive power or a designated State Corporation are treaties of an interdepartmental character. Whether a particular treaty falls into one or the other categories is a matter partly for the 1993 Russian Constitution, the jurisdiction of the State agencies concerned, and policy decisions taken by the parties to the treaty and/or the governments concerned.

---

[29] See A N Talalaev, Венская конвенция о праве международных договоров. Комментарий [*Vienna Convention on the Law of International Treaties. Commentary*] (1997).

[30] For the text of the 1978 Law, see W E Butler, *The Law of Treaties in Russia and the Commonwealth of Independent States: Text and Commentary* (2002) 218–29. All the former Soviet republics inherited this classification of international treaties and all, without exception, have incorporated the distinction into their respective laws on international treaties.

This tri-tiered classification of treaties, however, can be misleading with respect to the status of a treaty under international law because the classification into "tiers," especially insofar as embedded in Soviet and post-Soviet treaty legislation, has led to an inaccuracy of expression widely encountered in legislative and treaty practice. The problem is with the expression "in the name of"—a term of representation and, in civil law transactions, often accompanied by the words "and on behalf of." Only States and international organizations conclude treaties; what agency of the State or organ of an international organization and/or what natural persons act in their respective name is a matter of choice for the parties and often dictated by constitutional or other legislative provisions.[31] The expression is an abbreviated formulation of convenience—but is sometimes misunderstood to mean that the State organs and officials are somehow entering into a treaty in their own name, or that the State does not bear responsibility for and is not a party to the treaty concerned.

The true position under international law is not particularly contentious in international-legal doctrine and practice. The United Nations General Assembly confirmed the position, *inter alia*, in Resolution A56/83, of December 12, 2001, "Responsibility of States for Internationally Wrongful Acts":

Chapter II
Attribution of Conduct to a State

Article 4
Conduct of Organs of a State
1. The conduct of any State organ shall be considered an act of that State under international law, whether the organ exercises legislative, executive, or judicial, or any other functions, whatever position it holds in the organization of the State, and whatever its character as an organ of the central government or a territorial unit of the State.
2. An organ includes any person or entity which has that status in accordance with the internal law of the State.

---

[31] See A N Morozov, "Международные межведомственные договоры СССР: опыт и со временная практика Росссийской Федерации" ["International Interdepartmental Treaties of the USSR: Experience and Contemporary Practice of the Russian Federation"], Журнал ро ссийского права [*Journal of Russian Law*], no. 2 (2008) 106.

Article 5
Conduct of Persons or Entities Exercising Elements
of Governmental Authority
The conduct of a person or entity which is not an organ of the State under article 4 but which is empowered by the law of that State to exercise elements of the governmental authority shall be considered an act of the State under international law, provided the person or entity is acting in that capacity in the particular instance.

Morozov pointed out the implications:

The moment noted has significance not only from a theoretical, but a practical, point of view. The fact is that an international treaty imposes international-legal obligations on the State as a whole, and, consequently, also on its organs, namely the State as a whole acquired all those rights which have been established in a particular international treaty. As already indicated, namely the State and not the ministry or department according to international law bears responsibility for such an international treaty.[32]

The provision in Article 15(4) of the 1993 Russian Constitution that international treaties of the Russian Federation take precedence over an inconsistent law was known, as noted above, to Soviet law, but in Russia has been elevated for the first time to a rule of constitutional stature. The rule is repeated verbatim in dozens of other federal laws and codes, although by reason of its constitutional stature and generality, such repetition would appear to be superfluous. A literal interpretation of the provision requires that it extend to all treaties of the Russian Federation, including those that are intergovernmental and interdepartmental. The Plenum of the Supreme Court of the Russian Federation in its Decree of October 10, 2003 has concluded otherwise: "consent to the bindingness of an international treaty for the Russian Federation must be expressed in the form of a federal law" (point 5). It follows, declared the Plenum, that the "rules of an international treaty of the Russian Federation in force, consent to the bindingness of which was adopted in the form of a federal law, shall have priority in application with respect to laws of the Russian Federation" (point 8). Treaties

---

[32] Ibid.

of the Russian Federation whose binding force was not consented to in the form of a federal law (that is, not ratified)—which would be intergovernmental or interdepartmental treaties—have priority only with respect to subordinate normative acts issued by the agency of State power that concluded the said treaty.

Doctrine

The teachings and writings of Russian jurists have no formal place among the sources of Russian law. It is exceptional for Russian courts to cite the published works of jurists when issuing a decree or judgment, although such examples are known.[33] The State Duma of the Federal Assembly of the Russian Federation cited Russian doctrinal writings in general to support its understanding of the definition of a normative legal act in Russian law: noting the absence of a definition of a "normative legal act" in Russian legislation, the Duma said that "however, in legal doctrine it is accepted to proceed from the fact that … "; the definition of a normative legal act which the Duma derived from Russian legal doctrine has since been incorporated into a 2007 Order of the Ministry of Justice confirming the rules for drafting normative legal acts.

Insofar, however, as doctrinal writings are a subsidiary source of international law, they would be recognized in Russia as such in the domain of Russian foreign relations law and public international law, including the Russian law of treaties.

---

[33] See the Ruling of the Arbitrazh Court, City of Moscow, on the Enforcement of a Foreign Judicial Decision, of December 21, 2005, where English doctrinal writings were cited. The Ruling is translated in *Russian Law: Theory and Practice*, no. 1 (2008) 128–36. Dicey and Morris on *Conflicts of Law* was cited by the court in support of the proposition that the Common Law accepted the possibility that a foreign court judgment might be enforced in English courts without the existence of an international treaty authorizing such recognition and enforcement.

3

Contemporary Treaty-Making in the Russian Federation

Having considered the formal and informal sources of Russian treaty law, it is appropriate to consider how decisions are made to enter into an international treaty of the Russian Federation and what standard procedures are expected to be followed. The 1969 Vienna Convention on the Law of Treaties and Russian international legal doctrine offer general guidance, and certain requirements are imposed by the 1993 Russian Constitution, 1995 Law on treaties, edicts of the President and decrees or regulations of the Government, other federal laws, and subordinate legal acts of the Russian Federation.

That still leaves the issue of how, within a vast government, uniformity of approach and understanding is achieved with respect to treaty-making and how institutional memories are preserved with respect to past practices. One method of encouraging uniformity and explaining the reasons for certain policies and practices is the issuance of the "Recommendations on the Procedure for the Preparation of Materials Relating to the Conclusion and Termination of International Treaties of the Russian Federation."[1] These Recommendations were circulated internally by Letters of the Ministry of Foreign Affairs of the Russian Federation on April 1, 2009. They are summarized here with occasional interpolations, explanations, and annotations.

The Recommendations deal with the unseen part of treaty-making: the preparatory and implementing stages within the Russian State. These are important as an expression of the Russian understanding of international law and as a systemic response to how Russian State responsibility can best be ensured for the thousands of treaties concluded. In this sense the internal administration of treaty-making acts as a safeguard against ill-advised, or incompetently drafted, or inexperienced assumptions of legal risk by the State. The professed aim of the Recommendations is more modest: to

---

[1] Unpublished, but available on Consultant Plus, the text as of July 3, 2018.

establish a uniform approach to resolving the legal and technical-legal problems which arise when working with the materials relating to the conclusion or termination of an international treaty. They are a veritable manual for concluding treaties and are, in a real sense, the true source of the law of treaties in the Russian Federation.

Conclusion of Treaties

Powers to conclude treaties. What might be called "treaty-initiative" takes the form of a proposal submitted to the President or to the Government by federal agencies of executive power which have the competence to regulate issues that would be the subject-matter of a treaty or by organizations empowered to make such proposals by a federal law; for example, State corporations such as Rosatom or Roskosmos.

Advisability of concluding treaty. This is the fundamental policy determination of treaty-making, and under Russian law a variety of individuals and agencies may express views on whether a treaty ought to be concluded, including the federal agency submitting the proposal, the Ministry of Foreign Affairs, any other interested federal agencies, or organizations. Among the factors to be weighed are: that existing treaties in force do not regulate the respective matter satisfactorily; or potential parties to the treaty have expressed an interest in concluding it.

Proposals to Sign or Accede to Treaties Not Requiring Ratification. A proposal to sign or accede to a treaty which under Russian law is not subject to ratification is prepared by the lead department; it must be accompanied by a number of documents:

For proposals to be submitted directly to the President or to the Government: a draft accompanying letter to the Chairman of the Government or to the President which sets out the reasons for submitting the proposal and detailed references to the relevant federal law and concisely sets out the substance of the proposal and information about agreeing the proposal; a draft regulation of the Government or President; a draft treaty in the Russian language or attested copy of the treaty with, when necessary, a Russian translation of the text.

If the proposal is to sign a treaty whose text is already final (for example, other countries have signed the treaty; or an international conference has adopted the text, and so on), or to accede to a treaty, the set of documents must include an attested copy of the official text of such treaty in the Russian language.[2] If the treaty was not composed in the Russian language, in addition to an attested copy of the official treaty text in one foreign language (as a rule, English or French), the set of documents must include an attested translation of the treaty into Russian;[3]

In addition, an explanatory memorandum which sets out the reasons for concluding or acceding to the treaty, determines whether the treaty conforms to Russian legislation, considers possible financial, economic, and other consequences. Model formulations are suggested:

"Draft Agreement does not contain rules other than provided by legislation of the Russian Federation";

"Realization of the Agreement does not entail additional expenses from the federal budget."

If the treaty or draft thereof does not correspond to legislation, at a minimum the divergence with Russian law should be described in general. If additional expenses are involved, a detailed evaluation of such expenses should be set out and the sources from which it is planned to cover them. These matters are determined, as a rule, by the lead department.

If it is contemplated when signing or acceding to a treaty to enter a reservation or statement or to express objections to a reservation or statement made by another party(ies), the memorandum should include the reasons for this.

---

2 "Attestation" for these purposes is regulated by the "Procedure in Accordance with Which Copies of Official Texts of International Treaties are Attested by Federal Agencies of Executive Power," confirmed by the First Deputy Minister of Foreign Affairs, on October 24, 1994. This document provides that the "official texts" of international treaties are those examples signed in the name of the Contracting Parties. The Ministry of Foreign Affairs or other agency of federal executive power within whose competence are questions regulated by the treaty are the representing federal agency of executive power. Copies of an official text are attested by placing on the obverse side of the last sheet of the treaty the words "True Copy," and below the signature either of the Director of the Legal Department of the Ministry of Foreign Affairs or the head of the legal section of international affairs section or analogous subdivision of the representing federal agency of executive power. The copy is then sewn and sealed with the seal of the representing federal agency of executive power placed on the observe side of the final sheet below the signature referred to above. The text of a multilateral treaty officially published by the depositary is not attested.

3 Ibid. The translation into the Russian language of a treaty concluded only in foreign languages is attested and, after the Russian Federation has expressed consent to being bound by the treaty in the established procedure, the translation is regarded as official.

If the treaty or draft should be ratified, the explanatory memorandum must cite the specific details of the 1995 Law on treaties and provision of the treaty or to other federal laws which require ratification. Two model formulations are suggested:

> "The Draft Convention contains rules other than provided by legislation of the Russian Federation. In this connection after signature it will be subject to ratification on the basis of Article 15(1)(a) of the Federal Law "On International Treaties of the Russian Federation' ";
>
> "The Treaty affects questions of the defense capability of the Russian Federation. In this connection after signature it will be subject to ratification on the basis of Article 15(1)(d) of the Federal Law 'On International Treaties of the Russian Federation,' and also Article 15(2) of the said Law and Article 16(4) of the Treaty."

If the information is brief, it may be included in the letter to the President of the Russian Federation and an explanatory memorandum is not required.

Nearly all treaties will affect the interests of departments other than the lead department. In this case, the set of documents must include copies of letters from the agencies and organizations which agreed to the proposal being submitted, or, alternatively, if the documents are being submitted to the Government, copies of draft acts of the Government duly visaed by the executives of the respective agencies and organizations, or the deputies thereof, will suffice.

For proposals to be submitted by a federal agency of executive power to the Government for subsequent submission to the President (in instances when the submission of a proposal to the President to sign or accede to a treaty requires the preliminary consideration thereof by the Government): a draft accompanying letter to the Chairman of the Government setting out the reasons for the submission of the respective proposal (referring to specific provisions of the 1995 Law on treaties) and concisely setting out the substance of the proposal and information about agreeing it with other agencies of executive power; a draft accompanying letter from the Chairman of the Government to the President setting out the basic recommendations of the respective proposal with detailed references to the 1995 Law on treaties and information about the substance of the proposal submitted; a draft decree of the Government on the submission of the respective proposal to the President; a draft regulation of the President on signature of or accession to the treaty; the opinion of the Ministry of Justice of the Russian Federation on the draft decree of the Government; together with other relevant materials.

Preparation of draft treaty. Here treaty precedent plays a significant role. The suggestion is that "Russian treaty practice" should be used as guidance, drawing upon treaties published in the official gazettes, Internet Portal of the Russian Government, and other authoritative legal data bases.

Name, form, and structure of treaty. The most extensively used names of treaties, according to the Recommendations, are Convention, Treaty, Agreement, Protocol, Charter. Other names may be used, such as Memorandum on Cooperation, Memorandum on Mutual Understanding, Memorandum of Intent, if: (a) the foreign partners insist on this; or (b) the drafters have a common understanding that, irrespective of its name, the document is an international treaty; that is, creates rights and obligations regulated by international law.

Treaties may be drawn up as a single document, in which case the names above are usually used. Treaties in the form of an exchange of notes or letters are, as a rule, called an Agreement. In Russian treaty practice it is not acceptable to conclude treaties subject to ratification in the form of an exchange of notes or as interdepartmental treaties. A draft treaty will, as a rule, consist of the preamble, basic substantive part, and concluding provisions with, when necessary, annexes.

Title of treaty. The recommendation is that the title be concise and correspond strictly to the object or subject-matter of the treaty as determined in the text of the draft. Both parties are usually specified in the title of a bilateral treaty. In the case of an inter-State treaty, it is indicated that the treaty is concluded "between the Russian Federation and [official name of the other party]"; in the case of an intergovernmental treaty, "between the Government of the Russian Federation and the Government of [official name of the other party]"; in the title of a treaty of an inter-departmental character, "between [full name of the federal agency of executive power of the Russian Federation or State corporation] and the [full name of the department of the other State]." If the name "Russian Federation" is not part of the official name of the federal agency of executive power (Federal Customs Service), it is recommended to include the term "Russian Federation" in parenthesis after the name of the agency.

If the title of the treaty contains the name of another treaty in which the parties are mentioned, one may omit mention of the parties: for example, "Protocol on Making Changes in the Agreement between the Government of the Russian Federation and Government of the Chinese People's Republic on Visa-Free Group Tourist Trips of 29 February 2000," not repeating the names of the two governments.

Preamble of treaty. If a preamble to a treaty is proposed, it should proceed from the advisability of concisely consolidating the reasons or purposes which guided the parties when concluding the treaty. In a bilateral treaty it is suggested the preamble not exceed three or four provisions, but in a multilateral treaty the preamble may be longer. The preamble should not include obligations or the definition of terms used in the treaty. And, it is recommended that the preamble to treaties of an interdepartmental character not contain references to generally-recognized principles of international law or norms of international law, including the principles of the United Nations Charter or the Organization of Security and Cooperation in Europe regulating relations between States.

This last recommendation is a curious one, for it suggests that an interdepartmental treaty is not a treaty concluded under international law and that the State responsibility under the treaty is absent.

Preambles, it is suggested, should differ in matters other than length when they preface a bilateral treaty or a multilateral treaty. At the beginning of the preamble of an inter-State treaty it is indicated: "The Russian Federation and [official name of the other party]"; in the case of an intergovernmental treaty: "The Government of the Russian Federation and the Government of [official name of the other party]." For treaties of an interdepartmental character, however, the matter is more complex. The practice is to use the full name of the departments concerned from each side and then an accepted abbreviation of the departmental name.

Once the full name of the States-parties is given in the preamble of a bilateral treaty, subsequent references may be collectively to the "Contracting Parties" or individually to the "Contracting Party."

A multilateral treaty usually commences in the preamble with the "Contracting Parties" or the "Parties." In the case of so-called "diagonal" treaties—for example, concluded in the name of the State on one side and by the Government on the other—international treaty practice is not uniform. If the subject-matter of a treaty, for example, under Russian law is relegated to the competence of the Government but in the foreign power is beyond the competence of the Government, the treaty should be concluded at the inter-State level. If the subject-matter of the treaty is relegated to the competence of one department in one State but to two or more departments in the other party, the treaty must be concluded, at a minimum, at the intergovernmental level.

The preamble of a multilateral treaty should not enumerate the names of the parties. In a bilateral treaty the preamble should not indicate the personal names of those empowered to sign the treaty. The Recommendations suggest avoiding such formulations as: "The States-Parties of the present Treaty in the person of the Government ..." or the "Governments of the States-Parties of the present Treaty...".

In order to avoid any ambiguity created by the formulations, the Recommendations reiterate that "irrespective of the level of the conclusion of a treaty (inter-State, intergovernmental, inter-departmental), States are the participants thereof from the viewpoint of international law. The obligations placed on the 'Parties' under an intergovernmental treaty or treaty of an interdepartmental character are obligations of the respective States, and not only of those agencies in whose name the treaty was concluded."

When references are made in the preamble or the text of a treaty to documents, the names of such documents are cited in full, without abbreviations, indicating the date of their signature or adoption. This data must be verified against the respective documents.

Use of names of parties in treaty. It is not recommended to use the full names of the parties in the text of a treaty, but rather the term "Russian Party" (both words capitalized) or "Bangladesh Party," or, collectively, "Contracting Parties." If a treaty contains references to the rights and duties of State agencies, the full name of the State agencies should be given when first used and thereafter referred to as the "competent agencies of the Parties" or "competent agencies of the Party."

Basic text of treaty. The treaty, as a rule, is subdivided into Articles. Subdividing into points is permissible when the basic text is brief, only comprising several paragraphs or when the treaty is concluded by the exchange of notes or letters. The Article is the principal structural element of a treaty and contains a completed legal provision. When necessary, the Article may be subdivided into points, subpoints, or paragraphs, and subpoints, into paragraphs.

Articles bear a title or headnote reflecting their content. Points as a rule do not have headnotes. If the treaty text is divided into Articles, and in turn subdivided into points, the points do not have consecutive numbering in the text but are numbered anew within each Article. Subpoints are numbered anew within each point. When using letter designations for points or subpoints in treaty texts which are in different languages, use the letter of the same alphabet (for example, Latin letters). A voluminous and complex treaty will often be divided into Sections and Chapters, which will bear titles.

Definition of terms. It is recommended to define the basic terms used in the treaty and to devote a separate Article to this placed among the general provisions of the treaty. Such terms as "legislation" or "territory" when used in intergovernmental treaties should be used as phrases: "legislation of States of the Parties" or "national legislation of the Parties," and so on. In inter-State treaties the formulation should be "legislation of the Parties," and so on. The term "legislation" is always used in the singular.

Language of treaty. The basic text of the treaty should not set out the wishes and intentions of the parties.[4] The treaty provisions should be formulated as obligations, describing the rights and duties by using verbs and the present tense. For example: "The Korean Party transfers to the Russian Party … ". One should not use verbs in the future tense, or verbs of general vague content not enabling the concrete extent of the obligations of the parties to be determined (for example: "The Parties intended … ," "The Parties facilitate/promote measures … ," and the like). This does not, however, exclude the use of the English "shall" either in the English text or in translations of the Russian text into English, for even though the Russian may be drafted in the present tense, the use of "shall" is an indication of "being obliged," and not of the future tense.

The provisions of a draft treaty are formulated whenever possible by using the singular: for example, the construction "competent agency of each Party on the territory of its State in accordance with legislation of the last shall undertake … ," and not "competent agencies of the Parties in accordance with their national legislation on the territories of their States shall undertake … ".

Concluding provisions of treaty. The concluding part of a treaty should include provisions concerning entry into force, period of operation of the treaty, and the possibility of and procedure for termination. The possibility of provisional application of a treaty in full or in part is provided for only in exceptional instances when there is a real need to apply treaty provisions

---

[4] Issues of style, grammar, and proper usage arise frequently in practice and changes need to be agreed with the initiator of the treaty proposal. See S Ia Tsatkhlanov, "О некоторых аспектах заключения международных договоров Российской Федерации с иностранными государствами и международными организациями" ["On Certain Questions of the Conclusion of International Treaties of the Russian Federation with Foreign States and International Organizations"], in Ратификация международных договоров Российской Федерации [*Ratification of International Treaties of the Russian Federation*] (2007) II, 133.

prior to entry into force. A provision concerning provisional application should be so formulated that either the treaty as a whole or a specified part thereof are provisionally applied from a certain moment. Formulations should be avoided that do not precisely specify which provisions are subject to application. Under Article 23 of the 1995 Law on treaties, treaties provisionally applied which are subject to ratification must be submitted to the State Duma within six months from the day of the beginning of provisional application.

The concluding provisions mention ratification or confirmation if the treaty is subject to ratification or confirmation. This includes situations, except for interdepartmental treaties, when one of the parties considers ratification or confirmation of a treaty to be desirable or insists on this. If there are reasons to assume that the one or some parties need to perform various legal procedures for a treaty to enter into force (for example, one party has to ratify a treaty and the other party needs to confirm it, or one party needs to fulfill municipal procedures, and the other does not), as a rule the following formulation is used: "the treaty shall enter into force from the date of receipt of the last written notification concerning the fulfillment by the Parties of municipal procedures necessary for its entry into force."

It is recommended to include a provision concerning the making of changes or additions to a treaty only if a simplified procedure is introduced for this purpose (for example, by concluding protocols). The lack of such a provision in the treaty does not preclude the possibility of changes or additions because this would be consistent with norms of general international law. The treaty should not provide that "protocols on making changes in the treaty" will be an integral part of the treaty. Documents containing changes in a treaty are autonomous in each case (which often is not the case in commercial contractual practice). Only the changes themselves become an integral part of the treaty, but there is no need to indicate this in the treaty.

When concluding a bilateral treaty, the parties may determine the period of operation of the treaty. A common formulation provides the treaty will be in force for a period, say, of five years and will be automatically extended for another five-year period unless one of the parties informs the other about its intention to terminate the treaty at least six months before the expiration of the initial for any subsequent period. This means the treaty can be determined unilaterally only at the end of the initial or a subsequent period. By mutual agreement, however, the parties may terminate the treaty at any time.

The absence in a treaty of a time certain for the period of operation means the treaty is in force for an indefinite period unless it arises otherwise from other treaty provisions. For example: the Protocol between the Government of the Russian Federation and Cabinet of Ministers of Ukraine for Deliveries of Goods relating to Production Cooperation in 2005: the period of operation is confined to 2005 in the title of the treaty and the provisions of the Protocol provide for deliveries between January 1 and December 31, 2005. In this example, an expiration clause was not included in the treaty, but the title and periods of performance follow from the treaty provisions.

The concluding provision includes the place, date, number of original examples, and languages in which the texts of the treaty are drawn up. If the texts are drawn up in two or more languages and all texts have identical force, one may add that "in the event disagreements arise the texts in the English language may be used for the purpose of interpretation." But the formulation providing for the "preferential force" of any language should not be permitted if all the texts of the treaty have been declared to have identical force. The place and date of signature are usually not determined at the stage of submitting a proposal to conclude a treaty.

Treaties Concluded by Exchange of Notes or Letters

When concluding treaties in the form of an exchange of notes or letters, such notes or letters are identical, as a rule, in content. Usually the concluding paragraphs of the note or letter provides that the exchange thereof constitutes a treaty and commonly sets out the date for their entry into force. If it is proposed to conclude a treaty of an interdepartmental character by means of an exchange of letters (only the Ministry of Foreign Affairs of Russia may conclude interdepartmental treaties by an exchange of notes), such letters are, as a rule, identical in content. In the concluding part of the letter signed first, it is recommended to include a provision such as: "In the event of Your agreement with the aforesaid present Letter and Your positive reply in this question constitute an agreement between" [name of the federal agency of executive power of the Russian Federation] and the [name of the other contracting department]" followed by the precise name of the treaty, which shall enter into force from the date of the reply letter.

Draft Decisions to Sign or Accede to Treaties Not Requiring Ratification

These are key administrative matters within the Russian Federation to ensure that treaties undergo the proper review within the Government and that all interested or necessary parties on the Russian side concur with or at least have a voice in the decision to enter into a treaty with a foreign Government or department. If for any reason the provisions were not complied with, it is an interesting question whether "defects" in the administrative review of a draft treaty required by Russian law "taint" the validity of the treaty or whether the foreign Contracting Party or depositary have a duty to ascertain that all the procedures provided by law have in fact been complied with.

Insofar as such procedures can be known by foreign parties, due diligence or assurances may be appropriate.

Draft regulations are the legal "form" through which the Russian State controls decisions regarding treaty-making. Regulations of the President or Government concerning the possible signature of an inter-State or intergovernmental treaty contain a provision concerning the approval of the said draft by the federal department(s) submitting it, together with the agreement of all interested other federal departments, agencies of State power of subjects of the Russian Federation, and other relevant organizations—this is the coordination aspect of submitting a draft. The Draft regulation will seek authorization to sign the said treaty or to make changes in the course of negotiations which are not matters of principle. The introductory part of the draft regulation refers to the provisions of the 1995 Law on treaties on the basis of which the respective decision is adopted.

When a multilateral treaty is signed, the text of which is adopted within an international organization or at an international conference, or by way of accession to an existing treaty in force, a provision is included concerning the acceptance of the proposal submitted by the respective federal agency of executive authority(ies) agreed with the necessary interested departments, agencies of State power of subjects of the Russian Federation, and organizations concerning the signature of or accession to the treaty, together with a provision assigning the respective department to sign the treaty in the name of the Russian Federation or Government of the Russian Federation, or an assignment—given as a rule to the Ministry of Foreign Affairs—to notify the other parties or depositary about the accession.

If the proposal to sign a treaty is made through the Government to the President of the Russian Federation, the draft decree of the Government includes a provision to approve the proposal submitted by the respective department(s) duly agreed with all other interested departments, subjects of the Federation, and organizations, or a proposal to sign the treaty, or a proposal to recommend that the President sign the treaty. The introductory portion of the draft Decree of the Government should include a reference to the basis on which such a provision is included; that is, a reference to the 1995 Law on treaties. If the arrangement is a regulation of the President of Russia assigning the Government to sign or federal department(s) to do so, the draft regulation will provide for the acceptance of the Government's proposal, assign one or several departments to conduct negotiations with the authorization, when necessary, to agree changes in the draft treaty approved either by the Government or automatically approved because the changes do not involve matters of principle, or an assignment to sign the treaty or a provision to sign it at a higher level. The assignment to sign may designate a specific department or a concrete person, either by name or by position held in the respective agency.

Draft regulations of the Government relating to treaties of an interdepartmental character include a provision about acceptance of the proposal of the federal department(s) agreed with the Ministry of Foreign Affairs to conduct negotiations and sign the treaty. Draft decisions of the Government and/or President should specify in the title and text the precise nature of the action contemplated, for example: "on the Signature of an Agreement" if the treaty is subject to signature and entry into force after municipal procedures are completed; or "on the Conclusion of an Agreement"—if the treaty is subject to signature and entry into force without performing any additional municipal procedures (for example, on the day of signature or after the expiration of a certain period thereafter), or the treaty is concluded by an exchange of notes or letters; or "on accession to the Agreement"—in the event of accession to a treaty.

Agreeing Proposals to Sign or Accede to Treaties not Requiring Ratification and Submission to President or Government

In a complex State structure, the process of coordinating draft treaty proposals is crucial to obtaining input and feedback with respect to all the interests affected by a potential treaty. In Russia documents assembled to support a treaty proposal are sent for agreement to the Ministry of Foreign Affairs and to other interested federal agencies of State power and organizations. Insofar as such a proposal to sign or accede to a treaty affects questions relegated to the jurisdiction of a Federation, these materials are sent to be agreed with the agencies of State power of such a subject. If it happens that all eighty-five subjects of the Federation are affected by the proposal, all must have the opportunity to agree the proposal.

If proposals to sign inter-State or intergovernmental treaties would include rules other than provided by Russian legislation, after being agreed with the interested agencies and organizations, they are sent to the Ministry of Justice together with all the documents distributed to other departments, including the materials agreed. The Ministry of Justice, in other words, sees the entire flow of documents related to agreeing the treaty proposal. Those proposals which are subject to being submitted to the Government for subsequent submission to the President after being agreed with the relevant departments, likewise are submitted to the Ministry of Justice.

After obtaining all the necessary agreements and, when so required, the opinion of the Ministry of Justice, the proposal to sign or accede to a treaty is sent to the President or to the Government. The accompanying letter is signed by the executive of the federal agency of executive power and, should this person be absent, by the individual acting in place thereof, and all documents except for the materials of agreeing the proposal, attested copies of the treaty, and translation thereof, are visaed by this executive.

Powers to Negotiate and Sign Treaties

In a legal system where "formality" is an important feature, such as the Russian legal system, the powers to conduct negotiations and sign inter-State and intergovernmental treaties—including the signature of a letter subject to exchange—are formalized by the Ministry of Foreign Affairs of Russia. In order to receive such powers, the federal agencies of executive power send an application to the Legal Department of the Ministry of Foreign Affairs requesting the formalization of powers within the shortest possible time after the President or Government adopts the respective decision to sign a treaty, but no less than ten days before the proposed date to conduct negotiations, sign the treaty in Russia, or departure of a delegation abroad for this purpose. Exceptionally, the application to formalize powers may be submitted before the President or Government adopts the respective decision, but after the submission of the draft thereof for the consideration or the President or the Government. The powers duly formalized are issued to the respective individual only after the President or the Government adopts the respective decision.

The application represents an official letter to the Ministry of Foreign Affairs on the letterhead of the requested federal agency of executive power. The application should contain the full name of the person(s) requesting the powers, information concerning the posts they occupy, and in what capacity they have been included as part of the official delegation. The application also must indicate the full name of the forthcoming measure, the place and periods for holding it, and the full official name of the treaty being readied for signature. The full name and telephone number of the individual responsible for overseeing the process must be in the official application.

If the formalization of powers is being requested for a person who is not part of the leadership of the federal agency of executive power—that is, not the head or deputy head of the agency—the application must be signed by the deputy head or head of the respective agency.

When delegations are being sent to international conferences, meetings, or sessions of international agencies, an extract from the rules of procedure affecting the powers of a delegation must be appended to the application.

The federal agencies of executive power requesting the Ministry of Foreign Affairs to formalize powers attach to the letter copies of documents which are the grounds for the issuance of powers or specified in the letter the requisites (date of adoption and number) of these documents. The grounds for receiving powers are edicts, decrees, or regulations of the President or Government which have entered into legal force. If the respective decision of the President or Government has not been adopted, the date of submitting the draft to the President or Government and the position with respect to such consideration should be attached to the application. The powers may be formalized only for persons who are representatives of the requesting agencies that have been assigned by the President or Government to sign the treaty. Representatives of other departments may sign the treaty only on condition of making changes in the decision of the President or Government.

The position of Russia is that the President of the Russian Federation, Chairman of the Government, and Minister of Foreign Affairs do not need "in accordance with international law" powers to sign a treaty; powers are not formalized for them. Powers to conduct negotiations and sign interdepartmental treaties formalized in accordance with Article 13(c) of the 1995 Law on treaties are signed by the executives or acting executives of the federal agencies of executive power, sealed with the signature of the head or acting head of the legal subdivision of the respective agency, and attested by the seal of this agency.

The powers issued are transferred to the representative of the Contracting Party or secretariat of the international organization, as a rule, before the negotiations or sessions begin or before signature, or at the moment of signature. Powers are exchanged with the Contracting Party. In the case of a multilateral treaty, the powers are left with the depositary. The representatives of the Russian party certify that the other party has presented its powers in due form and in full.

Formalization of Treaty Texts for Signature

The text of treaties are printed, as a rule, on treaty paper and sewn into special folders. The texts of documents which are not treaties (statements, memoranda of intent, and so on) are not printed on treaty paper. The treaty text is placed within a red border on the treaty paper and printed using the usual rules, avoiding bold, italic, and underscored type. Room must be left on the final page for the date and place of signature, languages used, and space for signatures. Each annex is printed, as a rule, on a separate sheet. The text on treaty paper is formalized by the federal agency of executive power which submitted the proposal to sign to the President or to the Government. Texts of multilateral treaties signed within an international organization or other international forums are prepared, as a rule, by the respective structures of these organizations.

If a treaty is signed by the President, Head of Government, or Minister of Foreign Affairs, or in their presence, the federal agency of executive power which submitted the proposal to sign to the President or Government transfers the texts of the treaty formalized for signature, and the electronic version thereof, to the Legal Department of the Ministry of Foreign Affairs.

When the text of a bilateral treaty is printed, in Russian practice one should be guided by the "rule of alternate." According to this rule, the texts of the treaty in the Russian and foreign language(s) remaining with the Russian side (so-called "alternate of the Russian Party") which are printed on Russian treaty paper will mention throughout the entire text the Russian Party first. The alternate for the other Party will accordingly mention that Party first throughout the text.

If the language of the other Contracting Party is written from left to right (for example, Arabic or Persian), in the alternate of the Russian side the phrase "for the Government of the Russian Federation" written in the foreign language with space for the signature of the Russian empowered representative is placed on the right half of the signature page.

In accordance with international practice, the treaty texts in the Russian language, both those remaining with the Russian Party and the foreign Party, are printed by the Russian side. Equally, texts in the language of the Contracting Party may be printed by that Party. An arrangement to this effect is made with the Contracting Party responsible for preparing the treaty text for signature and must be reached in good time. In order to manufacture the text of the Russian alternate in the foreign language must be transferred on a sufficient number of sheets on Russian treaty paper, and the appropriate number of sheets of treaty paper must be obtained from the other side in order to prepare the Russian-language texts. One must be satisfied well in advance that the Russian alternate text of the treaty is properly formalized in the foreign language.

When the treaty is drawn up in different languages, the text must be verified in these languages by persons who have the respective linguistic knowledge and by the drafters. Different readings of the text must be eliminated. An act of verification stating that there are no discrepancies or inconsistencies in the texts of the treaty in the different languages is composed and signed by those performing the verification.

The text on treaty paper must be carefully verified for the absence of typographical mistakes. An act also is drawn up to confirm the checking; this confirms that the federal agency responsible for preparing the text has checked the text and not found any errors or misprints. This act is signed by the responsible agency and handed over to the Ministry of Foreign Affairs together with the signed treaty.

The examples of the treaty remaining with the Russian side which are in the Russian and foreign languages may be protected by a special ribbon and treaty folder to enable the treaty to be read or further worked with without damage to the treaty text. Those examples for the other Contracting Party are simply placed in a treaty folder given to the other side. After this, the State seals of the parties may be affixed to the inside cover of the treaty folders, being placed according to the alternate rule. Unless the parties have agreed otherwise, the State seals are placed, as a rule, before signature of the treaty. The placing of the seals is not necessary in accordance with Russian practice and encountered, rarely as a rule, at the insistence of the other side.

Any corrections in a text prepared for signature are not permitted, nor is the removal or damaging of ribbons or the State seals.

Signature of Treaties

The signatures in own hand are placed by the duly empowered individuals beneath the phrase, depending in the status of the treaty: "For the Russian Federation;" "For the Government of the Russian Federation;" or "For the [respective] federal agency of executive power." The posts held by these individuals are not, as a rule, specified with their signature. When necessary, more than one person may sign for the Russian side, in which case the powers are formalized for all representatives of the Russian side assigned to sign the treaty.

When signing reservations or statements relating to a multilateral treaty the persons empowered to sign the treaty are assigned to make, the signatures in own hand are affixed, as a rule, beneath their signatures on the signature pages and handed over to the depositary. If the treaty stipulates that the text is to be registered under Article 102 of the United Nations Charter with the Secretariat of the United Nations, the parties agree which of them will submit the treaty for registration. If the arrangement is that the Russian side will submit the treaty to the United Nations Secretariat, the Legal Department of the Ministry of Foreign Affairs of the Russian Federation is responsible for arranging this. In any event, once a treaty is signed abroad, the representatives of the federal agencies of executive power notify the Ministry of Foreign Affairs at once thereof.

Handing Over Treaty Text for Keeping

Within two weeks from the day of signature, the originals of inter-State and intergovernmental treaties, including those for which the

Government of Russia is the depositary) and attested copies of interdepartmental treaties are handed over for keeping to the Ministry of Foreign Affairs. They are sent to the Legal Department of Russia with an accompanying letter which sets out the full names and posts of the persons who signed on the Russian side and on the foreign side. Together with the treaty texts, the original powers received from the Contracting Party(ies) are transmitted, and any other documents received (instruments of ratification, instruments of accession, exchange of notes concerning corrections, and so on).

Attested copies of multilateral international treaties without the participation of the Russian Federation received from the depositary also are sent to the Legal Department of the Ministry of Foreign Affairs. When a treaty is concluded by an exchange of notes, letters, and the like, the original document of the party with which the treaty was concluded and the second copy of the Russian document are sent to the Legal Department of the Ministry. Federal agencies of executive power which concluded interdepartmental treaties of the Russian Federation whose authentic texts are drawn up in foreign languages send attested copies of these texts with a translation into Russian to the Legal Department. The act of checking texts drawn up in foreign and the Russian languages are sent together with the original of the treaty. Federal agencies of executive power send to the Ministry of Foreign Affairs all original texts of reservations and statements of States made with signing, ratifying, or acceding to treaties. Documents drawn up only in a foreign language which relate to the treaty are sent to the Legal Department together with an attested translation into the Russian language.

Expression of Consent to be Bound by Russian Federation

The expression is cumbersome, literally formulated "expression of consent to bindingness of treaty." After the signature of a treaty whose entry into force for Russia requires an expression of consent to be bound (ratification, confirmation, adoption, exchange of notifications), the federal agency of executive power which proposed to sign the treaty (lead department) is responsible for taking actions necessary to obtain such consent. If in the view of the lead department the expression of consent to be bound should be deferred until certain conditions have ensued (for example, larger number of parties to a multilateral treaty or changes in Russian legislation), it informs those concerned about this necessity and the reasons and circumstances which enable this deferral to be terminated. The lead department must monitor the situation and inform the Ministry of Foreign Affairs regularly about whether the conditions for consent have been satisfied. If the lead department comes to the view that the participation of Russia in the treaty is no longer advisable (changed circumstances), it should take measures to notify the intention of Russia not to become a party to the treaty.

Confirmation and Adoption of Treaty Not Needing Ratification

In instances provided by Article 20(1)(b) of the 1995 Law on treaties, a treaty not needing ratification may be confirmed or adopted in the procedure established for the signature of the treaty. The draft regulation of the President or Government concerning confirmation or adoption of inter-State or intergovernmental treaties containing a provision to confirm or adopt the treaty is included together with an assignment (usually to the Ministry of Foreign Affairs), to notify the other party or depositary about the decision taken. The introductory paragraph to the regulation or decree must include a reference to Article 20 of the 1995 Law on treaties.

One reason for seeking a further confirmation of the treaty is that changes of a principled character were made when signing the treaty in comparison with the draft approved by the Government or President or the treaty was signed without a respective decision of the Government or President authorizing signature.

Ratification of Treaty

The 1993 Constitution of the Russian Federation stipulates that the two chambers of the Federal Assembly shall ratify treaties, but does not specify which treaties are subject to ratification. That question is left to the 1995 Law on treaties, which provides:

Article 15. International Treaties of Russian Federation Subject to Ratification

1. International treaties of the Russian Federation shall be subject to ratification:

   (a) the performance of which requires changes of prevailing or the adoption of new federal laws, and also the establishing of other rules than those provided for by a law;

   (b) the subject of which is the basic rights and freedoms of man and citizen;

   (c) concerning the territorial demarcation of the Russian Federation with other States, including treaties on the course of the State boundary of the Russian Federation, and also the demarcation of the exclusive economic zone and continental shelf of the Russian Federation;

   (d) on the basic principles of inter-State relations, regarding questions affecting the defense capability of the Russian Federation, regarding questions of disarmament or international control over armaments, regarding questions of ensuring international peace and security, and also peace treaties and treaties on collective security;

   (e) on the participation of the Russian Federation in inter-State unions, international organizations, and other inter-State associations, if such treaties provided for the transfer to them of the effectuation of part of the powers of the Russian Federation or establish the legal bindingness of decisions of their organs for the Russian Federation.

2. International treaties of the Russian Federation likewise shall be subject to ratification when during the conclusion of which the parties have stipulated subsequent ratification.

Other federal laws of the Russian Federation require ratification of treaties, including the following:

Federal Law "On the Procedure of Providing Military and Civilian Personnel by the Russian Federation for Participation in Activity Relating to the Maintenance or Restoration of International Peace and Security" of 23 June 1995;[5]

---

[5] СЗ РФ (1995) no. 26, item 2401, as amended June 4, 2014: "In the event of the conclusion of an international treaty of the Russian Federation on the provision of military and

Federal Law "On Precious Metals and Precious Stones," of 26 March 1998;[6]
Federal Law "On Military Duty and Military Service," of 28 March 1998;[7]
Federal Law "On Cultural Valuables Moved to the USSR as a Result of the Second World War and Situated on the Territory of the Russian Federation," of 15 April 1998;[8]
Federal Law "On the Status of Military Servicemen," of 27 May 1998;[9]
Budget Code of the Russian Federation, of 31 July 1998;[10]

civilian personnel by the Russian Federation in order to participate in activity relating to the maintenance or restoration of international peace and security, this treaty is subject to ratification in the procedure established by a federal law if for the realization of such treaty the allotment is necessary of additional budget appropriations or the treaty provides for the provision of military formations of the Armed Forces of the Russian Federation for participation beyond the limits of the territory of the Russian Federation in international enforcement actions with the use of armed forces, and also on other grounds established by federal laws" (Article 4).

[6] СЗ РФ (1998) no. 13, item 1463, as amended June 6, 2019: "International treaties of the Russian Federation in the domain of the extraction, production, and use of precious metals and precious stones shall be subject to obligatory ratification in the procedure established by legislation of the Russian Federation" (Article 24(3)).

[7] СЗ РФ (1998) no. 13, item 1475, as amended May 29, 2019: "Citizens permanently residing beyond the limits of the Russian Federation and having expressed the wish to undergo military service upon call-up for military posts replacing soldiers, seamen, sergeants, and senior officers in the Armed Forces of the Russian Federation, other forces, military formations, and agencies may be placed on military recording in the procedure determined by the Statute on Military Recording on condition of the conclusion and ratification by the Russian Federation of respective international treaties" (Article 8(8)).

[8] СЗ РФ (1998) no. 16, item 1799, as amended July 23, 2008: "International treaties of the Russian Federation concerning moved cultural valuables, and likewise any other international treaties of the Russian Federation concerning the cultural legacy thereof, shall be subject to ratification" (Article 23).

[9] СЗ РФ (1998) no. 22, item 2331, as amended February 25, 2019: "For citizens who underwent military service in military units of the Armed Forces of the USSR, other military formations of the USSR and States-Participants of the Commonwealth of Independent States before the acceptance of the said military formations under the jurisdiction of the Russian Federation and transferred for military service to forces and other military formations, and organizations of other States previously part of the USSR, the social guarantees and contributory compensations provided by the present Federal Law, federal laws, and other normative legal acts of the Russian Federation shall be preserved on condition of the conclusion and ratification in the established procedure of respective international treaties of the Russian Federation" (Article 2(3)).

[10] СЗ РФ (1998) no. 31, item 3823, as amended June 2, 2016: "Treaties on State external borrowings of the Russian Federation with international financial organizations whose constitutive documents were not previously ratified on the grounds provided by Article 15 of the Federal Law of 15 July 1995 'On International Treaties of the Russian Federation' shall be subject to ratification" (Article 109); "A treaty on the restructuring and/or writing off of a debt of a foreign State to the Russian Federation, shall be subject to ratification, except for restructuring and/or writing off of this debt within the framework of participation of the Russian Federation in international financial organizations and financial clubs on conditions common and uniform for all participants of the said organizations and clubs, and also except for the restructuring and/or writing off of the debt of a foreign State and/or foreign juridical person to the

Federal Law "On Internal Sea Waters, Territorial Sea, and Contiguous Zone of the Russian Federation," of 31 July 1998;[11]

Federal Constitutional Law "On the Procedure for the Acceptance into the Russian Federation and Formation Therein of a New Subject of the Russian Federation," of 17 December 2001;[12]

Federal Law "On Technical Regulation" of 27 December 2002.[13]

The full package of documents that must accompany a proposal to the President of the Russian Federation or Chairman of the Government regarding ratification, confirmation, adoption, or accession (we use the term "ratification" here to encompass all four expressions of consent to be bound) replicate, with additions, the basic procedures outlined above with respect to confirmation of a treaty by the Government. For ratification proposals sent to the President or to the Head of the Government (excluding instances in which ratification occurs without signature of the treaty—International Labour Organization conventions, for example), must be accompanied by a letter setting out concisely information about the treaty and the agreeing thereof by other departments of the State. In this case the letter is signed by the Minister of Foreign Affairs and the executive of the federal agency of executive power which proposed ratification of the treaty. The package of documents includes a draft decision (in the form of a regulation) of the President to appoint his official representative(s) to explain the proposal for ratification to the chambers of the Federal Assembly; a draft letter to the

Russian Federation provided by the federal law on the federal budget for the next financial year and planning period" (Article 127(2)).

[11] СЗ РФ (1998) no. 31, item 3833, as amended December 27, 2018: "Foreign citizens and stateless persons, foreign juridical persons, and also associations of juridical persons not having the status of a juridical person of foreign States and international organizations may effectuate the use of natural resources of internal sea waters and the territorial sea, and also other activity in internal sea waters and in the territorial sea, including from on board a flying apparatus, in the procedure provided by the present Federal Law, other federal laws, and international treaties of the Russian Federation subject to ratification" (Article 20(2)).

[12] СЗ РФ (2001) no. 52(I), item 4916, as amended October 31, 2005: "With regard to individual questions connected with the acceptance into the Russian Federation of a foreign State or part thereof as a new subject, special protocols subject to ratification simultaneously with the ratification of the international treaty may be signed by the Russian Federation and the particular foreign State" (Article 7(3)).

[13] СЗ РФ (2002) no. 52(I), item 5140, as amended July 29, 2017: "technical document—document which was adopted by an international treaty of the Russian Federation subject to ratification in the procedure established by legislation of the Russian Federation, or in accordance with an international treaty of the Russian Federation ratified in the procedure established by legislation of the Russian Federation . . . " (Article 2).

Chairman of the State Duma referring to the legal grounds for submission of the draft law (Article 86 or 104 of the 1993 Russian Constitution); the draft federal law, including the text of any Russian reservation and objections to any reservation made by other parties to the treaty. If there is a Russian reservation, statement, or objection, the text of that is included in the draft law.

We observe, however, that the documents must include an explanatory memorandum which, *inter alia*, sets out any divergence between the treaty provisions and Russian law. There also must be a List of acts of federal legislation subject to change or amendment in connection with the adoption of the federal law on ratification to being deemed to have lost force, suspension, change, addition, or adoption. The List should include subordinate acts as well, and if no laws or other acts are subject to repeal, change, or adoption by reason of ratification of the treaty, that should be indicated too.

The package of documents must include a financial-economic substantiation of the proposal to ratify the treaty—setting out any expenditures which realization of the treaty would entail. Even if no expenses are involved, this document must be part of the package. An attested copy of the official text of the treaty in the Russian language must be submitted; if an authentic text of the treaty in the Russian language does not exist, then an attested copy in one of the foreign languages and an attested Russian translation thereof. All materials relating to agreeing the treaty text with other departments are required, including the letters sent and the visaed draft decree of the Government and federal law, together with the opinion of the Ministry of Justice—which is routine for any draft normative legal acts, including decrees of the Government and federal laws.

If the treaty is to be submitted by federal agencies of executive power to the Government for subsequent submission to the President (in instances when a proposal to the President concerning treaty ratification requires preliminary consideration thereof by the Government), most of the same procedures are repeated with respect to the Head of Government and a draft decree of the Government produced, duly agreed by all interested departments, and the accompanying letter signed by the Minister of Foreign Affairs and executive of the federal agency of executive power which initiated the proposal to sign the treaty. The draft decree cites the provisions of the 1995 Law on treaties on the basis of which a decision to submit is based

(Articles 16(3), 20, and 21). The Government approves a draft opinion on the draft federal law to ratify a treaty, which opinion must be agreed with the Ministry of Finances, Ministry of Economic Development, and Ministry of Justice of the Russian Federation.

Before the entire package of documents is sent to the Ministry of Foreign Affairs, the lead department checks the treaty in the Russian language and in other languages for mistakes and misprints. An act is formalized which lists any mistakes or misprints identified, or confirms that there are none. This act also is sent to the Ministry of Foreign Affairs. If any misprints or other errors were identified, the Ministry of Foreign Affairs undertakes actions provided by international law to make corrections. Documents confirming the correction of errors is later included with the attested copy of the treaty.

After agreeing the proposal with the interested departments and organizations and having received a positive opinion from the Ministry of Justice, the head of the federal agency of executive power which prepared the proposal, or acting head, signs the accompanying letter, visas the documents attached thereto (except the materials agreeing the text, attested copies of the treaty, and translation thereof). These materials are all sent on to the Ministry of Foreign Affairs for submission respectively to the President or to the Government.

When the materials are sent by the relevant executive branch of the State to the State Duma with respect to ratification of a treaty, a new cycle of expert evaluation begins by the Legal Administration of the Duma on behalf of the Council of the State Duma or on behalf of the Duma Committee which is assigned by the Duma Council to consider the matter.[14] Within the Legal Administration a decision is made as to which subdivision of the Legal Division will be responsible for evaluating the draft, usually the Section for International Law and Analysis of Foreign Legislation pursuant to the Statute on the said Section adopted August 4, 2004. When necessary, other sections of the Legal Administration may become involved. Linguistic expert evaluation is undertaken of the draft Law on ratification, but not on the text of the international treaty itself. The Legal Administration prepares an Opinion on the draft ratification law and text of the treaty which is circulated to deputies of the State Duma. All the materials assembled by the

---

[14] See Articles 189 and 190, Reglament of the State Duma; trans. in W E Butler, *Russian Public Law* (3rd edn.; 2013) 375–6.

initiating agencies, Ministry of Foreign Affairs, Ministry of Justice, and others are re-verified as part of the parliamentary exercise. Attention is paid to the form of the draft law and the conferral of a registration number for the draft law. A view to taken on whether the international treaty conforms to the 1993 Constitution of Russia, pre-existing international legal obligations of the Russian Federation, and the consequences of ratifying the treaty. The positions taken by the Constitutional Court of the Russian Federation are considered.

If the Legal Administration of the State Duma believes that the treaty would be contrary to the Constitution, it must specify precisely in what respect and set out the argumentation in support of this view.[15]

Language of Treaty Subject to Ratification

Among the documents that are required to be submitted, when there is a proposal to conclude a treaty subject to ratification, is an attested copy of the official text of the treaty in the Russian language. If an authentic text of the treaty in the Russian language does not exist, then an attested copy of the official treaty text in one of the foreign languages is included together with an attested translation of the treaty into the Russian language. The legal service or the international relations service of the federal agency of executive power which is preparing the proposal for ratification attests to the quality of translating the treaty text into Russian. The attesting is done by placing the inscription "True copy" for copies of the official text or "Translation true" on the last page on the text or reverse side thereof, the armorial seal and signature of the executive of the respective service or deputy thereof, indicating full name and post). The attesting must be so arranged that it is impossible to replace sheets of the text of the document. The copy of the official text of the treaty in the Russian or foreign language for the purposes of submitting the text for ratification is attested by the Legal Department of the Ministry of Foreign Affairs immediately before submission to the Government or to the President.

---

[15] On the internal proceedings in the State Duma on the part of the Legal Department with regard to treaty ratification, see N V Lavrenova, "О некоторых вопросах ратифик ации международных договоров государственнй Думой Федерального собрания Российской Федерации" ["On Certain Questions of the Ratification of International Treaties by the State Duma of the Federal Assembly of the Russian Federation"] in n. 4, II, 105–15.

Notification of Fulfillment of Municipal Procedures

When a federal law on ratification of a treaty of the Russian Federation is adopted and has entered into legal force, or confirmation, adoption, or accession to a treaty which does not require ratification has been provided by the President or the Head of Government of the Russian Federation, the Ministry of Foreign Affairs sends notification to the Contracting Party(ies) or to the depositary without the lead department taking the initiative to seek this. If the municipal procedures do not involve ratification, confirmation, and so on, once these have been completed, the Ministry of Foreign Affairs will send due notification to the Contracting Party(ies) on the basis of the decision of the Government or the President concerning signature of the treaty at the request of the lead department. Such a notification should: (a) cite the decision of the President or Government which is grounds for sending the notification; (b) confirm that no changes of a principled character have been made in the treaty in comparison with the draft version approved by the President or Government; and (c) confirm that there are no grounds for requiring ratification of the treaty.

Decision Not to Become Party to Treaty

If, after the signature of a treaty but before the treaty has entered into force, it is determined that the participation of the Russian Federation in the treaty is inadvisable, with a view to removing from the Russian Federation the obligation provided by international law to refrain from actions which would deprive the treaty of its object and purpose, notification is to be sent to the other participants in the treaty and/or to the depositary about the intention of the Russian Federation not to become a party to the treaty. The conclusion that Russian participation in a treaty is not advisable is made by the federal agency of executive power which submitted the proposal to sign the treaty to the President or to the Government of the Russian Federation, having regard to the views of the Ministry of Foreign Affairs and other interested agencies of State power and organizations. The actual decision to send the notification of the Russian Federation not to become a participant is taken by the President or by the Government, depending on which decided to sign, upon the recommendation of the federal agency of executive power which recommended signature either singly or jointly with the Ministry of Foreign Affairs.

The conclusion that Russia's becoming a participant in a treaty is inadvisable is made by the federal agency of executive power which originally submitted the proposal to sign and now believes it to be in the interests of Russia not to become a party, which prepares a formal proposal to this effect and accompanying documents for proposals to be submitted directly to the President or to the Government: (a) a draft accompanying letter to the President or Chairman of the Government setting out information concerning the content and coordination of the proposal; (b) a draft regulation of the President or Government to accept the proposal and send notification to other participants and/or the depositary and an indication that the draft regulation does not contain rules other than provided by legislation or the Russian Federation or additional expenditures from the federal budget; (c) an attested copy of the treaty, and if the text is in a foreign language—an attested copy of the treaty in the foreign language and an attested translation into Russian. The official text of the treaty may be attested by the federal agency of executive power which is preparing the proposal or by the Legal Department of the Ministry of Foreign Affairs, and the translation by the federal agency which is preparing the proposal; (d) the materials relating to agreeing the proposal, including copies of letters from the agreeing agencies and organizations that they concur with the proposal and copies of draft acts of the Government visaed by the executives or deputies thereof of the agreeing agencies and organizations.

If the decision to sign the treaty was taken by the President upon the recommendation of the Government, the proposal not to become a participant of the treaty contains a different set of accompanying documents: (a) a draft accompanying letter to the Chairman of the Government which sets out the content and agreeing of the proposal; (b) a draft decree of the Government on submitting a proposal to the President on sending notification to the other participants of the treaty and/or depositary about the intention of Russia not to become a party; (c) a draft letter of the Chairman of the Government to the President which sets out the content of the proposal; (d) a draft regulation of the President to accept the proposal of the Government to notify other treaty participants and to assign the Ministry of Foreign Affairs to send such notification; (e) the opinion of the Ministry of Justice of Russia on the draft decree of the Government; (f) the texts of the treaty, in translation as necessary, and materials on agreeing the proposal.

When all the necessary materials have been assembled, the head or acting head signs the accompanying letter to the President or Chairman of the Government.

Termination of Provisional Application of Treaty

Unless provided otherwise by the treaty, or the parties to the treaty have decided otherwise, the provisional application of a treaty or part thereof terminates upon the notification of the other parties which are temporarily applying the treaty about the intention of the Russian Federation not to become a party thereto. The proposal to terminate provisional application is accompanied by the same package of documents as withdrawal from participation with minor distinctions in their wording to reflect the formulation of the draft decree of the Government or regulation of the President.

Termination or Suspension of Treaties

If federal agencies of executive power consider it necessary to terminate or suspend the operation of a treaty as a whole or in part, they send a substantiated proposal to the Ministry of Foreign Affairs. In Russia's view, an international treaty may be terminated in accordance with the provisions of the treaty itself and by agreement of the parties in accordance with norms of international law (in essence, by concluding a new treaty to this effect), or terminated or suspended unilaterally—called denunciation—by sending notification to the other State party or to the respective depositary. If another treaty is to be the means of termination or suspension, the general rules apply in Russia for the conclusion of a treaty.

The decision to denounce or suspend a treaty is adopted by the agency of State power which adopted the decision for the Russian Federation to be bound by the treaty. If the treaty was ratified by a federal law, the proposals for denunciation are prepared in the same way as the federal law originally. If consent to a treaty being binding was given by the President or by the Government of the Russian Federation, appropriate draft regulations are prepared in the usual way and provision is made for notification to be made to the other party or the depositary, and a department (usually the Ministry of Foreign Affairs) is assigned to undertake this. Reference must be made to Article 36 of the 1995 Law on treaties.

Example. On March 4, 2019 by Edict of the President of the Russian Federation "On the Suspension by the Russian Federation of the Fulfillment of the Treaty between the Union of Soviet Socialist Republics and the United States of America on the Elimination of Their Intermediate-Range and Shorter-Range Missiles" of December 8, 1987 the said treaty was suspended until "the elimination by the United States of America of violations permitted by them of obligations under the said Treaty or until the termination of the operation thereof." The Ministry of Foreign Affairs was directed to send notification about suspension of the fulfillment of the treaty. The Edict entered into force on the day of signature; that is, March 4, 2019.[16]

On July 3, 2019 the President of the Russian Federation signed the Federal Law "On Suspension by the Russian Federation of the Fulfillment of the Treaty between the Union of Soviet Socialist Republics and the United States of America on the Elimination of Their Intermediate-Range and Shorter-Range Missiles"[17] of December 8, 1987. The said treaty was suspended and, according to Article 2 of the Federal Law, might be renewed by a decision adopted by the President of the Russian Federation. The Federal Law entered into force from the day of official publication; official publication occurred on the same day of signature, the Federal Law having been placed on the official Internet-Portal of Legal Information, www.pravo.gov.ru.

Commentary. This example shows temporary suspension by the President of Russia in March 2019 and full suspension by the Federal Assembly in July 2019, presumably because the "violations permitted" were not eliminated. The principle of notification was observed; it will be noted that notification, or receipt thereof, or confirmation of receipt thereof, has no bearing on when the Edict or Federal Law, and therefore suspension, took effect.

If a treaty is to be terminated because full performance of obligations has been completed by the parties, the Ministry of Foreign Affairs of Russia is so advised by the federal agency of executive power, with a recommendation to officially terminate the treaty.

Denunciation or suspension of interdepartmental treaties is made by the federal agencies of executive power which concluded such treaties, by

---

[16] СЗ РФ (2019) no. 10, item 950.
[17] СЗ РФ (2019) no. 27, item 3531.

agreement with the Ministry of Foreign Affairs, other interested departments, and agencies of State power of respective subjects of the Federation and with the authorization of the Government. In order to obtain the authorization of the Government, the federal agency of executive power needs to substantiate the advisability of denunciation or suspension and evaluate the financial, economic, and other consequences of termination or suspension of the treaty.

Monitoring Realization of Treaty

Although all international treaties of the Russian Federation, irrespective of whether inter-State, intergovernmental, or interdepartmental, are the responsibility of the State, the 1995 Law on treaties (Article 32) requires that the President of Russia, Government of Russia, and federal agencies of State power and empowered organizations, including agencies of State power of subjects of the Russian Federation, ensure that international treaties of the Russian Federation are duly fulfilled or realized. Some departments have adopted Reglaments to this effect. One is the Reglament of International Activity of the Federal Agency for Fishing, adopted October 15, 2010, No. 921.[18] "Activity" for these purposes is activity connected with official membership of the Russian Federation in international fisheries organizations and participation in bilateral and multilateral international treaties relegated to the jurisdiction of the Agency. The Reglament is intended to fulfill the provisions of the 1995 Law on treaties, including ensuring the execution in the established procedure of decisions of treaty-law issues. The Agency prepares for this purpose a "Plan of International Cooperation" that enumerates the measures to be conducted within the respective calendar year. The representatives of the Agency representing the Russian Federation in international organizations and intergovernmental commissions are obliged to inform the Government of the Russian Federation, leadership, Administration of International Cooperation, and other interested structural subdivisions of the Agency, Ministry of Foreign Affairs, and, when necessary, other departments, about the realization of treaties of the Russian Federation,

---

[18] See the Order of Rosrybolovstvo, October 15, 2009, No. 921, "On Confirmation of the Reglament of International Activity of the Federal Agency for Fishing," as amended August 25, 2015. Available on Consultant Plus.

the current state of affairs, and matters arising in the course of their representation work.

Investment Protection Treaties

The materials addressed above concern all treaties, subdivided into inter-State, intergovernmental, and interdepartmental, irrespective of subject-matter. The Russian State is the party on the Russian side responsible for their fulfillment. In Russian judicial practice, ratified international treaties take precedence over provisions of federal laws which differ from treaty provisions.

Russian State practice, however, has gone further with respect to individual categories of treaties—investment protection treaties in particular. The materials above are based on a set of Recommendations issued by the Ministry of Foreign Affairs of the Russian Federation and circulated to all federal agencies of State power, departments, and organizations. One may anticipate that the Recommendations are normally complied with and that failure to comply risks not formal sanctions but, in all likelihood, rejection of the treaty proposal unless and until compliance is obtained. The Government of the Russian Federation has, however, confirmed this by Decree of September 30, 2016, No. 992, the Reglament "On the Conclusion of International Treaties of the Russian Federation Relating to Questions of the Encouragement and Defense of Investments."[19] The Reglament determined the "peculiarities" of holding negotiations and concluding international treaties of the Russian Federation with regard to the encouragement and defense of investments.

One of the main "peculiarities" is that with respect to these treaties the lead department in the Russian Federation is the Ministry of Economic Development of the Russian Federation. Negotiations to conclude investment protection treaties are conducted "in accordance with a plan for negotiations annually confirmed" by the Ministry of Economic Development,

---

[19] СЗ РФ (2016) no. 41, item 5836. The Decree confirmed the "Reglament on the Conclusion of International Treaties of the Russian Federation with Regard to Questions of the Encouragement and Defense of Investments." The 2016 Decree replaced the Decree of the Government of the Russian Federation of June 9, 2001, No 456, "On the Conclusion of Agreements between the Government of the Russian Federation and Governments of Foreign States on the Encouragement and Mutual Defense of Capital Investments," as amended April 11, 2002 and December 17, 2010. СЗ РФ (2001) no. 25, item 2578; (2002) no. 15, item 1445; (2010) no. 52, item 7137.

having regard to proposals of the Ministry of Foreign Affairs. When preparing the plan, the Ministry of Economic Development is guided by criteria for determining the advisability of holding negotiations and concluding investment protection treaties set out in Annex 1 to the Reglament. There are several criteria:

(a) the interest of Russian investors in the conclusion of such a treaty; this is determined by the existence of recourses to the Ministry of Economic Development by associations or individual entrepreneurs or employers on this matter;

(b) the volume of mutually accumulated investments and the dynamic of investment flows between Russia and the other party;

(c) the volume of existing and potential investments by Russian investors and investment projects of Russian investors planned to make in the other party and *vice versa*.

The investment climate in the other party is determined by using the assessments of international organizations and the existence of prohibitions, limitations, and other barriers obstructing the effective undertaking of investments by Russian investors in the other country. Another factor is the general state of relations between the Russian Federation and the other party, and the level of mutual obligations of the two States arising from other investment protection treaties or other treaties. The final factor is the possibility of Russian investors receiving preferences and advantages as part of negotiating an investment protection treaty, having regard to an analysis of the other party having concluded analogous treaties with other States, associations of States, international organizations, or "other formations possessing the right to conclude international treaties."

General approaches. The "general approaches" to concluding investment protection treaties are set out in Annex 2 to the Reglament. The purposes of such treaties are to "attract foreign investments or capital investments) to the economy of the Russian Federation by forming stable, transparent, and predictable conditions" for undertaking and defending such investments and creating effective mechanisms "for the defense of Russian investors and their investments abroad."

Sphere of application of treaty. The Reglament requires that the treaty apply to measures which are taken or will be taken by the parties to the treaty, including at the federal, regional, and municipal levels, and determines the conditions for allowing investments and the activities of investors (especially the conditions and procedure for the founding, creation, or registration of juridical persons, branches, representations, individual entrepreneurs undertaking other forms of investing assets, obtaining authorizations, hiring workers, the procedure for the suspension or termination of juridical persons, branches, representations, and individual entrepreneurs, including bankruptcy, and the conditions and procedure for the possession, use, and disposition by investors of assets in other forms). The treaty should apply to investments of investors which were undertaken after the entry of the treaty into force and those undertaken by agreement of the parties before the entry of the treaty into force and which exist on the territory of the party on the date of entry into force of the treaty. On the other hand, the treaty should not apply to any situations, claims, or disputes which existed, arose, or ceased to exist before the treaty entered into force.

The Reglament provides that an investment protection treaty should apply throughout the territory of each party and to the exclusive economic zone and continental shelf (when these exist), which are determined in accordance with international law. The applicability of the treaty extends to assets determined therein which are contributed by an investor of one party on the territory of the other party, the investment being connected with receiving profit, or directed toward receiving profit, on the territory of the party receiving the investment. Investments made on the territory of the other party must comply with the legislation of the other party to the treaty, but this may not affect the obligations of the other party with respect to the regime granted to investments of the said persons under the contract. Moreover, the treaty should apply to assets which are contributed on the territory of any party by natural persons who are citizens of the other party to the treaty and juridical persons which were founded or created on the territory of the other party to the treaty. If natural persons are or were citizens of the party to the treaty on whose territory these investments are or were undertaken at the time of making such investments, the treaty would not apply to them.

Nor should the treaty apply to investments of juridical persons of a party to the investment protection treaty who do not undertake active business activity on the territory of this party to the treaty, or to juridical persons of a party to the treaty which belong to or are controlled by persons of the other party to the treaty on whose territory the investments are or were undertaken, or to juridical persons which belong to or are controlled by persons of a third State. Nor would an investment protection treaty apply to services and other types of activity supplied or undertaken in performance of State powers by agencies of State power of the party to the treaty or organizations to which such powers have been transferred by this party. Services and other types of activity supplied or undertaken not for the purpose of deriving profit and in the absence of competition on the part of other economic subjects are relegated to the category of the said services and other types of activity.

Conditions for allowing investments and investor activity. The Reglament provides that an investment protection treaty will provide for the general rule of national regime and most-favored nation regime with respect to investments and that the regime granted to these investors on the territory of the party to the treaty were investments that were or are being undertaken, subject to any exceptions agreed in the negotiations. The choice of which regime would operate lies in the discretion of the investors, depending upon which is more favorable.

However, the Reglament cautions, the regime provided by the treaty should not affect existing or future legislation of the Russian Federation relating to investing in economic societies and sectors of the economy which are natural monopolies or which have strategic significance for ensuring the defense of the country and security of the State, privatization, differences in taxation between residents and non-residents, new sectors of services and types of activity which were not supplied or undertaken on the territory of the Russian Federation at the time of concluding the treaty. This last is a bizarre requirement, for it imposes a restraint on investment activity impossible to predict.

An investment protection treaty also should not provide for the possibility of extending the treaty provisions to investors of the parties to the treaty and their investment preferences provided by Article V of the General Agreement on Trade and Services (GATS).

Although one might expect the principle of national regime to extend to these matters, the Reglament provides that an investment protection treaty should guarantee to an investor of either party the right and possibility to contest or review measures of the other party to the treaty in a judicial or administrative proceeding which affect his investments in accordance with the procedure established by legislation of the other party. And the treaty should provide that the general application of the treaty embodied in normative legal acts affecting investments of investors must be applied by the other party on whose territory the investments are made is reasonable, objective, and unbiased. Although no precise reference is made to Article 15(3) of the 1995 Law on treaties, the Reglament provides that the treaty must oblige each party to ensure the publication of its measures of general application affecting the investors from the other party in official publications no later than the date of their entry into force—a requirement that is actually more stringent than that provided by Russian legislation or required by Russian judicial practice.

Defense of investors. Investment protection treaties must provide a general prohibition against a party undertaking the expropriation of investments by investors of the other party, except when expropriation is undertaken in accordance the following conditions:

(a) the existence of public interests (see below);
(b) complete compliance with the procedure provided by legislation of the respective party to the treaty, in which case the procedure must be officially published or otherwise be generally accessible before the date of the expropriation;
(c) non-discriminatory;
(d) payment to the investor of prompt, adequate, and effective compensation for damage caused to the investor by the expropriation.

The Reglament cautions that the fact of causing damage to an investor of the party to the investment protection treaty does not automatically means that these investments were subjected to expropriation. The treaty should provide that, when determining the fact of expropriation, the character, nature, and aims of the measures or complex of measures actually achieved and declared by the other party are taken into account. Moreover, the treaty should be clear that a violation by a party of other obligations under the treaty determined by using the mechanism for dispute settlement provided by the treaty does not mean automatic violation with respect to expropriation. Security measures applied to investments by investigative and judicial agencies of the other party to the treaty on whose territory the investments were made should not be regarded as expropriation. The position is similar in relation to measures connected with the establishment and recovery of taxes and charges, provided that these taxes and charges are not arbitrary and do not provide differentiated rates depending on the origin of the investor or capital, taking into account tax treaties between the parties to the investment protection treaty.

Requisition should not be equated to expropriation when such measures are applied in the event of natural disasters, accidents, epidemics, epizootics, and analogous emergency circumstances and the property requisitioned was returned to the investor without unsubstantiated delay when the circumstances ceased and compensation was paid to the investor for the market value of the damage caused to such property. Measures of customs regulation also should not be relegated to expropriation.

Similarly, the Reglament provides that the issuance of enforcement licenses with respect to intellectual property should not be considered to be expropriation, provided that such issuance is not contrary to obligations assumed by the party to the treaty on whose territory such enforcement was undertaken within the framework of the World Trade Organization.

Compensation payable to an investor by reason of expropriation should be in full for damage caused by the expropriation and the amount determined by the application of the real market value of the investments, having regard to the duration and consequences of the expropriation measures. This would include the objective reduction of value of expropriated investments if the fact of a planned or undertaken expropriation was generally known. Where a payment of compensation is delayed, interest accrues at a rate established on a market basis. The compensation is to be paid in the currency in which the investments were initially made, and the investor must have the possibility to convert this payment of compensation into a freely convertible currency of his choice. With respect to damage caused by investments of an investor of one party to the treaty on the territory of the other party as a consequence of military action, armed conflicts, revolts, civilian disorders, and the like, the treaty must provide for the granting to the investor of a regime no less favorable than the regime granted to investors of the other party to the treaty or any third State.

An investment protection treaty should make provision for the transfer of rights under insurance against political or non-commercial risks between the investor and empowered agency or organization of the party to the treaty without prejudice to the arrangements between the parties to the treaty with respect to the regime granted to the other party. Moreover, the investors of each party to the treaty should be granted the freedom of remittance of payments from the territory of that party to the treaty connected with the investments, including amounts paid as compensation for damage caused. These remittances should be in any currency at the investor's discretion and be convertible into any freely convertible currency of the investor's choice. However, nothing in the treaty should prevent the parties from introducing measures on a non-discriminatory basis to limit remittances provided by the legislation of each party to the treaty in the event of bankruptcy, defense of the rights of workers, creditors, bookkeeping, and taxation. Limitations might be introduced on international remittances within the framework of rights and duties in accordance with the Charter of the International Monetary Fund or balance of payments difficulties.

Settlement of investment disputes. An investment protection treaty must provide that the disputes arising between an investor of the parties to the treaty are to be resolved in the procedure provided by the treaty, by legislation of the other party to the treaty, or by a written arrangement between the investor and the other party to the treaty. Consultations are the first mechanism of peaceful settlement to be proposed by the parties to the dispute. Notification of the proposal to commence consultations must be given and details set out in the treaty as to the content of such notification. A mechanism also should be inserted in the treaty for the exchange of information (addresses, etc). A notification which does not contain the information required in the Reglament is not considered to be duly made.

If consultations have not commenced within 180 days from sending due notification to the other party or have begun but not led to a mutually advantageous result, consideration of the dispute may be referred to a State court of one of the parties or arbitration may be provided for in the treaty. However: "any arbitration organs not expressly specified in the treaty shall not have the competence to consider disputes connected with the treaty. Any arbitration organs, *ad hoc* or permanently operating, shall not have the powers to use arbitration rules not provided by the treaty" (point 46).

The Reglament contains detailed requirements regarding the consideration of peaceful settlement of investment disputes. The request to transfer a dispute to arbitration, for example, should not expand or change the essence of claims set out in the notification to propose to commence consultations or to consider claims not mentioned at all in the notification. The parties must have the possibility at any moment to agree on an interpretation of individual provisions of the treaty in accordance with a procedure determined in the treaty. At any time during the dispute, whether during consultations or arbitration, a party to the dispute must have the possibility to send a notification to the other party proposing to commence consultations on individual provisions of the treaty, and if the dispute is in arbitration, the arbitrators must be duly notified as well. The investment protection treaty may provide that any interpretation of the treaty provisions reached by the parties to the treaty is binding on the parties, investors of the parties, and agencies to which, under the treaty, the disputes have been transferred for consideration between the parties to the treaty or between a party to the treaty and an investor from the other party to the treaty.

The Reglament cautions that nothing in the treaty, including the most-favored-nation regime, should give to the investors of parties to the treaty the right to resort to peaceful settlement mechanisms differing from those expressly provided in the treaty unless both parties have agreed otherwise in written form. If the investor chooses arbitration ad hoc, unless the parties agree otherwise, the provisions of the UNCITRAL Arbitration Rules should apply subject to certain requirements contained in the Reglament.

Arbitration awards adopted in accordance with the treaty are binding on the parties and must be enforced in accordance with their legislation. The investment protection treaty should not prevent the parties to a dispute from settling such disputes in an extra-judicial procedure, including by way of conciliation, mediation, or similar procedures if both parties agree to use them.

General exceptions. The Reglament mentions a number of what are called "general exceptions"—measures that might be taken by the parties to an investment protection treaty on a non-discriminatory basis and would presumably override the treaty provisions. The list of such measures includes: measures necessary to protect human life and health, flora and fauna, the environment, exhausted natural resources, public morality and public order, rights of consumers, objects of cultural, historical, or archaeological heritage, personal data and other confidential information whose dissemination is restricted in accordance with legislation of the parties to the treaty applying the respective measures, and also measures directed toward combating corruption, money laundering, money received by criminal means, and terrorism. Nor should the treaty prevent the parties from undertaking prudential measures as provided in point 2 of the Annex relating to financial services in the GATS.

Nor should the treaty prevent the parties from taking measures to defend material "security interests in connection with extraordinary situations in international relations, including war, deliveries for needs of the armed forces and law enforcement agencies, fissionable materials, or materials used to obtain them" (point 61). Measures necessary to fulfill obligations arising from the United Nations Charter should also not be obstructed by the investment protection treaty, and the parties should immediately notify one another about such measures if they may affect the investments of their investors.

Furthermore, the Reglament provides that the measures relating to security, war, and the United Nations "may not be the subject-matter of arbitral examination in the event disputes arise between the investor of one party to the treaty and the other party to the treaty" (point 63).

Other obligations. The investment protection treaty should not obstruct investors being granted a regime more favorable than established by the treaty if such regime is established by their legislation or by international agreements to which all the parties to the investment protection treaty are parties. Nor should the investment protection treaty be used to reduce ecological or labor standards, or to mitigate anti-terrorist, corruption, or money-laundering legislation.

An investment protection treaty is seen as an appropriate vehicle for the exchange of information between the parties concerning legislation and investment policies, consultations regarding the interpretation, application, or review of the treaty, including by means of creating a joint committee composed of representatives of the parties and a Statute on the formation of such a committee.

The investment protection treaty should provide that nothing in the treaty should be construed as obliging a party to the treaty to divulge confidential information.

Disputes between parties to investment protection treaty. Consultations between the parties are the preferred method of dispute settlement. If a dispute arises relating to the interpretation or application of the treaty, any party may send to the other a notification to propose to commence consultations. If consultations are not begun within a designated period, the treaty may provide for referral of the dispute to arbitration.

If the treaty does provide for arbitration, the arbitral tribunal should be formed of three members, one of whom is the chairman. The treaty should contain a procedure for the appointment of arbitrators, including the chairman if the arbitrators cannot agree on the chairman.

The treaty should provide that the award of the arbitrators is final and binding. Each party should bear its own expenses and share with the other party half of the expenses of the chairman of the tribunal; the arbitrators would have the right to determine that one party should bear a larger portion of the expenses.

Concluding and other provisions. The Reglament is silent on whether investment protection treaties should be ratified. Given the judicial interpretation of Article 15(4) of the 1993 Russian Constitution, most States will prefer to insist on ratification if their own legislation does not so require. The Reglament requires a minimum period of ten years for the duration of an investment protection treaty during which it may not be dissolved by a party unilaterally. Renewal is automatic unless a party gives no less than twelve months' notice beforehand that the treaty should expire. After the treaty expires, its provisions should apply to investments which were made before the date of termination of its operation and existed on the date of termination for the next ten years unless the parties agree otherwise when terminating the treaty.

The Reglament emphasizes in its final provisions two points:

[1]. The presence or absence "in the present document of any provisions does not predetermine the concrete content of a treaty" (point 78).

[2]. The Reglament "may not be used when interpreting the provisions of treaties which were concluded before the entry into force of the Decree of the Government of the Russian Federation of 30 September 2016, No. 992" or were concluded after the entry into force of the said Decree.

4
Publication and Registration of Treaties in Russia

The publication of international treaties has always been a matter of more than ordinary concern in Soviet and post-Soviet international legal practice and doctrine. The October 1917 Russian Revolution was dedicated in part to exposing the perfidious secret diplomacy engaged in by the Allied and the Central Powers during World War I, including by Imperial Russia. Dekret No. 1 "On Peace" abolished secret diplomacy and provided for the publication of secret treaties whose texts were found in Imperial Russian State archives, to the discomfiture and embarrassment of the parties on both sides in the War.

Lenin's exposure of the secret treaties and simultaneous espousal of self-determination as a principle of diplomacy was consistent with his analysis of "Imperialism as the Highest Stage of Capitalism." In his view, the leading European capitalist powers had managed to stave off inevitable revolution by "bribing the working class" with pensions and other forms of social security and higher wages than would otherwise have been possible through the pursuance of colonial policies in what from the 1960s onward was known as the "third world." Colonies enabled the capitalist States to import cheap raw materials by impoverishing or enslaving the working class and peasantry in those parts of the world and "pay off" their own working class with some of the proceeds. Deprive the capitalist States of this source of wealth, Lenin believed, and the ruling classes would have no alternative to victimizing their own workers, which in turn would lead to discontent and ultimately revolution. On this theory, self-determination was the key to breaking the capitalist hold on cheap raw materials and labor because, once independent, the former colonies would seek a fair return for their goods and labor, raise prices in the metropolitan country, and hasten the spark of revolution on a worldwide basis.

The secret treaties in various ways agreed sundry redivisions of territory in Europe, Africa, the Middle East, and elsewhere. Their existence and provisions were unknown to the general public, including in the United States, which entered the War too late to become involved in them and would have been disadvantaged by their provisions. President Woodrow Wilson seized upon the disclosure of the secret treaties and diplomacy behind them exactly two months later, on January 8, 1918, in the formulation of his Fourteen Points for a postwar settlement and world order, which provided in Point I for: "Open covenants of peace, openly arrived at, after which there shall be no private international understandings of any kind but diplomacy shall proceed always frankly and in the public view."[1]

A secret treaty concluded in 1915 between Italy and Russia appeared in the press. Lenin attacked the treaty after the February 1917 Revolution in Russia because Italy would have been generously rewarded after the War with territories settled by Germans (Tyrol) and Croatians and Serbs (Dalmatia).[2] Once in power, the Government of the RSFSR published more than 100 secret treaties found in the Imperial Russian archives.[3] The *New York Times* and the *Manchester Guardian* were among the western newspapers that published a number of texts.[4] Among the treaties of greatest concern to the Allied Powers was an agreement of September 5, 1914 in which they had obliged themselves (including Russia) not to make a separate peace. The Government of the Soviet Russia in the person of its People's Commissar for Foreign Affairs, Leon Trotsky (1879–1940), sent the first

---

[1] The Soviet release of the secret treaties was said to have had a "profound effect" on President Wilson, duly reflected in the salient positioning of the abolition of secret diplomacy in the first of the Fourteen Points. See P Johnson, *Modern Times: The World from the Twenties to the Nineties* (1991) 22. Secret treaties were actually prohibited by the United States on June 14, 1790, establishing that all treaties made by the United States "from time to time be published and annexed to their code of laws, by the Secretary of State." A rare Congressional Resolution, only one physical copy being recorded at the American Antiquarian Society.

[2] V I Lenin, "Одна из тайных договоров" ["One of the Secret Treaties"], in I I Kul'kov (ed.), Ленин о международной политике и международном праве [*Lenin on International Politics and International Law*] (1958) 281.

[3] E A Korovin (ed.), Международное право [*International Law*] (1951) 108.

[4] G F Kennan, *Soviet-American Relations, 1917–1920: Russia Leaves the War* (1967) I, 92. The Russian Soviet Government inaugurated a series of "Russian Revolutionary Pamphlets" in January 1918 devoted to secret treaties. The first contained an introduction by the People's Commissar of Foreign Affairs, Leon Trotsky. See L Trotsky, "Secret Diplomacy," *Secret Diplomatic Documents and Treaties from the Archives of the Ministry of Foreign Affairs of the Former Russian Government*, I (Petrograd, January 1918) 3–4. Trotsky wrote: "The Workmen's & Peasants' Government absolutely abolishes all secret diplomacy with its appurtenances of intrigue, cipher code, and trickery." Ibid, 4. The materials were set out in sections: Agreement regarding Constantinople and the Straits of February 19/March 4, 1915; diplomatic notes concerning the Straits of March 5 and 7, 1915; an Agreement with Italy in 1915; annexation agreements with France of January 30, 1917; the role of Japan with correspondence of April 28/May 11, 1916; offering territories to Greece on November 22, 1914; discussions of Romania entering the War; and secret telegrams sent from the Russian plenipotentiary in London in July 1917.

formal notification to the Allied Governments, including the United States, of the establishment of Soviet power and drew attention to a "formal proposal for an armistice" contained in Dekret No. 1 "On Peace." The Note was in the French language.[5] On the same day that the Soviet Note was sent to the Allied Powers and the United States, the RSFSR Government began to make public the secret treaties found in the Archives of the Imperial Russian Ministry of Foreign Affairs. On the preceding day Trotsky cautioned that the Bolsheviks intended to publish the treaties:

> [The secret treaties] are even more cynical in their contents than we supposed, and we do not doubt that when the German Social Democrats obtain access to the safes in which the secret treaties are kept, they will show us that German imperialism in its cynicism and rapacity yields in nothing to the rapacity of the Allied countries.[6]

Although the initial concern was what the Allies perceived as a breach of the 1914 agreement not to seek a separate armistice by the Government of the RSFSR, the implications of denouncing secret diplomacy and treaties went far beyond the immediate military situation. Not only by secret treaty had the Allied and Central powers undertaken to "re-divide" colonies and other dependent territories, but existing capitulations and extraterritoriality arrangements were called into question. At the peace negotiations in Versailles initiated in 1918, several delegations sought the termination of capitulations, among them Siam, China, and Persia. The RSFSR itself entered into bilateral treaties terminating the capitulations arrangements previously agreed with the Imperial Russian Government.[7]

Although the Bolsheviks concentrated upon exposing the treaties concluded on the eve of or during World War I, the practice of secret treaties was well established in international law and diplomacy. Such treaties date back to at least the year 499, when one of the Kings of Bourgogne, Godegisile, concluded a secret agreement with Clovis, King of the Franks, concerning military assistance.[8] The earliest recorded Russian secret treaty

---

[5] See V Rjéoutski, D Offord, and G Argent, "French as a Diplomatic and Official Language in Imperial Russia," *Jus Gentium: Journal of International-Legal History*, IV (2019) 419–93. The Government of the RSFSR resorted immediately to the *lingua franca* of diplomacy of the international community.

[6] J Degras (ed.), *Soviet Documents on Foreign Policy* (1951) I, 7–8.

[7] See J B Quigley, Jr, *Soviet Legal Innovation and the Law of the Western World* (2007) 133–7.

[8] See E Grosek, *The Secret Treaties of History* (2nd edn.; 2007) 3.

was concluded on October 12(22), 1675 between Tsar Aleksei Mikhailovich and the Holy Roman Emperor Leopold I (1640–1705) concerning concerted actions against Turkey and Poland and continuing the war against France and Sweden.[9] In all, Grosek records 158 secret treaties concluded by Russia before October 26, 1917 and seventy-six known to have been concluded by the RSFSR and USSR between October 26, 1917 and the year 2000. Presumably these statistics are minimum figures and understate the true number.[10]

For the law of treaties, the enduring impact of these developments was not the abolition of "secret diplomacy"—which continues in practice down to the present—but the introduction of a requirement, transformed in practice into a behest—embodied in Article 18 of the Covenant of the League of Nations:

> Every treaty or international engagement entered into hereafter by any Member of the League shall be forthwith registered with the Secretariat and shall as soon as possible be published by it. No such treaty or international engagement shall be binding until so registered.

The Harvard Draft on the Law of Treaties (1935) sought to improve on this formulation in the belief that the word "treaty" in Article 18 of the League Covenant did not include all international agreements, in any event plainly did not extend to treaties between non-Members of the League or between Members and non-Members of the League, and did not impose an obligation upon a State which left the League of Nations. The authors of the Harvard Draft sought to erect another barrier against secret treaties.[11]

The architects of the Harvard Draft reported that the formulation in Article 18 of the Covenant that a treaty was not binding until registered had generated "no considerable dissatisfaction," although the Permanent Court of International Justice had given effect to "unregistered treaties or engagements" to "which Members of the League of Nations were parties."

---

[9] Ibid, 38.

[10] Some arrangements take the form of a Memorandum of Understanding, which has its own legal status and may or may not constitute a proper treaty. See A Aust, *Modern Treaty Law and Practice* (3rd edn.; 2013) 28–54.

[11] The Commentary to Article 17 of the Harvard Draft, which dealt with the registration and publication of treaties, noted: "The purpose of Article 18 of the Covenant was clearly to prevent the conclusion by Members of the League of secret treaties." See J P Grant and J Craig Barker (comps), *The Harvard Research in International Law: Original Materials* (2008) II, 915.

The commentators were unwilling at the time to refrain from "any endeavor to state its effect more definitely ... ".

When the United Nations succeeded the League of Nations in 1945, the United Nations Charter contained a similar provision. Article 102 read as follows:

1. Every treaty and every international agreement entered into by any Member of the United Nations after the present Charter comes into force shall as soon as possible be registered with the Secretary and published by it.
2. No party to any such treaty or international agreement which has not been registered in accordance with the provisions of paragraph 1 of this Article may invoke that treaty or agreement before any organ of the United Nations.

Soviet international lawyers considered the introduction of the registration and publication of treaties to be a significant contribution of their country to international law which led directly to the inclusion of Article 18 in the Covenant of the League of Nations and the establishment of the *League of Nations Treaty Series* (LNTS) and its successor, the *United Nations Treaty Series* (UNTS): "Incontestable facts testify that the institution of the registration of treaties in international law arose under the impact of acts of the Soviet Government with regard to the publication of secret treaties."[12]

The provision of Article 18 of the League Covenant for all practical purposes did not operate insofar as registration of a treaty with the League of Nations was a precondition for the treaty entering into force. The sanction of not entering into force was not accepted in State practice,[13] and only

---

[12] See V M Chkhikvadze (ed.), Курс международного права в шести томах [*Course of International Law in Six Volumes*] (1968) IV, 153; G I Tunkin and Rein Müllerson, "Закон о международных договорах СССР" ["Law on International Treaties of the USSR"], Советское государство и право [*Soviet State and Law*], no. 2 (1979) 30. See also I I Lukashuk, in V N Kudriavtsev (ed.), Курс международного права в семи томах [*Course of International Law in Seven Volumes*] (1990) IV, 45: "The Great October Socialist Revolution played an important role in the struggle against secret treaties." In all, the League of Nations registered 4,834 treaties published in 205 volumes. See A Aust, "Law of Treaties," in J P Grant and J Craig Barker (eds.), *The Harvard Research in International Law: Contemporary Analysis and Appraisal* (2007) 312.

[13] This is a harsher view than usually encountered in the literature. Figures are available on the registered treaties, but no reliable statistics on treaties not registered for whatever reason. Germany registered treaties from 1920, the United States registered some between 1926 and 1934 and, from 1934, most treaties.

some treaties were submitted to the League of Nations for registration—far from all. Neither could secret treaties be abolished, although they could be abrogated by a party thereto. Notwithstanding its declared hostility to secret treaties, the RSFSR and later the Soviet Union did conclude secret treaties, among them an armistice with Latvia in 1920 and a trade agreement with Turkey in 1932, together with the Soviet-German agreements of 1939 and Yalta arrangements involving the Far East in 1945.[14]

The formulation of Article 102 of the United Nations Charter was more realistic with respect to the sanction for non-registration—it being supposed that the United Nations, with an immense backlog of treaties for publication, could not conceivably give effect to a treaty regime in which treaties did not enter into force until publication or that publication was a precondition of entry into force. Funding issues and challenges in publishing large-scale charts, maps, and other annexes are among the factors that have contributed to the backlog in the UNTS.

The publication of international treaties, unlike legislation in many national legal systems, although desirable, is not a prerequisite under international law for the validity of the treaty. Neither publication in official gazettes nor registration with, and subsequent publication by, an international organization is essential—from the standpoint of international law—to the legal effect of an international treaty unless the treaty so stipulates. On the other hand, publication is not a pure formality. The international community has come to accept, in disapproving of secret treaties, that publication in principle at least is essential for reasons of publicity, reference, information and use, and as part of what might be called the international democratic process.

The early Soviet legislation on the conclusion, ratification, and denunciation of treaties contained no provisions regarding their publication until 1924. From 1921 the People's Commissariat for Foreign Affairs of the RSFSR published the Сборник действующих договоров, соглашений и конвенций, заключенных РСФСР с иностранными государствами [Collection of Treaties, Agreements, and Conventions in Force Concluded by the RSFSR with Foreign States] (1921–23) on a chronological basis using not the year in which the treaty was concluded, but the year when it entered into force. Only some treaties were included. The USSR continued the

---

[14] These examples were cited in Lukashuk (n. 12) 45.

publication from 1924 at intermittent intervals until the dissolution of that country.

Official Publication of Treaties and Treaty-Related Normative Legal Acts

RSFSR Legislative Practice: 1917–22

Treaties differ from national legislation in a number of general respects. The authentic text of a treaty is that signed by the parties in however many originals or examples are agreed. Whether the texts signed and ultimately approved or ratified, if such is required, are printed for general information, and/or are gazetted in an official gazette as a condition of entry into force or application within a national legal system, is a matter for agreement of the parties or regulated by national legislation.

The initial Bolshevik attitude toward secret diplomacy and secret treaties as a product of such diplomacy had nothing to do with the law of treaties, although exposure of the secret treaties led, as noted above, to changes in the international legal regulation of treaties. Publication of secret treaties was a prelude to their abrogation, to their becoming non-treaties. Some were in force at the time; others were ideas, proposals, or drafts for discussion. Bringing them to "general information" by way of publication was not a factor in their ratification or entry into force; it was rather a factor in their exposure and termination. Publication here was to discredit the treaties, not in any way to introduce them into the municipal legal system of the RSFSR.

Within three days following the October Revolution, with revolutionary legislation already being enacted, no later than October 29, 1917 (November 11) the Council of People's Commissars adopted a dekret, signed by Lenin, "On the Procedure for the Confirmation and Publication of Laws." Each draft law was to be considered for consideration of the Government by the respective people's commissariat over the signature or the respective people's commissar or by the legislative proposals department attached to the Government over the signature of the section head. After confirmation by the Government, the draft dekret in its final version was signed in the name of the Russian Republic by the Chairman of the Council of People's Commissars and published for general information. The dekret entered into force upon publication in the official newspaper of the Workers' and Peasants' Government unless specified otherwise in the enactment or introduced into operation by telegraph; in the last event, entry into force was the moment of receipt in each locality upon publication there of the respective telegram. The publication of legislative decrees of the Government through the Ruling Senate of the Provisional Government was abolished.[15] The following day the full name of the official gazette was designated as the medium through which "all laws, dekrets, decrees, and regulations" of the Government enter into legal force: Газета временного рабочего и крестьянскьго правительства [newspaper of the Provisional Workers' and Peasants' Government].[16]

No mention was made of treaties in these enactments, nor had the fledgling RSFSR Government concluded any. Once treaties began to be concluded, irrespective of whether the texts were published, the ratification or approval enactments—as documents of municipal origin—would fall within this general legislation and be subject to publication. Communication was the major concern at the time: communicating to the addressees of legislation and to the general public the orders and instructions of the authorities. Telegraph was used to transmit the texts of legislative enactments, together with numerous official and unofficial newspapers, journals, and other serial publications.[17]

As time passed, the need was felt for more detailed regulation and systematization of the practice of publishing legislation. When, for example, in a country with up to eleven time zones, did dekrets and decrees of the All-Russian Central Executive Committee and Council of People's Commissars enter into legal force? The first definitive answer was provided on November 23, 1918, when entry into force was linked to publication in the Известия Всероссийского Центрального исполнительного комитета советов[18]

---

[15] СУ РСФСР (1917–18) no 1, item 12; trans by W E Butler, in *Soviet Statutes & Decisions*, XII, no 1 (1975) 29–30.

[16] СУ РСФСР (1917–18) no 3, item 40; trans in ibid, 31.

[17] See, for example, the Direction of the Presidium of the All-Russian Executive Committee to all Soviets of Deputies on the Duty of All Newspapers to Print Decrees of the People's Commissariat for Military Affairs, especially those on universal compulsory military training and on the procedure for appointing to posts in the Army. Translated in ibid, 34.

[18] СУ РСФСР (1918) no 86, item 903, based on a draft submitted by the Section for the Publication of Laws of the People's Commissariat of Justice. Translated in Butler (n. 15) 40. This enactment was "clarified" on October 8, 1920 to add Экономическая жизнь [Economic Life] as an official gazette and to provide that if the dekret or decree stipulated transmission by telegraph, entry into force occurred upon receipt of the telegram. Ibid, 45–6. On December 7, 1918 the Council of People's Commissars decreed to recommend to people's commissars that "when citing old dekrets to indicate the respective number of the issue [and] item" of the СУ РСФСР. The decree is translated in ibid, 41.

[News of the All-Russian Central Executive Committee of Soviets] or in the СУ РСФСР. This approach proved to be unrealistic, for considerable time could elapse between publication of the respective gazette in Moscow and its receipt in the localities. On March 27, 1919 the date of entry into force was changed in the localities from the moment of publication in Moscow to the date of receipt of either the printed gazette or of a telegraph notification (or any other form of notification) by the respective executive committee of the local soviet or Soviet institution to which the enactment was addressed. Registration of receipt was required, as was posting of the enactment (for example, on a municipal bulletin board on the street and/or in the headquarters of local government, or in enterprises, and the like) for general information.[19] All these developments would, of course, affect the texts of treaties and the enactments confirming or ratifying them.

In November 1919 a reform was instituted in the Government of the RSFSR to unify the provision of legal advice to people's commissariats. Whether this was a cosmetic reform intended to streamline government or resulted in layoffs of legal personnel is ambiguous. On November 19, 1919 the Council of People's Commissars decided to close all legal sections, bureaus, organs, and the like, and the posts of jurisconsults and jurists, in the people's commissariats for foreign affairs, trade and industry, nationality affairs, post and telegraph, State control, and provisions both at the center and in the localities. Instead, certain people's commissariats were allowed, by special permission, to have individual jurisconsults at their disposal.[20] With respect to international-legal matters, this reform will have prejudiced the People's Commissariat for Foreign Affairs in its competence and ability to advise on treaties and related matters, passing this mostly to the People's Commissariat of Justice.

The Civil War in Russia frustrated the realization of procedures for the editing and printing of legislative and governmental acts. Having

---

[19] This decree was never published in the official gazette, its existence being disclosed in the publication of archival sources. The text originated in the Legal Section of the Supreme Council, duly amended by the People's Commissariat of Justice. See Декреты советской власти [Dekrets of Soviet Power], IV, 652.

[20] The decree was first published in 1973. The purpose of the enactment was to centralize legal advice in the People's Commissariat of Justice. On the same date the People's Commissariat of Justice was to reorganize its apparatus so as to meet the needs of the other people's commissariats for legal advice and to abolish the post of individual jurisconsults and legal sections in all institutions of the Republic even if prior consent to the existence of these posts and sections had been previously obtained. Trans. in Butler (n. 15) 43.

"acquired experience" in these activities, further centralization and professionalization was introduced and the People's Commissariat chosen as the appropriate vehicle. All legislative and "most important" governmental proposals originating in individual departments were to be submitted to the Legislative Proposals Section of the People's Commissariat of Justice no later than three days before submission to the Council of People's Commissars unless pressing urgency required a more expeditious approach. The Legislative Proposals Section had three days after receipt of the proposal to prepare comments; once these were submitted to the originating department, when either accepted the comments or declined to do so and passed its version to the Council of People's Commissars, the Legislative Proposals Section had the right to be present with a consultative vote at the session of the Council of People's Commissars. Moreover, the People's Commissariat of Justice had to approve official publication unless the enactments entered into force by telegraphic transmission.[21]

USSR Legislative Practice: 1922–58

The abolition of secret diplomacy (ostensibly) and the renunciation of secret treaties concluded by the Imperial Russian Government sat uneasily with the commitment to publish treaties entered into, Soviet treaty practice in general, and the failure to adopt enactments clarifying the need or place to publish treaties. After the Treaty of the Union was concluded on December 30, 1922, the newly formed Union of Soviet Socialist Republics introduced legislation determining the allocation of responsibilities among the legislative and executive branches of State for treaty policy. This was first addressed in the 1924 USSR Constitution, Article 1 of which provided in part:

1. To the jurisdiction of the Union of Soviet Socialist Republics in the person of its supreme agencies shall be subject:
   ...
   (d) declaration of war and conclusion of peace;
   (e) ratification of international treaties ...

---

[21] See the decree of December 20, 1920, trans. in Butler (n. 15) 46–7.

The phrase "supreme agencies" was addressed in Article 8 of the 1924 Constitution; in descending order they were: (1) the Congress of Soviets; (2) in intervals between sessions of the said Congress—the Central Executive Committee; (3) in intervals between sessions of the Central Executive Committee, the Presidium of the Central Executive Committee; and (4) the Council of People's Commissars as the executive and administrative organ of the Central Executive Committee. On a literal reading of Article 1 of the Constitution, neither the Presidium of the Central Executive Committee or the Council of People's Commissars were considered to be "supreme agencies," and therefore did not have the right to ratify treaties. In practice, however, both bodies were involved in treaty-making and occasionally in ratification.

The Central Executive Committee of the USSR on November 12, 1923 confirmed the Statute on the Council of People's Commissars of the USSR conferring jurisdiction to consider treaties and agreements with governments of foreign States and to confirm those not requiring ratification.[22] On the same date the Statute on the People's Commissariat of Foreign Affairs of the USSR was confirmed, setting the tasks for the People's Commissariat of fulfilling decrees concerning the conclusion of treaties with foreign States, directing the implementation of treaties, and watching over the fulfillment of treaties (Article 2).[23] Nothing was said about treaty publication, although the official gazettes sometimes published the texts of treaties and on most occasions the normative legal acts ratifying or confirming treaties. By 1925 the situation was acknowledged to be unsatisfactory.[24]

This omission was addressed in the decree of the Central Executive Committee dated August 22, 1924 "On the Procedure for the Publication of Laws and Regulations of the Government of the USSR," which provided as follows in point 11:[25]

11. Treaties, agreements, and conventions concluded by the USSR with foreign States shall be subject to publication in the Собрание

---

[22] Trans in Butler, *Soviet Statutes & Decisions*, III, no 4 (1967) 51.

[23] Ibid, 52.

[24] Some relief was given by a treaty series inaugurated by the People's Commissariat for Foreign Affairs, but this appeared with tardiness, included merely a small number of treaties concluded by Soviet Russia and the USSR, published treaties only upon entry into force (which in some cases was many years, even decades, after signature or accession); in all the set amounted to just over forty volumes and ceased publication in the early1990s.

[25] Trans. in Butler (n. 15) 81.

законов и распоряжений Рабоче-Крестьянского Правительства Союза ССР [Collection of Laws and Regulations of the Workers'-Peasants' Government of the Union of Soviet Socialist Republics] in the following procedure:

(a) treaties, agreements, and conventions subject to ratification by the Government of the USSR or which enter into force upon the exchange of declarations between the Parties which have signed them shall be subject to publication only after the exchange of instruments of ratification or declarations;

(b) treaties, agreements, and conventions entering into force upon their signature by the Parties or upon the expiry of a certain period after signing or upon their publication in official organs of the USSR, shall be published upon their being concluded.

Note. Treaties, agreements, and conventions subject to publication shall be sent to the Section for the Publication of Laws by the People's Commissariat for Foreign Affairs with the visa of the People's Commissar or of the Deputy People's Commissar, without which publication may not occur.

On January 8, 1926 the aforesaid decree was amended (Article 1) to distinguish between "decrees of a legislative character" and "other decrees," together with "international treaties, agreements, and conventions"; the former would be published in Section One of the gazette, and the rest in Section Two of the gazette. For some years Section One of the gazette was published in six languages, whereas the materials in Section Two were published, as a rule, only in the Russian language.

Mention of publication came in the decree on the Procedure for the Submission of International Agreements Concluded in the Name of the USSR for Approval, Confirmation, and Ratification of the Government of the USSR, adopted October 2, 1925, but only with respect to the publication of a decree of the Council of People's Commissars concerning accession of the USSR to an international treaty in force, with no mention of publication of the treaty itself.

This omission in early Soviet legislation may perhaps be attributable to a full agenda of other items and inexperience in treaty-making. The Soviet Union did not join the League of Nations until September 18, 1934, although it did work closely with several League commissions and committees prior to joining. Nonetheless, Soviet and post-Soviet international legal doctrine have credited Dekret No. 1 of Soviet Russia with influencing the introduction of treaty registration and publication by the international community.

With the adoption of the 1936 Constitution of the USSR and gradual implementation of the new constitutional terminology, the Collection of Laws and Regulations was discontinued pursuant to the Law on the Procedure for the Ratification and Denunciation of International Treaties of the USSR, of August 20, 1938[26] and replaced by the Ведомости Верховного Совета CCCP [Gazette of the Supreme Soviet of the USSR], initially issued in tabloid format. The decree of August 22, 1924, as amended to 1928, remained in force however for another two decades.

The gazette (or Vedomosti) of the Supreme Soviet was published by the USSR until the dissolution of the Union on or about December 25, 1991 (there were some adjustments in title at the very end). Wartime conditions made appearance of the gazette episodic during World War II, and for many of the early postwar years publication was either suspended or classified and circulated to a select limited list of recipients. The Supreme Soviet itself met, as a rule, twice a year for two or three days at a time, and its proceedings and enactments were published in casebound book form.

USSR Legislative Practice: 1958–91

As part of the post-Stalin reforms, on June 19, 1958 the Presidium of the USSR Supreme Soviet adopted an edict with provided with respect to treaties:[27]

4. Treaties, agreements, and conventions concluded by the USSR with foreign States and ratified in the established procedure, and the respective edicts concerning ratification, shall be published in Ведомости

[26]   Trans. in Butler (n. 22) 55–6.
[27]   Trans. in Butler, *Soviet Statutes & Decisions*, XII, no. 2 (1975–76) 110. The text of the edict was not available to Triska and Slusser, who cited a press release summarizing the edict. See J Triska and R Slusser, *The Theory, Law, and Policy of Soviet Treaties* (1962) 108. By an edict of May 6, 1980, No 2025-X, the 1958 edict was adopted in a new version. On the same day the Presidium of the USSR Supreme Soviet adopted Decree No 2026-X "On the Organization of Work for the Publication of Laws of the USSR, Decrees and Other Acts of the USSR Supreme Soviet, and Edicts and Decrees of the Presidium of the USSR Supreme Soviet." See Ведомости Верховного Совета CCCP [Gazette of the USSR Supreme Soviet] (1980) no 20, item 375. This decree provided that international treaties of the USSR are to be published in Section One of the gazette (point 7).

upon the recommendation of the USSR Ministry of Foreign Affairs to the Presidium of the USSR Supreme Soviet.

Note that this formulation applied only to "ratified" treaties, and the formulation "upon the recommendation" meant that the publication of such treaties was within the discretion of the Ministry of Foreign Affairs to "recommend" or not. In practice, only some treaties were published in the gazette, although most edicts ratifying treaties were so published.

This left the question of treaties not subject to ratification. The decree of the USSR Council of Ministers "On the Procedure for the Publication and Entry into Force of Decrees and Regulations of the Government of the USSR" of March 20, 1959 provided:[28]

4. Treaties, agreements, and conventions concluded by the USSR with foreign States and not subject to ratification, and also the respective decrees of the Government concerning their confirmation, shall be published in the Собрание постановлений Правительства СССР [Collection of Decrees of the Government of the USSR] upon the recommendation of the USSR Ministry of Foreign Affairs.

On May 6, 1980 the following paragraph was added to point 4 of the 1958 edict:[29]

International treaties of the USSR whose authentic texts have been drawn up in foreign languages shall be published in Ведомости in one of these languages with an official translation into the Russian language.

Some treaties were published in the mass media, although this was at the discretion of the Government and there was no time limit placed on their appearance. The mass media chosen were usually the Government newspaper Известия [Izvestia] or Правда [Pravda].

With the adoption in 1977 of a new Constitution of the USSR to replace that of 1936, followed in 1978 by constitutions in each of the fifteen union republics, the USSR Supreme Soviet on July 6, 1978 enacted the Law on the Procedure for the Conclusion, Execution, and Denunciation

---

[28] Trans. in Butler (n. 27) 112.
[29] Ведомости Верховного Совета СССР [*Gazette of the USSR Supreme Soviet*] (1980) no 20, item 374.

of International Treaties of the USSR (hereinafter: 1978 USSR Law on treaties).[30] The enactment of the Law had been expressly foreshadowed in the concluding speech of Leonid Il'ich Brezhnev (1906–82) at the Extraordinary Seventh Session of the USSR Supreme Soviet on October 6, 1977 convoked to adopt the USSR Constitution,[31] but the drafting of the 1978 Law on Treaties had been, it is believed, underway for some time in the Permanent Commission for Foreign Affairs of the USSR Supreme Soviet and its working groups. At the time of its enactment, the Soviet Union had not ratified the 1969 Vienna Convention on the Law of Treaties;[32] nonetheless, the 1978 USSR Law on treaties represented to a considerable extent the codification in Soviet, now Russian, law of the 1969 Vienna Convention.

The publication of international treaties, unlike normative-legal acts in many national legal systems, is not a prerequisite under international law for their validity. Neither publication in official gazettes (whether in printed form or online) nor registration with, and subsequent publication by, an international organ is essential from the standpoint of international law to the legal effect of an international treaty unless the treaty itself so stipulates. Oral treaties are possible and indeed known in the history of international law. Neither, on the other hand, is publication a mere formality. The international community has come to accept, in principle at least, that publication is essential for reasons of publicity, reference, information, and use, and as part of what might be called the international democratic process.

But treaty publication may have another dimension, and in Russian legal doctrine at this stage of its history the position was taken that publication was tantamount to the treaty becoming part of Russian domestic law. This was said to happen from the moment of publication, even though the treaty at the international level between the States parties entered into force in accordance with the treaty. This position dated back to the 1920s and was widely shared in the Soviet international legal community. It was a position that contained its own dilemmas: what of secret treaties; what of oral treaties; what of delays in publication or simple non-publication ever of an official text or an official translation?

The 1978 USSR Law on treaties treated the domestic publication of treaties as follows:

---

[30] Ведомости Верховного Совета СССР [*Gazette of the USSR Supreme Soviet*] (1978) no 28, item 439; trans in W E Butler, *International Legal Materials*, XVII (1978) 1115–22; W E Butler, *Basic Documents on the Soviet Legal System* (1983) 285–92.

[31] The Communication was published in Известия [Izvestia], October 8, 1977, 2, col 3.

[32] The Soviet Union acceded to the 1969 Vienna Convention on April 29, 1986.

(1) *Interstate* international treaties concluded in the name of the USSR which have entered into force for the USSR, decisions concerning the signature of which were adopted by the Presidium of the USSR Supreme Soviet, international treaties of the USSR concluded in the name of the Presidium of the USSR Supreme Soviet, ratified treaties, and treaties to the accession of which was effectuated on the basis of decisions of the Presidium of the USSR Supreme Soviet, were published upon the recommendation of the USSR Ministry of Foreign Affairs in the official gazette of the USSR Supreme Soviet noted above, published weekly. Treaties appeared in Section One of the gazette, which was reserved for normative materials.[33]

(2) *Intergovernmental* treaties concluded in the name of the USSR which have entered into force for the USSR, decisions concerning the signature of which were adopted by the USSR Council of Ministers, treaties concluded in the name of the Government of the USSR and are not subject to ratification, and treaties, the accession to which was carried out on the basis of decisions of the USSR Council of Ministers, were published upon the recommendation of the USSR Ministry of Foreign Affairs in the official gazette of the Government, the Собрание постановлений Правительства СССР [Collection of Decrees of the Government of the USSR], published roughly at fortnightly intervals.[34]

(3) *Interdepartmental* treaties were, according to the 1978 USSR Law on treaties, those concluded with foreign States or international organizations in the name of "the ministries, State committees, and departments of the USSR" (Article 2). Pursuant to the 1978 USSR Law on treaties, the USSR Council of Ministers adopted on August 28, 1980 Decree No. 743 "On the Procedure for the Conclusion, Performance, and Denunciation of International Treaties of the USSR of an

---

[33] See point 5, decree "On Organizing the Work for Publication of Laws of the USSR, Decrees, and Other Acts of the USSR Supreme Soviet, and Edicts and Decrees of the Presidium of the USSR Supreme Soviet," adopted May 6, 1980. Ведомости СССР (1980) no 20, item 375; trans in W E Butler, *Collected Legislation of the USSR and Union Republics* (loose-leaf service; 1979–91).

[34] See Article 25(2), 1978 USSR Law on treaties. From January 1981 the gazette of the Government, known by its initials SP SSSR, was published in two Sections: Section One and Section Two. The latter was devoted solely to the text of agreements, conventions, protocols, and other international treaties concluded by the Government of the USSR with foreign States. See Известия [Izvestia], August 21, 1980, 8, col 8.

Interdepartmental Character."[35] With respect to publication, the decree provided that:

13. International treaties of the USSR of an interdepartmental character which have entered into force for the USSR shall be published by decision of the ministries, State committees, and departments of the USSR on whose name such treaties were concluded unless there is another arrangement on this question.

Nothing was said about where such publication might occur. The 1978 USSR Law on treaties (Article 25) simply provided that "the procedure for the publication of international treaties of the USSR of an interdepartmental character shall be determined by the USSR Council of Ministers." Unless there is another decree or regulation which has not come to light, the Council of Ministers gave no further details.

Constitutional changes in the late Soviet period required that the edict of June 19, 1958, as amended, be replaced by the Law on the Procedure for the Publication and Entry into Force of Laws of the USSR and Other Acts Adopted by the Congress of People's Deputies of the USSR, USSR Supreme Soviet, and Organs Thereof, adopted July 31, 1989, No. 307-1. Article 5 of the Law dealt with international treaties and retained the previous procedure for publication, introducing some changes in the title of the official gazette:

5. International treaties concluded in the name of the USSR and ratified by the Supreme Soviet of the USSR which have entered into force for the USSR shall be published in the Ведомости Съезда народных депутатов СССР и Верховного Совета СССР [Gazette of the Congress of People's Deputies of the USSR and Supreme Soviet of the USSR] upon the recommendation of the Ministry of Foreign Affairs of the USSR.

International treaties of the USSR whose authentic texts have been drawn up in foreign languages shall be published Ведомости in one of these languages with an official translation into the Russian language.

This Law was never repealed but presumed to have lost force *de facto* with the dissolution of the Soviet Union. On November 29, 1990, the

---

[35] СП СССР (1980) no 22, item 136.

Constitutional Supervision Committee of the USSR on its own initiative raised the question whether the rules permitting the application of unpublished normative acts affecting the rights, freedoms, and duties of citizens were in accordance with the 1977 USSR Constitution and "international acts." In Opinion No. 12 (2-12), the Constitutional Supervision held that:[36]

1. The publication of laws and other normative acts concerning the rights, freedoms, and duties of citizens; that is, bringing them by one means or another to general information, is an obligatory condition of the application of these acts. Article 4 of the USSR Law "On the Procedure for the Publication and Entry into Force of Laws of the USSR and Other Acts Adopted by the Congress of People's Deputies of the USSR, USSR Supreme Soviet, and Organs Thereof," points 1, 2, and 5 of the Decree of the USSR Council of Ministers of 20 March 1959, No. 293, "On the Procedure for the Publication and Entry into Force of Decrees and Regulations of the Government of the USSR," and other normative provisions in that part thereof in which they directly or indirectly permit the entry into force of unpublished normative acts affecting the rights, freedoms, and duties of citizens do not conform to the USSR Constitution and international acts concerning human rights and in that part lose force from the moment of adoption of the present Opinion.

2. On the basis of Article 22 of the Law of the USSR "On Constitutional Supervision in the USSR" previously adopted but not published normative acts affecting the rights, freedoms, and duties of citizens shall be subject to publication by the respective State agencies within a three-month period from the day of adoption of the present Opinion. Acts which are not published upon the expiry of this period shall lost force.

In a decree of February 15, 1991, No. 16(2-12), "On the Procedure for the Realization of the Opinion of the Committee of 29 November 1990 'On Rules Permitting the Application of Unpublished Normative Acts concerning Rights, Freedoms, and Duties of Citizens,'" the Constitutional Supervision Committee of the USSR noted that the process of publishing unpublished acts was seriously being dragged out. Partly this was because

---

[36] Ведомости СНД СССР и ВС СССР [Gazette of the Congress of People's Deputies of the USSR and USSR Supreme Soviet] (1990) no 50, item 1080.

of the large number of such acts, many of which required additional analysis in substance. But the majority of unpublished acts would lose force from March 1, 1991, including some which provided individual categories of citizens with lawfully established privileges, guarantees, and compensations; if these were repealed, serious prejudice might be caused to the rights of these citizens. Therefore, the Committee ruled that from March 1, 1991 those unpublished acts or parts thereof which "limit the rights of citizens or place duties on them or established legal responsibility" would lost force. Those acts unpublished which establish rights of citizens, including privileges, guarantees, and compensations, would not terminate on March 1. But these acts, the Committee said, must be inventoried and declassified, so that there could be free access to them. Any acts adopted after November 29, 1990—the date of the Opinion of the Constitutional Supervision Committee—which affected the rights, freedoms, and duties of citizens were legally invalid and not subject to application.[37]

Treaties passing through the Government of the USSR instead of the parliament required new legislation which would reflect constitutional changes (including the renaming of the "Government" to the "Cabinet of Ministers") and the Opinion of the USSR Constitutional Supervision Committee. This was accomplished by the enactment of the decree of June 22, 1991, No. 389, "On the Procedure for the Publication of Decrees of the Cabinet of the USSR Cabinet of Ministers and International Treaties."[38] The formulation with respect to the publication of international treaties remained, however, the same:

> International treaties which have entered into force for the USSR and concluded in the name of the USSR, decisions concerning the signature of which have been adopted by the Cabinet of the USSR Council of Ministers, treaties concluded in the name of the Government of the USSR and not subject to ratification, treaties, accession to which or the adoption of which was effectuated on the basis of decisions of the Government of the USSR, shall be published upon the recommendation of the Ministry of Foreign Affairs of the USSR in the Собрание постановлений Правительства СССР [Collection of Decrees of the Government of the USSR].

---

[37] Ibid, (1991) no. 9, item 207.
[38] СП СССР (1991) no. 18–19, item 74. The decree of March 20, 1959 was repealed by the decree of June 22, 1991, No. 389.

International treaties of the USSR, the authentic texts of which have been drawn up in foreign languages, shall be published in one of these languages with an official translation into the Russian language.

Although the Opinion of the Constitutional Supervision Committee invoked the 1977 USSR Constitution and international acts to strike down Article 4 of the Law of July 31, 1989, this Opinion will have affected treaties in at least two respects: directly with respect to laws or decrees ratifying international treaties, and indirectly, the texts of treaties themselves as normative-legal acts.

Other mediums for the domestic publication of treaties existed in the Soviet Union. The series of volumes issued by the Ministry of Foreign Affairs of the USSR, continued by the Russian Federation, ended in about forty-three volumes but contained a small percentage of all Soviet treaties.[39] The Ministry of Foreign Trade published a monthly journal, Внешняя торговля [Foreign Trade], which often contained the texts of trade agreements and protocols. Numerous subject collections of treaties were issued for departmental use, often with restrictive cyphers limiting their circulation to internal use. There were and remain retrospective collections of diplomatic documents, including treaties, and pedagogical collections for reference or instructional use.[40]

None of the enactments on Soviet treaties explained what guidelines the Ministry of Foreign Affairs should apply when deciding to recommend publication of international treaties to which the USSR was a party, assuming that the parties to the treaty have not themselves stipulated publication in one forum or another.

The publication of treaties is associated with the process of treaty registration. Introduced in the Covenant of the League of Nations, the desirability of registering treaties is widely recognized to owe much to the Soviet Russian exposure of secret diplomacy. The 1978 USSR Law on treaties merely provided that the Ministry of Foreign Affairs of the USSR had responsibility for registering international treaties with the United Nations

---

[39] Сборник действующих договоров, соглашений и конвенций, заключенных СССР с иностранными государствами [Collection of Treaties, Agreements, and Conventions in Force Concluded by the USSR with Foreign States] (1925–).

[40] Many, but far from all, are listed in the four-volume bibliography of Soviet and Russian publications on international law. See D I Fel'dman (ed.), Международное право. Библиография 1917–1972 [International Law. Bibliography 1917–1972] (1976) and subsequent volumes.

Secretariat or with other international organizations. In the case of interdepartmental treaties, the decree of the USSR Council of Ministers of August 28, 1980 provided, pursuant to the 1978 USSR Law on treaties, that:

> 14. The registration of international treaties of the USSR of an interdepartmental character which will be deemed subject to registration shall be effectuated by the ministries, State committees, and departments of the USSR in whose name such treaties were concluded in the respective international organizations according to the rules operating in these organizations.

Within the framework of socialist economic integration being pursued from approximately 1970 onward, the Council for Mutual Economic Assistance (Comecon) registered many interdepartmental agreements,[41] but there was no generally available medium for publication of the texts.

Russian Federation Doctrine and Practice on the Publication of Treaties

Although the United Nations Charter (Article 102) required that organization to register and publish treaties submitted to its Secretariat, no norm of international law requires individual States to publish treaties themselves. Russian law does so require and elevated the requirement in 1993 to the constitutional level.

Prior to the adoption of the 1993 Russian Constitution but after the dissolution of the former Soviet Union, the President of the Russian Federation issued an edict of January 11, 1993, No 11, "On the Procedure for the Publication of International Treaties of the Russian Federation."[42] The edict provided that international treaties of the Russian Federation, except for interdepartmental treaties, were "subject to official publication in the monthly Бюллетень международных договоров [Bulletin of International Treaties] of the Publishing House 'Legal Literature' of the

---

[41] See the Procedure for the Mutual Transfer by COMECON Members of International Cooperation Agreements Through the COMECON Secretariat, approved by the COMECON Executive Committee on December 16, 1969. W E Butler (ed. and trans.), *A Source Book on Socialist International Organizations* (1978) 9–12.

[42] СЗ РФ (1993) no. 3, item 183; (1995) no. 49, item 4777.

Administration of the President of the Russian Federation and, when necessary, also in the newspaper Российские вести [Russian News]." In addition, international treaties might be brought to general information by other mass media and publishers.[43] Although the edict remains in force, as amended in 1995, the newspaper mentioned no longer exists, but the edict provided the foundation for the appearance of the monthly bulletin of international treaties.

Article 15(3) of the 1993 Russian Constitution requires that laws are subject to official publication and unpublished laws shall not be applied. As for other normative legal acts, if they affect the rights, freedoms, and duties of man and citizen, they may only be applied if they have been published for general information. The question is whether international treaties of the Russian Federation are to be considered, for the purposes of Article 15(3), either the equivalent of federal laws (over which they have priority under Article 15(4) of the Constitution) or "normative legal acts" which also require publication if they concern human rights. A distinction is drawn in Article 15(1) of the Constitution between "legal acts" (which treaties would undoubtedly be) and "normative legal acts" in Article 15(3).[44]

Official publication of international treaties of the Russian Federation is regulated, pursuant to Article 15(3) of the 1993 Constitution, by the 1995 Federal Law on International Treaties of the Russian Federation (Articles 5(3) and 30).[45] The procedure for the publication of federal laws ratifying international treaties or the texts of international treaties is governed by the Federal Law on the Procedure for the Publication and Entry into Force of Federal Constitutional Laws, Federal Laws, and Acts of Chambers

---

[43] This provision was challenged in the Supreme Court of Russia on the grounds that it consolidated "the possibility of applying international treaties of the Russian Federation published in other publications and served as grounds for applying provisions of an international agreement with respect to her not officially published, which would lead to a violation of her rights." The Supreme Court held that this provision did not restrict the operation of the requirement of official publication as a "direct condition of the application of normative acts and international treaties affecting the rights, freedoms, and duties of man and citizen." See the Decision of the Supreme Court of the Russian Federation, April 20, 2011. Available on Consultant Plus.

[44] Marochkin observed that because international treaties are part of the Russian legal system, "it is logical to conclude that this requirement [of publication] involves the treaties as well." On the view that treaty obligations override even the Constitution, Article 15(3) would not apply. See V S Ivanenko, "Международные договоры, Конституция и правовая система Российской Федерации: эволюция соотношения и тенденции взаимодействия" ["International Treaties, Constitution, and Legal System of the Russian Federation: Evolution of the Correlation and Trends of Interaction"], in Российский ежегодник международного права 2009 [*Russian Yearbook of International Law 2009*] (2010) 27.

[45] СЗ РФ (1995) no 29, item 2757, as amended; trans in Butler, *Russia & The Republics: Legal Materials* (loose-leaf service; 2006–).

of the Federal Assembly, which provides in a paragraph added October 21, 2011, as amended to May 1, 1919,[46] that Federal constitutional laws, federal laws, international treaties which have entered into force for the Russian Federation and international treaties which are provisionally applied by the Russian Federation (except for treaties of an interdepartmental character), resolutions of the United Nations Security Council providing for the introduction, change, suspension, or repeal of enforcement measures, and acts of chambers of the Federal Assembly adopted with regard to questions relegated to the jurisdiction of the chambers by Article 102(1) and Article 103(1) of the Constitution of the Russian Federation, edicts and regulations of the President of the Russian Federation, decrees of the Constitutional Court of the Russian Federation, rulings of the Constitutional Court of the Russian Federation concerning an explanation of Decrees of the Constitutional Court of the Russian Federation, and also other decisions of the Constitutional Court of the Russian Federation by which this procedure for placement (or publication) is provided, are to be placed (or published) on the "Official Internet-Portal of Legal Information."

Officially published international treaties of the Russian Federation which do not require the enactment of municipal acts in order to be applied operate in the Russian Federation directly (self-executing). If implementing legislation is required, then application of the treaty will await such enactment (non-self-executing).

Those treaties which have been ratified and entered into force are, upon the recommendation of the Ministry of Foreign Affairs of the Russian Federation, published in the gazette Собрание законодательства Российской Федерации [Collection of Legislation of the Russian Federation]. Only a comparatively low number of treaties receive the recommendation of the ministry for publication in this gazette. A larger number of treaties which have entered into force for Russia—likewise upon the discretionary recommendation of the Ministry of Foreign Affairs—appear in the monthly Бюллетень международных договоров [Bulletin of International Treaties], often with arrears. Alternatively, and also requiring the discretionary recommendation of the ministry, treaties are published on the "Official Internet-Portal of Legal Information" (www.pravo.gov.ru).

---

[46] СЗ РФ (1994) no. 8, item 801, as amended to May 1, 2019.

As for treaties which make provision before entry into force for provisional application by the Russian Federation of the entire treaty or parts thereof, or an arrangement concerning the provisional application of the treaty in other form, may upon the recommendation of the ministry be published at once in either the aforesaid bulletin or online.

Interdepartmental treaties are an exception to all of the foregoing. These are published, if at all, not by decision or recommendation of the Ministry of Foreign Affairs, but by decision of the federal agencies of executive power or duly empowered organizations in whose name such treaties were concluded. The site of publication will normally be the official publications of those agencies.

The Supreme Court of the Russian Federation and Supreme Arbitrazh Court of the Russian Federation (until its abolition in February 2014) were emphatic in their endorsement of the requirement of official publication. The decree of the Plenum of the Supreme Court of the Russian Federation of October 31, 1995, No 8, "On Certain Questions of the Application by Courts of the Constitution of the Russian Federation When Effectuating Justice" provided:

> Courts should have in view that by virtue of Article 5(3) of the Federal Law of the Russian Federation "On International Treaties of the Russian Federation" the provisions of officially published international treaties of the Russian Federation not requiring the publication of municipal acts for application operate in the Russian Federation directly. In other instances, together with the international treaty of the Russian Federation, the respective municipal legal act adopted for the effectuation of the provisions of the said international treaty should be applied.[47]

A later decree of the Plenum of the Supreme Court reiterated that on the basis of the meaning of Article 15(3) and (4) of the Constitution of the Russian Federation and Article 5(3) of the Federal Law "On International Treaties of the Russian Federation," those international treaties which have entered into force and which have been published officially in the Собрание законодательства Российской Федерации or in the Бюллетень международных договоров or placed on the "Official Internet-Portal of Legal Information" (www.pravo.gov.ru) in the procedure

---

[47] Point 5, para. 3. Available on Consultant Plus.

established by Article 30 of the said Federal Law may be applied by courts directly. International treaties of the Russian Federation of an interdepartmental character are to be published by decision of federal agencies of executive power or empowered organizations in the name of which such treaties have been concluded in the official publications of those agencies.[48]

The Supreme Arbitrazh Court in a decree of the Plenum of June 11, 1999, No 8, "On the Operation of International Treaties of the Russian Federation with Regard to Questions of Arbitrazh Procedure," instructed lower courts:

> An arbitrazh court shall apply international treaties of the Russian Federation which have entered into force and were duly brought to general information ... An international treaty of the Russian Federation is brought to general information by means of publication.[49]

In a case involving an exporter from the Kyrgyz Republic who transferred goods to a Russian purchaser in January 2001, Russian customs admitted the goods duty-free but then sought VAT, citing an intergovernmental Agreement between Russia and Kyrgizia of October 10, 2000, which entered into force on January 1, 2001, having been ratified on December 27, 2000 and the Law on ratification was published in the official gazette of January 1, 2001. The text of the Agreement, however, was not officially published until July 2, 2001. The arbitrazh court at the regional level held that the recovery of VAT was illegal because the text of the treaty had not been published at the time the export/import occurred even though the law on ratification had been published. The Supreme Arbitrazh Court affirmed this decision and rejected the protest of the Procuracy to the contrary.[50] A similar position was taken by the Presidium of the Supreme Arbitrazh Court in a decree of December 21, 2004 with regard to the application of a treaty and protocols thereto involving the import of goods from Moldova.[51]

The Case of I D Ushakov, decided by decree of the Constitutional Court of the Russian Federation on March 27, 2012, offers considerable insight into how the Russian judiciary approaches the interface between international

---

[48] Point 4, para. 3. Trans. in W E Butler, *Russian Public Law* (3d edn.; 2013) 49–50.

[49] Point 1, paras. 1 and 3. Available on Consultant Plus. Although the Supreme Arbitrazh Court was abolished in February 2014, its decrees remain in force unless specifically repealed. The present decree remains in force and was amended by the Supreme Court of the Russian Federation on June 27, 2017.

[50] See the decree of the Presidium of the Supreme Arbitrazh Court, May 15, 2002, No 1851/02. Available on Consultant Plus.

[51] Case No 9466/04. Available on Consultant Plus.

treaties of the Russian Federation and the requirement of official publication as a condition of municipal application of a treaty.

Case of I D Ushakov

Ushakov returned to the Russian Federation from China on July 10, 2010 and brought in with him certain goods for personal use. He declared these goods when crossing the customs boundary of the Russian Federation and paid duty in the sum of 1,529.78 rubles pursuant to a decree of the Government of the Russian Federation of November 29, 2003, No 718. The customs agency later conducted a "verification" of the calculation of the customs payment and discovered that the duties should have been levied under the Treaty on the Customs Code of the Customs Union, concluded on November 27, 2009, which entered into force on July 6, 2010 but was provisionally applied from July 1, 2010 pursuant to a separate treaty between Russia and Kazakhstan of May 28, 2010 implementing an Agreement between Russia, Belarus, and Kazakhstan of June 18, 2010.

The customs agency brought suit against Ushakov for the additional customs duty before a justice of the peace in Russia; Ushakov refused to pay, and the justice of the peace ruled against Ushakov in a ruling of May 5, 2011; that decision was upheld by a district court on September 1, 2011. Rejecting Ushakov's position that the treaty of June 18, 2010 had never been officially published, the appellate instance pointed out that the said treaty was subject to provisional application on the territory of the Russian Federation from July 1, 2010 and therefore was in force when Ushakov crossed the customs boundary of the Russian Federation.

Ushakov requested the Constitutional Court of the Russian Federation to determine that Articles 5(3), 23(1), and 30 of the 1995 Federal Law "On International Treaties of the Russian Federation," read together, were unconstitutional because, in his view, they would permit the provisional application of international treaties of the Russian Federation affecting the rights, freedoms, and duties of man and citizen before the treaty entered into force without official publication, with the result that citizens could not be familiar with them, foresee the consequences of their application, and appropriately adjust their behavior to the rules contained in the treaty provisionally applied.

The Ushakov decision is of interest at two levels. First, the Constitutional Court addressed the general requirement of publication of treaties in the

Russian Federation. Second, the Court considered the implications of a "gap" identified in the Ushakov situation as to whether the requirement of official publication extended to a treaty not yet in force but subject, by agreement of the parties, to provisional application.

With respect to official publication of treaties in general as a condition of their application within Russia, the Court observed:

> The requirement of official publication of international treaties of the Russian Federation which have entered into legal force has constitutional-legal significance in principle because, being an integral part of the legal system of the Russian Federation and possessing priority over Russian laws with respect to application, international treaties of the Russian Federation exert direct effect on normative-legal regulation in the Russian Federation, including the content of the rights and freedoms of man and citizen, the value significance of which is determined by the prescriptions of Articles 2, 17, and 18 of the Constitution of the Russian Federation.
>
> Official publication of an international treaty of the Russian Federation which has entered into force ensures the full and precise bringing, in the name of a competent State agency, of the content of such treaty to the information of an indefinite group of persons by means of placing the authentic text in a printed publication specified in a law and thereby correlating them with the rules established by laws and other normative legal acts of the Russian Federation and makes it possible to evaluate the consequences of the municipal application thereof. For these purposes Article 5(3) of the Federal Law "On International Treaties of the Russian Federation" specially stipulates that the provisions of officially published international treaties of the Russian Federation directly operate without requiring the issuance of municipal acts for application.
>
> The courts of general jurisdiction are oriented to the application of international treaties of the Russian Federation which have entered into force merely on condition of their official publication, and the Decree of the Plenum of the Supreme Court of the Russian Federation of 10 October 2003, No. 5, "On the Application by Courts of General Jurisdiction of Generally-Recognized Principles and Norms of International Law and International Treaties of the Russian Federation," point 4 of which, in particular, directs attention to the fact that, proceeding from the sense of Article 15(3) and (4) of the

Constitution of the Russian Federation and Article 5(3) of the Federal Law "On International Treaties of the Russian Federation" those international treaties that have entered into force may be applied by courts directly which have been officially published in the Собрание законодательства Российской Федерации [Collection of Legislation of the Russian Federation] or the Бюллетень международных договоров [Bulletin of International Treaties] in the procedure established by Article 30 of the said Federal Law. This approach also is adhered to by the Supreme Arbitrazh Court of the Russian Federation, which assumes that arbitrazh courts must apply international treaties of the Russian Federation which have entered into force and been duly brought to general information (point 1, Decree of the Plenum of the Supreme Arbitrazh Court of the Russian Federation, 11 June 1999, No. 8, "On the Operation of International Treaties of the Russian Federation with Regard to Questions of Arbitrazh Procedure").

Thus, it follows from the provisions of the Federal Law "On International Treaties of the Russian Federation" contained in Article 5(3), Article 24(2), Article 30, and Article 31(1) that international treaties of the Russian Federation which have entered into force, including those affecting the rights, freedoms, and duties of man and citizen, are subject to obligatory official publication in the established procedure, without which—by virtue of the requirements arising from inter-related Articles 1(1), 2, 15(1)(3) and (4), 17(1), 18, and 19(1) of the Constitution of the Russian Federation—they may not be considered to be satisfying the principles of a rule-of-law State, legal equality, and legal certainty as essential constitutional criteria for the defense of the rights and freedoms of man and citizen on the territory of the Russian Federation.[52]

It follows from the above that, in the view of the courts of general jurisdiction and arbitrazh courts, a treaty of the Russian Federation which has entered into legal force but has not been officially published does not exist and will not be applied by the courts.

---

[52] Decree of the Constitutional Court of the Russian Federation of March 27, 2012, No 8-П, "Re: Verification of the Constitutionality of Article 23(1) of the Federal Law 'On International Treaties of the Russian Federation' in Connection with the Appeal of Citizen I D Ushakov." СЗ РФ (2012) no 15, item 1810. The decree of the Plenum of the Supreme Arbitrazh Court of June 11, 1999, as amended June 27, 2017, remains in force although the Supreme Arbitrazh Court was abolished in 2014.

Article 23(1) of the Federal Law "On International Treaties of the Russian Federation," however, provides that "An international treaty or part of a treaty may, before entry into force, be applied by the Russian Federation provisionally if such has been provided for in the treaty or if an arrangement was reached concerning this with the parties who have signed the treaty." This provision in essence reproduced Article 25(1) of the 1969 Vienna Convention on the Law of Treaties. The Russian Federation, the Constitutional Court observed, uses provisional application in practice when the treaty is of special interest for the parties and they wish to implement the treaty provisions without awaiting ratification and entry into force.

The Constitutional Court pointed out that the Russian Federation has the right to agree to provisional application of a treaty in full or in part, to stipulate a maximum period for provisional application, or to condition its provisional application on conformity to the Constitution of Russia, laws, or other normative acts. Consent to provisional application means that the treaty becomes an integral part of the legal system of Russia and is subject to application equally with treaties already in force—otherwise the concept of provisional application would make no sense. Likewise, it would follow that if the Russian Federation were to decide not to become a party to the treaty, provisional application would terminate.

The Russian legislation regulating the official publication of treaties did not at the time of Ushakov address the issue of provisionally applicable treaties. The failure to do so, in the view of the Constitutional Court, constituted a departure "from the principles of a rule-of-law State, legal equality, and legal certainty as essential constitutional criteria" for the protection of human rights on the territory of Russia. Only official publication of the authentic text of a treaty was a proper guarantee of duly bringing the text to the information of the general public. This meant that publication of the official text on the internet site of the Commission of the Customs Union, or a reference to the relevant treaties and agreements in a Letter of the Federal Customs Service, could not "compensate for the lack of due official publication of the text thereof." Article 23(1) of the Federal Law "On International Treaties" was not unconstitutional in and of itself; the failure to officially publish in the gazettes duly assigned for this purpose a treaty provisionally which had not entered into legal force was, however, unconstitutional.

In two similar cases the Constitutional Court of the Russian Federation on April 3, 2012, took the same view with respect to treaties provisionally in force, citing its decision in the Ushakov case as a precedent, terminating the constitutional proceedings, but ordering a review of the earlier lower court decisions which recovered customs duties inappropriately.[53]

On July 12, 2012, with specific reference to the case of I D Ushakov in the Constitutional Court, the President of the Russian Federation issued Edict No 970, "On Official Publication of International Treaties of the Russian Federation to be Provisionally Applied." The edict required that the official publication of international treaties of the Russian Federation to be provisionally applied and affected the rights, freedoms, and duties of man and citizen and establishing rules other than provided by legislation of the Russian Federation be undertaken on the Internet Portal by the Ministry of Foreign Affairs in accordance with a List of such treaties.[54] The provisions of the edict were incorporated into the 1995 Law on treaties by an amendment of December 25, 2012.

Russian jurists who have delved into the archives of Russian courts have determined that the "everyday court practice" with respect to applying published treaties only "is contradictory." Marochkin cited a case from the archives of the Tiumen regional arbitrazh court in which a treaty was applied before official publication on the ground that publication was not a municipal requirement for the treaty to enter into legal force.[55] An analogous case in another region and court resulted in the court being unwilling to apply the same treaty. Judicial practice, in other words, in the lower courts was inconsistent on the question of official treaty publication. Decisions of this nature and delays in the official publication of treaties persuaded some Russian jurists that entry into force, and not official publication, should become the criterion for a court applying a treaty.[56]

Secret and Unpublished Treaties

Although the categories of "secret" and "unpublished" treaties overlap, they are not necessarily the same. "Unpublished" treaties may equate

---

[53] See the Rulings of April 3, 2012, No 476-O (Re: Karpov) and No 477-O (Re: Gorodenko and Smirnova). Available on Consultant Plus.

[54] СЗ РФ (2012) no. 29, item 4069.

[55] S Y Marochkin, *The Operation of International Law in the Russian Legal System: A Challenging Approach* (2019) 131.

[56] This argument was made by V Ia Suvorova, "С какого момента международный договоры Российской Федерации подлежат исполнению и применению" ["From What Moment are International Treaties of the Russian Federation Subject to Performance and Application?"], Русский юридический журнал [*Russian Legal Journal*], no. 1 (2010) 143–9.

to "unregistered" treaties, having in view the requirement of the United Nations Charter (Article 102) that "every treaty and every international agreement entered into by any member of the United Nations" after the Charter entered into force on October 24, 1945 "shall as soon as possible be registered" with the United Nations Secretariat and published by it. The terminology of obligation is unambiguous in Article 102; there is a legal duty to register by parties to every treaty and to every international agreement, and there is a duty of the United Nations Secretariat to publish the registered treaties. The Charter provides for no exceptions, although the delay in treaty publication by the United Nations does not take full advantage of modern technologies and has exceeded several years in duration, although this has been reduced in recent years to between fourteen and eighteen months.

The sanction is: no party to any such unregistered treaty may invoke that treaty before any organ of the United Nations. In effect, from the standpoint of the United Nations, the treaty does not exist.[57]

The treaty law of the Russian Federation has taken an analogous approach. The Supreme Court of the Russian Federation has made clear in its decree of October 10, 2003, No 5, and in individual cases, that an international treaty of the Russian Federation which has not been officially published will not be applied by a Russian court.

What, then, of international treaties of the Russian Federation whose discussion, drafting, consideration within Russian agencies of power and administration, conclusion, and ultimate existence falls within the category of classified information whose divulgence would be a serious criminal offense.

The Law of the Russian Federation on State Secrecy of July 21, 1993, as amended to July 29, 2018, defines a "State secret" as information defended by the State in the field of, *inter alia*, foreign policy activity (Article 2).[58] The List of information comprising a State secret constitutes the aggregate of categories of information, in accordance with which information is relegated to a State secret and duly classified. The said List was confirmed by edict of the President of the Russian Federation on November 30, 1995,

---

[57] However, the International Court of Justice (an organ of the United Nations) is said not to "apply the provision strictly, or perhaps at all ... The sanction in Article 102(2) would appear from the practice of the principal organs of the United Nations to be more honored in the breach than in the observance." See Aust (n. 10) 303.
[58] The Law itself was not published officially until 1997. СЗ РФ (1997) no. 41, 8220-35.

No 1203.[59] Depending upon the subject-matter of a treaty, many, perhaps most, items on the List could fall into the category of classified information. Treaties, however, are specifically mentioned in certain categories:

70. Information concerning negotiations between representatives of the Russian Federation and representatives of other States on elaborating a unified position of principle in international relations if, in the opinion of the participants of the negotiations, divulgence of this information may prejudice the security of the Russian Federation and other States [as amended April 17, 2017].

71. Information concerning the preparation, conclusion, ratification, preparation for denunciation, content, or fulfillment of treaties, conventions, or agreements with foreign States, the premature dissemination of which may prejudice the security of the State [as amended April 17, 2017]. . . .

75. Information divulging the essence or volume of economic cooperation of the Russian Federation with foreign States in wartime, interaction with military-mobilization agencies of foreign economic organizations of States-Participants of the Commonwealth of Independent States on these questions [as amended April 17, 2017].

Among the powers of agencies of State power and officials in the domain of classifying and defending information as a State secret, the President of the Russian Federation may conclude "international treaties of the Russian Federation on the joint use and defense of information comprising a State secret" (Article 4(2)). The Government of the Russian Federation is empowered to "conclude intergovernmental agreements, take measure for the fulfillment of international treaties of the Russian Federation on the joint use and defense of information comprising a State secret, adopt decisions on the possibility of the transfer of the bearers thereof to other States or international organizations" (Article 4(3)).

---

[59] СЗ РФ (1995) no. 49, item 4775, as amended to January 14, 2019. The procedure for drawing up and adding or deleting items from the List is set out in the decree of the Government of the Russian Federation on Confirmation of the Rules for Drafting the List of Information Relegated to a State Secret, of July 23, 2005, No. 443. СЗ РФ (2005) no. 31, item 3224, as amended to March 18, 2016. Treaties are not specifically cited in the Law on State Secrecy itself; the List presumably clarifies the laconic provision in the Law on State Secrecy: "information in the domain of foreign policy and the economy on the foreign policy and foreign economic activity of the Russian Federation, the premature divulgence of which may prejudice the security of the State" (Article 5(3)).

Certain information is not subject to being relegated to a State secret and classified. Although treaties are not mentioned specifically in this connection, information "concerning facts of a violation of legality by agencies of State power and officials thereof" may not be classified as a State secret. Officials who adopt decisions to classify such information are subject to criminal, administrative, or disciplinary responsibility, depending on the material and moral harm caused to society, the State, and citizens. Treaty violations could fall into this category of a "violation of legality."

Russian legislation provides for three degrees of secrecy: "special importance," "top secret," and "secret." The rules for determining the level of classification of information have been determined by decree of the Government of the Russian Federation "On Confirmation of the Rules for Relegating Information Comprising a State Secret to Various Degrees of Secrecy," of September 4, 1995, No 870.[60] Foreign policy activity, including treaties, is present in all three levels of classification. The Rules provide that the degree of secrecy of information comprising a State secret "should conform to the degree of gravity of prejudice which may be caused to the security of the Russian Federation as a consequence of the dissemination of the said information" (point 2). These indicators of prejudice to security, both quantitative and qualitative, are determined in accordance with "normative-methods documents" confirmed by executives of agencies of State power and by the heads of the State Corporations Rosatom or Roskosmos—both corporations having treaty-making capacity. Also involved is the Inter-Departmental Commission for the Defense of State Secrecy.[61]

There is no issue under international law with how individual States choose to manage their foreign policy deliberations, including treaty-making. The issue is the ultimate outcome of a treaty (a) being concluded but not registered and published with the United Nations and (b) being concluded but not divulged or published within the States-parties to the treaty. Plainly the considerations a century ago that led the League of Nations and its successor the United Nations to ameliorate the consequences of secret treaties have receded into the past. Many believed during World War I that the lack of transparency with respect to all international

---

[60] СЗ РФ (1995) no. 37, item 3619, as amended to March 18, 2016.
[61] See the Statute on the Inter-Departmental Commission for the Defense of State Secrecy, confirmed by edict of the President of the Russian Federation, October 6, 2004, No. 1286, as amended August 3, 2018.

treaties contributed to the outbreak of war. In the instances of both World Wars I and II, the reaction to secret treaty-making came immediately in the postwar settlement arrangements—the Covenant of the League of Nations and the United Nations Charter.

In reviewing Russian legislation on State secrecy, the question would be whether the formulation "information about" contained in points 70, 71, and 75 above encompasses the final texts of the treaties themselves. Whatever the answer to that finer point, there is discretion with the Ministry of Foreign Affairs and other State agencies as to whether treaties, once concluded, should obligatorily be published. Sometimes the discretion is exercised positively or negatively; in other situations a decision is avoided, and the treaty sits in limbo until its publication fate is resolved. If, for example, the parties to an interdepartmental treaty agree not to publish the treaty text, it will not be published and few will know of the document's existence—although this would appear to be a violation of the United Nations Charter. Indeed, the discretion given to ministries and departments, or the possibility of parties to agree not to divulge the existence or publish a treaty, would seem to constitute a violation of Article 102 of the United Nations Charter.

There are two dimensions to the situation. The first is that a treaty under Russian law could be formally and officially "classified" as a State secret. At least one Russian jurist is on record as saying that "international treaties, the decision concerning consent to whose bindingness is subject to adoption in the form of a federal law" cannot be secret or classified "for official use."[62] This statement refers to ratified treaties and assumes that the Federal Assembly of the Russian Federation will not refrain from publishing a federal law on the ratification of a treaty and the text of the treaty itself. This leaves open not only interdepartmental treaties, but also intergovernmental treaties.

Apart from an international obligation to register and publish international treaties, domestic complications may arise when ministries and departments are not aware that treaties may have been concluded or entered into force and therefore may be remiss in implementing the treaty obligations. Insofar as such treaties are not included on the Government Internet

---

[62] B I Osminin, Принятие и реализация государствами международных договорных обязательств [*Adoption and Realization by States of International Treaty Obligations*] (2006) 383.

Portal, there literally may be ignorance of the existence of the treaties within the precincts of government. Or foreign partners may be unaware that the Russian side has completed the necessary internal procedures needed for an international treaty to enter into force.

On July 3, 2018 the Ministry of Foreign Affairs issued an "Information on Sending Notification concerning the Fulfillment of Municipal Procedures Necessary for the Entry of International Treaties into Force."[63] The aim was to ensure compliance with a uniform practice when preparing and sending such notifications to foreign partners. The "Information" constituted a "request" to be guided by the following:

> A written notification is sent concerning the fulfillment of such procedures under a bilateral treaty or to the depositary of a multilateral treaty (Note of the Ministry of Foreign Affairs of Russia or embassy of the Russian Federation to the respective foreign State or representation of the Russian Federation attached to an international organization, and with respect to international treaties of an interdepartmental character—letter of the federal agency of executive power of the Russian Federation, and so on).
>
> The decision of the respective agency of power of the Russian Federation (federal law, regulation of President of the Russian Federation, decree or regulation of the Government of the Russian Federation) is the grounds for sending the notification concerning fulfillment by the Russian party of municipal procedures. The initiative for sending such notification belongs to the federal agency of executive power which submitted the proposal to sign the treaty to the President of the Russian Federation or to the Government of the Russian Federation.[64]

Such a notification may be sent only when the treaty is not subject to ratification or confirmation and upon signature no changes or additions of a principled character were made in comparison with the text of the draft approved by the President or Government of the Russian Federation. The Ministry of Foreign Affairs requested that when seeking such a notification the following information be provided or indicated: (a) that the treaty is not subject to ratification pursuant to Russian legislation; (b) no changes or additions have been made in the text; (c) the date and number of the decision of the President or Government concerning signature of the treaty.

---

[63]   Available on Consultant Plus.
[64]   Unpublished. Available on Consultant Plus.

The Information noted that interdepartmental international treaties as a rule enter into force on the day of signature. If, however, the treaty provides that it enters into force after the exchange of notifications concerning the fulfillment of municipal procedures, the respective notification is sent through departmental channels, for example, in the form of a letter, unless provided otherwise in the treaty. The draft of such a notification is subject to being agreed with the Ministry of Foreign Affairs of Russia in accordance with the edict of the President of the Russian Federation "On the Coordinating Role of the Ministry of Foreign Affairs of the Russian Federation on Conducting a Unified Foreign Policy Line of the Russian Federation" of November 8, 2011, No 1478.[65] Copies of all notifications sent and received are to be provided to the Legal Department of the Ministry of Foreign Affairs, which has responsibility for a single State system or the registration and recording of international treaties of the Russian Federation pursuant to the 1995 Law on Treaties (Article 26).

Registration of Treaties in Russia

Note has been taken above of the requirements that treaties be registered, in their own time, with the League of Nations or with its successor, the United Nations. The League of Nations registered 4,834 treaties.[66] By 2019 in the range of 70,000 treaties had been submitted to the United Nations for registration, with a rejection rate of *circa* 10 percent for various reasons. The United Nations has its own detailed regulations on registration prepared by the United Nations Secretariat.[67]

As a complex federated State, the Russian Federation has its own problems with keeping up with the its own treaty engagements, and its internal rules differ in key respects with those of the United Nations—including the registration of materials that would not be accepted by the United Nations Secretariat; that is, acts which are not necessarily treaties. Presumably the Soviet Union had analogous internal enactments, but if they existed, they are still not a matter of public record and were probably classified. The same might be said of Imperial Russia. Whatever the internal registration provisions were, treaties from the Imperial and Soviet periods in many instances

---

[65] СЗ РФ (2011) no. 46, item 6477.
[66] Aust (n. 10) 297.
[67] These are summarized and the full text reproduced at Appendix P in Aust, ibid, 298–300, 443–7.

remain in force for Russia as the legal-continuer of the Soviet Union and would, one must suppose, be subject to registration somewhere besides the League of Nations or the United Nations.

It remains unclear when the registration system of treaties began in the Russian Federation. Reference was made to registration in the 1995 Law on treaties (Article 26), but the present system is based on the Order of July 27, 2007, No 12828, of the Ministry of Foreign Affairs "On Confirmation of the Rules of State Registration and State Recording of International Treaties of the Russian Federation."[68] The Order (hereinafter: 2007 Order) makes no mention of replacing or repealing earlier enactments, but was introduced twelve years after the 1995 Law on treaties.

The 2007 Order distinguishes between the "registration" and the "recording" of a treaty. In either case, the requisite entry is made in the "Unified State System for the Registration and Recording of International Treaties of the Russian Federation." This Unified System is within the jurisdiction of the Ministry of Foreign Affairs,[69] where it is kept by the Legal Department. Treaties which have entered into force for the Russian Federation are subject to State registration. Registered treaties, and likewise signed treaties which have not entered into force for Russia, treaties with regard to which Russia has consented to be bound in a form provided by international law and Russian legislation other than signature (ratification, confirmation, adoption, accession), are subject to being recorded in the system.

State registration involved the conferral of a registration number on the treaty in an electronic system, the number being conferred by the Legal Department within ten working days from the date of receiving the documents (notes, letters, and so on) confirming the entry of the treaty into force for the Russian Federation. The registration number is not placed on the original text of the treaty or attested copies thereof, but kept only within the electronic system.

The State recording of treaties also is an electronic entry in the form of a record card. In the case of a bilateral treaty the entry consists of the:

(a) full official name of the treaty;
(2) name of the contracting Party;

---

[68] Registered in the Ministry of Justice of the Russian Federation, August 23, 2007, No. 10041. Entered into force September 28, 2007. Available on Consultant Plus.

[69] See point 6(23), Statute on the Ministry of Foreign Affairs of the Russian Federation, July 11, 2004, as amended; trans. in Butler (n. 48) 232.

(3) level of signature of the treaty (inter-State, intergovernmental, interdepartmental);

(4) date(s) and place(s) of signature of the treaty;

(5) office, surname, forenames (or patronymic) of persons who signed the treaty;

(6) information concerning the powers of the person who signed the treaty on the Russian side (date of issuance of powers), and grounds for issuance of powers (requisites of act of President of Russian Federation, Government of Russian Federation, executive of federal agency of State power of Russian Federation);

(7) information concerning operation of treaty (operates, does not operate; is applied provisionally);

(8) information on need to fulfill municipal procedures for entry of treaty into force after signature thereof (subject to ratification, adoption, confirmation);

(9) dates of ratification of treaty by parties (for Russian party the number of the federal law on ratification is indicated);

(10) date and place of exchange of instruments on ratification of the treaty;

(11) requisites of documents (notes, letters, and other notifications) on fulfillment by parties of municipal procedures necessary for entry of the treaty into force;

(12) date of entry of treaty into force;

(13) concise information on period of operation provided by the treaty, conditions for entry into force; extension, suspension of operation, termination;

(14) information on extension, suspension of operation, termination of treaty (requisites of document—note, letter, or other notification—on extension, suspension of operation, termination of the treaty; date from which and for what period a treaty is prolonged or the operation thereof suspended, date of termination of operation of treaty);

(15) place of keeping the original treaty (Historical-Documentary Department of ministry or Archive of federal agency of executive power of Russian Federation in whose name the treaty of an interdepartmental character was concluded);

(16) source of official publication of the treaty;

(17) subdivision of ministry responsible for overseeing questions regulated by the treaty;

(18) federal agency of executive power of the Russian Federation or other Russian agency or organization within whose competence are questions regulated by the treaty;

(19) other information relating to the treaty.

In the case of a multilateral treaty, the:

(1) full name of the treaty;

(2) number of the dossier in which information is kept in the Legal Department of the ministry relating to the treaty;

(3) level of signature of the treaty (inter-State, intergovernmental, interdepartmental);

(4) date and place of adoption of text of treaty, and opening thereof for signature;

(5) office, surname, forenames (or patronymic) of person who signed the treaty from the Russian side;

(6) information concerning the powers of the person who signed the treaty (date of issuance of powers), and grounds for issuance of powers (requisites of act of President of Russian Federation, Government of Russian Federation, executive of federal agency of State power of Russian Federation);

(7) depositary of treaty;

(8) date of entry of treaty into force;

(9) concise information on period of operation provided by the treaty, conditions of entry into force, extension, suspension of operation, and termination;

(10) date of suspension of operation and termination of treaty;

(11) date of signature of treaty from the Russian side;

(12) requisites of act on the basis of which the Russian party signed or expressed consent in other form to the bindingness of the treaty (federal law, act of President of Russian Federation, Government of Russian Federation, or executive of federal agency of executive power of the Russian Federation);

(13) requisites of document (instrument of ratification, note, letter, or other notification) confirming the expression of final consent of the Russian party to the bindingness for it of the treaty (ratification, adoption, confirmation, accession);

(14) requisites of act on the basis of which the Russian party expressed final consent to the bindingness for it of the treaty (federal law, act

of President of the Russian Federation, Government of the Russian Federation, or executive of federal agency of executive power of the Russian Federation);

(15) date of entry of the treaty into force for the Russian Federation;

(16) information concerning reservations, objections to reservations, removal of reservations, statements, other communications made by the Russian party when signing or adopting the treaty and/or when expressing final consent to the bindingness thereof;

(17) requisites of the document (note, letter, or other notification) concerning suspension of the operation of a treaty by the Russian party, withdrawal from it by the Russian party;

(18) date of suspension of the operation of the treaty by the Russian party, withdrawal from it by the Russian party;

(19) dates of signature of the treaty by States, international organizations, and also giving by them for keeping to the depositary of documents (instruments of ratification, notes, letters, and other notifications) concerning ratification, adoption, confirmation of the treaty, accession thereto, suspension of operation of the treaty, withdrawal from it;

(20) information concerning reservations, objections to the treaty, removal of reservations, statements, other communications in connection with the treaty of States, international organizations who signed or in other form expressed their consent to the bindingness thereof;

(21) subdivision of the ministry overseeing questions regulated by the treaty;

(22) federal agency of executive power of the Russian Federation, other Russian agency or organization within whose competence are questions regulated by the treaty;

(23) place of keeping the treaty with respect to which the Russian party effectuates the functions of depositary (Historical-Documentary Department of the ministry, Archive of the federal agency of executive power of the Russian Federation in whose name the treaty of an inter-departmental character was concluded);

(24) source of official publication of the treaty;

(25) other information relating to the treaty.

The original treaty or attested copy thereof is sent for keeping to the ministry within fourteen calendar days from the date of signature or receipt from the depositary of an attested copy and official translation thereof.

Within three working days of receipt of the treaty or attested copy thereof in the ministry, these materials are forwarded to the Legal Department of the ministry, which within ten working days undertakes the State recording of the treaty and then within fourteen working days from receipt thereof hands these materials over to the Historical-Documentary Department of the ministry.

Nothing is said in these materials about registration of Russian treaties with the United Nations Secretariat. Moreover, the assumption of the 2007 Order is that a "treaty is a treaty," with no indication of the recording or registration of doubtful or marginal documents (memorandum of understanding, and so on)—issues that have challenged the United Nations Secretariat.

In any event, the registration of international treaties of the Russian Federation, although required by Russian legislation, is not a requirement for their recognition or application by Russian courts or arbitral tribunals. The registration number is not known or routinely cited or mentioned in Russian doctrinal writings or inquired into by Russian courts or arbitral tribunals. Registration and recording requirements appear to be primarily an exercise in internal housekeeping.

5
Constitutional Legislative History and Treaties in the Russian Legal System

In 1977 the Union of Soviet Socialist Republics adopted a new Constitution to replace that of 1936, as amended, and for the first time included a Chapter 4 entitled "Foreign Policy." With respect to international law, the Constitution provided as follows:

> *Article 29.* Relations of the USSR with other States shall be built on the basis of observing the principles of mutual recognition of sovereign equality; mutual renunciation of the use or threat of force; inviolability of frontiers; territorial integrity of States; peaceful settlement of disputes; non-interference in internal affairs; respect for human rights and basic freedoms; equality and the right of peoples to decide their own destiny; cooperation between States; good-faith fulfillment of obligations arising from generally-recognized principles and norms of international law and from international treaties concluded by the USSR.[1]

The formulation of Article 29 was curious insofar as it enumerated what most would consider to be principles of international law but in the last clause refers to "generally-recognized principles and norms" as though those previously enumerated did not fall into that category. Nor was anything said about the stature of international treaties with respect to the municipal legal system even though the priority of treaties was well-established in some branches of Soviet law.

When the USSR was dissolved on or about December 25, 1991, the Russian Federation was left with its own RSFSR Constitution of April 12, 1978, as amended, which contained provisions on foreign policy that

---

[1] W E Butler (comp., trans., and ed.), *Basic Documents on the Soviet Legal System* (1983) 9.

replicated those of Article 29 of the USSR Constitution. Article 28 of the 1978 RSFSR Constitution provided:

> *Article 28.* The foreign policy activity of the Russian Federation shall be based on recognition of and respect for State sovereignty and the sovereign equality of all countries, the inalienable right to self-determination, principles of equality and non-interference in internal affairs, respect for territorial integrity and inviolability of existing boundaries, renunciation of the use and threat of force, economic and any other methods of pressure, principles of the peaceful settlement of disputes, respect for human rights and freedoms, including the right of national minorities, good-faith fulfillment of obligations and other generally-recognized principles and norms of international law [as amended April 21, 1992, No. 2708-1].

Chapter 5 of the 1978 RSFSR Constitution, devoted to the "Rights and Freedoms of Man and Citizen," was issued in a new version on April 21, 1992, Article 32 of which provided as follows:

> *Article 32.* Generally-recognized international norms relating to human rights shall have preference over laws of the Russian Federation and shall directly generate rights and duties of citizens of the Russian Federation.

Both Articles 28 and 32 made reference to "generally-recognized norms of international law" and Article 28 added "principles." Neither amendment referred to international treaties of the Russian Federation.

It was the USSR and RSFSR formulations to which the drafters of the 1993 Russian Federation Constitution reacted, favorably or unfavorably, in the myriad of draft constitutions which circulated in Russia from 1990 to the final version of December 12, 1993. This chapter considers several of these chronologically, with commentary on their respective sources and approach to drafting, concentrating primarily on whether only ratified treaties should enjoy priority (if at all) and whether generally-recognized principles and norms of international law and international treaties of Russia are part of Russian law or part of the Russian legal system (if at all). Italics, unless otherwise indicated, are supplied by the present writer.

Official Parliamentary and Presidential Draft Constitutions

Work on preparing a new Constitution for the Russian Federation was undertaken in 1990 by a Constitutional Commission of the RSFSR. An early draft was published for discussion by the Constitutional Commission pursuant to a Decree of the Congress of People's Deputies dated June 16, 1990. The date of the draft itself is not indicated but is presumed to be earlier than September 1990; in any event, the formulation differs from that of September 28, 1990.

Draft of Constitutional Commission: Decree of June 16, 1990[2]

Article 3. Supremacy of Law

...

(3) Generally-recognized principles and norms of international law and ratified international treaties of the Russian Federation shall comprise part of its law. If other rules have been established by an international treaty of the Russian Federation than by a law, the rules of this international treaty shall apply.

...

Article 11. Russian Federation in the World Community

The Russian Federation is a fully-fledged member of the world community, complies with principles and norms of international law and international treaties concluded by it, may participate in international organizations and other associations and collective security systems, and aspires to universal and just peace, mutually advantageous international cooperation, and the resolution of global problems.

---

[2] The text appears in Конституционное совещание: Стенограммы. Материалы. Документы. 29 апреля – 10 ноября 1993 г. [Constitutional Assembly: Transcripts. Materials, Documents. 29 April – 10 November 1993] (1995-). 21 vols. under the general editorship of S A Filatov, V S Chernomyrdin, S M Shakhrai, Iu F Iarov, A A Sobchak, and V F Shumeiko. See ibid, I, 498, 500.

Commentary. According to this version, only ratified international treaties comprise part of the "law" of the Russian Federation (but not legal system). The next sentence is a non-sequitur, as it confers priority on all treaties of the Russian Federation, whether part of the law of Russia or not. In other words, the requirement of "ratification" is excluded in the second sentence of the formulation.

The Commission Working Group and Group of Experts prepared a draft dated September 28, 1990 which contained the following provision:

Draft Constitution of Working Group of Constitutional Commission: September 24, 1990[3]

Article 1.6. Supremacy of Law and Constitution

...

[3]. International treaties and agreements recognized by the Russian Federation shall be an integral part of the law of the Republic.

Commentary. The formulation is "primitive," but compared to many drafts, it recognizes the problem of the interface between international law and Russian law. Nothing is said of priority of treaties, no requirement of ratification is imposed, and how Russia may "recognize" a treaty is left open but, as a matter of international law, not helpful.

Constitutional Commission Working Draft: September 28, 1990[4]

Article 1.11. Russian Federation in an Open World Community

1. In its foreign policy the Russian Federation, respecting the rights and freedoms of peoples, shall be guided by generally-recognized

[3] Published from the Archive of the Constitutional Reform Fund, opis 1, delo 188, 40. Published in O G Rumiantsev (ed.), Из истории создания Конституции Российской Федерации [*From the History of the Creation of the Constitution of the Russian Federation*] (2007–10), VI, 81 (6 vols. in 10).

[4] Published from the Archive of the Constitutional Reform Fund, opis 2, delo 2, folios 430–46; see Rumiantsev (n. 3) V, 186. Precisely the same formulation was retained in a draft

principles and norms of international law. It shall aspire to universal and just peace based on general human values; to close, business-like, and mutually-advantageous cooperation with all countries. The Russian Federation shall aspire to actively participate in the resolution of global problems.

2. Favoring the creation of an open international community based on the rule of law, the Russian Federation may join international organizations, collective security system, alliances, and inter-State formations, delegating to them a respective part of its powers.

Commentary. This early version said nothing about international treaties, confining itself to be "guided" by generally-recognized principles and norms of international law. This was more a general statement of an approach to foreign policy and, as such, in the spirit of the 1978 RSFSR Constitution, which at the time was still in force.[5]

Constitutional Commission Draft Published for National Discussion: November 12, 1990[6]

Article 1.6. Supremacy of Law and the Constitution

...

(3) International treaties, a participant of which is the Russian Federation, shall comprise a part of the law of the Federation. If other rules are contained in an international treaty of the Russian Federation than in Russian legislation, the rules of the international treaty shall operate. International treaties of the Russian Federation

---

of October 11, 1990, except that the headnote of Article 1.11. was changed to read: "Russian Federation—Part of Open World Community." Ibid, V, 207.

[5] A virtually identical formulation was proposed by a Draft Constitution (Basic Law) of the Russian Federation, submitted on November 10, 1990 by the Chairman of the Supreme Soviet of the Iakut-Sakha SSR, which suggests a degree of borrowing among the drafts being circulated. This version is published in Rumiantsev (n. 3) V, 442.

[6] This working draft was published in Конституционный вестник [Constitutional Herald], no. 4 (1990) 55–120; as a special issue of Аргументы и факты [Arguments and Facts], no. 47 (November 1990), both publications noting that all prior versions were of a "deeply preliminary character." Also published in Rumiantsev (n. 3) I, 596–663.

shall create rights and duties for persons subject to the jurisdiction of the Russian Federation.

Article 1.11. Russian Federation—Part of the World Community

(1) In its foreign policy, the Russian Federation, respecting the rights and freedoms of peoples, shall be guided by generally-recognized principles and norms of international law. It shall aspire to a universal and just peace based on general human values, close, business-like, and mutually-advantageous cooperation with all countries. The Russian Federation shall actively participate in the resolution of global problems.

...

Commentary. This version contains no changes from that of September 28, 1990, which seems to have been when it first appeared.

Draft Constitution Prepared by Constitutional Commission of RSFSR: July 8, 1991[7]

Article 5. Supremacy of Law

...

(4) International and inter-republic treaties, a participant of which is the Russian Federation, shall comprise part of its law. If other rules are contained in an international or inter-republic treaty of the Russian Federation, the rules of the respective treaty shall operate rather than in the legislation thereof.

...

Article 11. Russian Federation in the World Community

(1) The Russian Federation shall be a fully-fledged member of the international community, comply with generally-recognized principles and norms of international law, and aspire to a universal and just

---

[7] State Archive of the Russian Federation, fund 126, opis 1, delo 370; published in Rumiantsev (n. 3) VI, 383.

peace, mutually-advantageous cooperation, and the settlement of global problems.

Commentary. This was the only formulation identified to equate international and inter-republic treaties, and it would have given both categories of treaty priority over Russian law. Generally-recognized principles and norms of international law are mentioned, but not in relation to the municipal Russian legal system.

Draft Constitution Variant "0": April 9, 1992

A draft Constitution, Variant "0", was submitted on April 9, 1992,[8] but contained no provisions on the place of international law or international treaties in the legal system of the Russian Federation. In Article 42 of the Draft, however, reference was made to the territory of the Russian Federation not being changed other than by a "special federal law adopted in accordance with an international treaty." Article 42(3) further stipulated that the constitutional system of the Russian Federation is "based on the principle of the priority of the rights and freedoms of man and citizen," among others.

Draft Constitution of Constitutional Commission: April 8, 1993[9]

Article 3. Supremacy of Law

. . .

[4]. Generally-recognized principles and norms of international law and international treaties of the Russian Federation shall constitute *part of the law* thereof. If other rules have been established by a *ratified* international treaty of the Russian Federation than by a law, the rules of the international treaty shall be applied [rejected by Soviet of Nationalities].

---

[8] This version prepared by a Working Group chaired by S M Shakhrai is published in Rumiantsev (n. 3) V, 769–802.
[9] Printed from the State Archive of the Russian Federation, fund 10026, opis 1, delo 312, folios 69–137; published in Rumiantsev (n. 3) vol. 4(1) 326.

Commentary. Why the upper chamber of the Congress of People's Deputies rejected this point as a whole has not been determined. The formulation equated generally-recognized principles and norms of international law and international treaties to Russian legislation, and would have given priority to international treaties with respect to such "Russian law" only to ratified treaties.

Draft Constitution of Supreme Soviet Group of Specialists: June 4, 1993

Article 3. . . .

[4]. Generally-recognized principles and norms of international law and international treaties of the Russian Federation shall comprise part of its legal system.

Commentary. This draft was submitted by a group of specialists chaired by M L Zakharov and was based on the draft prepared by the Constitutional Commission and a draft prepared at the initiative of the President of the Russian Federation. The formulation omits the word "integral" part of the legal system, but moves in the direction of the final version of Article 15(4) of the 1993 Russian Constitution.

On May 5, 1993 the Constitutional Commission sent to President Eltsin a draft Basic Provisions of the Constitution prepared by the Constitutional Committee and approved by the Sixth Congress of People's Deputies. This version took into account amendments of the President, proposals of subjects of legislative initiative, and individual provisions of an initiative draft Constitution published on April 30, 1993 in two leading publications.

In spring 1993 another draft Constitution circulated which contained provisions that did not conform to a draft submitted by the President of the Russian Federation to the Constitutional Commission. With respect to international law, however, both versions provided as follows:

Article 11. Russian Federation in the World Community

The Russian Federation is a fully-fledged member of the world community, observes generally-recognized principles and norms of international law and its international treaties and may participate in international organizations and other associations and collective security systems, and aspires to a universal and just peace, mutually-advantageous international cooperation, and the settlement of global problems.

Commentary. This text in spirit is an adaptation of the 1978 RSFSR Constitution, essentially programmatic in character, and virtually devoid of normative content.

In the interval between May 5 and July 12, 1993, further changes were made in the draft Constitution. The draft approved by participants of the Constitutional Assembly as of July 12, 1993 contained Article 15[4] in the version as it exists today in the 1993 Russian Constitution approved by national referendum in December 1993. The sole difference in the two texts of this paragraph (or point) of Article 15 is that the paragraphs were unnumbered in the version of July 12, 1993. This draft appeared in a printed version labeled "draft" and dated "Moscow, Kremlin, 12 July 1993."[10]

This above draft, however, was a Presidential version. The Congress of People's Deputies continued to work on their version and produced a "Constitution (Basic Law) of the Russian Federation" the basic provisions of which were approved by the Sixth Congress of People's Deputies of the Russian Federation, taking into account the proposals of subjects of the Russian Federation, other subjects of the right of legislative initiative, and also the variant of the draft Constitution of the Russian Federation discussed at the Constitutional Assembly (as of August 1993).[11]

Parliamentary Draft of September 1993

Article 3. Supremacy of Law

...

(4). Generally-recognized principles and norms of international law and international treaties of the Russian Federation shall constitute *part of the law* thereof. If other rules have been established by a *ratified* international treaty of the Russian Federation than by a law, the rules of the international treaty shall be applied.

Commentary. This is exactly for the formulation of April 1993 and rejected by the Soviet of Nationalities. The only change is that the points of Article 3 are now numbered.

---

[10] Reproduced in Rumiantsev (n. 3) IV(3), 144.
[11] Reproduced in Rumiantsev (n. 3) IV(3), 357–8. This draft is published as of September 1993.

Draft Constitution of Constitutional Assembly: November 2, 1993[12]

This draft of the Constitution contains Article 15(4) as it finally appeared in the text submitted to the national referendum.

Unofficial Constitutional Drafts

This was a period when political parties, citizens groups, law faculties, and individual specialists on constitutional law submitted full-fledged draft constitutions or drafts devoted to specific sections of a Constitution. Collectively, they constitute an interesting source of thinking at the time about the place of international law, if any, within the constitutional structure of the Russian Federation. On November 5, 1990 an "initiative group of people's deputies of the RSFSR 'Communists of Russia'" submitted a draft "Constitution (Basic Law) of the Russian Soviet Federated Socialist Republic" which contained no provisions on international law.[13]

Draft Constitution of "Agrarian Union," "Fatherland," and "Communists of Russia": April 1, 1992[14]

Article 39. Fundamental Principles of Policy in Domain of Human Rights

The rights, freedoms, and duties of citizens of the RSFSR shall be established and exercised in accordance with obligations of the RSFSR under international treaties and agreements.

---

[12] From a personal archive. This variant of the draft was published only in Rumiantsev (n. 3) V, 1047.

[13] For the draft, see Rumiantsev (n. 3) V, 400–35; the same group submitted a more considered draft on March 25, 1991, which likewise contained no provisions on international law. See ibid, 504–52.

[14] Published from the Archive of the Constitutional Reform Fund, opis 2, delo 3, folios 587–620; published in Rumiantsev (n. 3) V, 694–738.

Commentary. So far as materials disclose, this was the first occasion on which the "Communists of Russia" associated themselves with a provision on international law, probably the influence of the other two groups. This clause does nothing to embed international law in the Russian legal system or, for that matter, Russian law and confines itself to a purely declaratory statement that Russia will comply with its international obligations—which Russia must do in any event irrespective of draft Article 39.

Draft Constitution of International "Reform" Fund: March 11, 1993[15]

Article 2
The Constitution of the RF, laws, and international treaties which have entered into force shall possess the highest legal force with respect to all other normative acts.

…

Article 7
The RF shall comply with generally-recognized principles and norms of international law and participate in international organizations and other associations whose activity is not contrary to the purposes of the preservation of a universal and just peace.

Commentary. This draft places the Constitution, laws, and international treaties on the same level and places them above all other normative acts, but does not address the possible conflict between them, should such occur, unless one regards the sequence in which they are enumerated as establishing a hierarchy—in which case international treaties cede place to laws. Article 7 is programmatic and contains no concrete obligations.

---

[15] Published in Независимая газета [Independent Newspaper], March 11, 1993; and in Rumiantsev (n. 3) V, 911–25.

Draft Constitution of Liberal-Democratic Party of Russia: April 1993[16]

> *Article 22.* The relation of the Russian Federation to other States shall be built on the basis of comply with the following principles: sovereign equality; non-interference in internal affairs; territorial integrity; indissolubility of boundaries; mutual renunciation of the use or threat of force; peaceful settlement of disputes; respect for human rights and freedoms; equality and rights of peoples to dispose of their own fate; cooperation between States; good-faith fulfillment of obligations arising from international treaties concluded by the Russian Federation.

Commentary. This formulation appears in Chapter 4 of the draft devoted to foreign policy. Although the article enumerates principles—all of which are regarded as principles of international law—no mention is made of their status in this respect. This clause is indebted to the formulations in the 1978 Constitution of the RSFSR.

Doctrinal Contributions to Constitutional Drafting

From time to time materials on a draft Constitution were prepared to assist those considering the drafts. The Legal Section of the Apparatus of the Supreme Soviet of the Russian Federation, for example, drew up a document entitled "Some Questions and Answers on the Constitution of the Russian Federation," published in 1993 but not precisely dated within that year. The questions were unnumbered. That relating to international law read as follows:

> [Question]: What is the correlation of international norms of law and the Constitution of the Russian Federation in the domain of human rights and freedoms?

---

[16] Archive of Constitutional Reform Fund, opis 2, del 3, folios 1159–62; published in Rumiantsev (n. 3) V, 937.

[Answer]: In accordance with Article 32 of the Constitution of the Russian Federation, generally-recognized international norms relating to human rights have preference over a law of the Russian Federation and directly generate rights and duties of citizens of the Russian Federation.

Commentary. This text is reproduced from an archival version but was published in a booklet entitled Некоторые вопросы и ответы о Конституции Российской Федерации [Some Questions and Answers on the Constitution of the Russian Federation] (Moscow, 1993).[17] This was the version of Russian law at the time, and it is unclear what version of Article 32 the document refers to, but there is no reference to treaties and no definition of general principles of international law; the notion of priority, however, is in evidence, as is the concept of direct effect—although not all human rights norms in international conventions are necessarily norms of direct effect.

Doctrinal contributions took various forms and were submitted in the form of articles, transcripts of round tables or seminars, memoranda, critiques of conceptual approaches, and even formal proposals containing specific suggestions for the inclusion or exclusion of individual provisions. The Institute of State and Law of the Russian Academy of Sciences had addressed the conception of a new Constitution for the USSR as early as spring 1990. A new Soviet constitution should contain general provisions on the foreign and economic policy of the State and, in particular, consolidate at the constitutional level the "primacy of international law."[18]

After the Soviet Union was dissolved in December 1991, the central authorities in the Russian Federation struggled to maintain the integrity of the Federation. The conclusion of the Treaty of the Federation on March 30, 1992 was an early concern. It was suggested that the conclusion of the Treaty of the Federation had changed "the character and nature of the legal

---

[17] Printed respectively from the Archive of the President of the Russian Federation, f. 92, op. 4, delo 456, folio 46; State Archive of the Russian Federation, fund 10026, opis 1, delo 313, folios 108–13; published in Rumiantsev (n. 3) IV(2), 67, 819.
[18] See "Концепция новой конституции Союза ССР" ["Conception of a New Constitution of the USSR"], Советское государство и право [*Soviet State and Law*], no. 4 (1990) 15–21; reprinted in Rumiantsev (n. 3) V, 102.

system of the Russian Federation."[19] A four-tiered structure of the legal system had been created, of which the first consisted of:

(1) Constitution of the Russian Federation and Treaty of the Federation; Fundamental Principles of Legislation; laws, federal codes, subordinate acts (edicts of the President of Russia, Presidium of the Supreme Soviet of the Russian Federation, normative acts of the Government, law-application acts of branch ministries and departments); agreements on delegating powers of Russia to subjects of the Federation; inter-State treaties of Russia and governmental agreements; acts connected with the realization of international treaties, conventions, acts of the Commonwealth of Independent States, and others.[20]

The authors observed that "generally-recognized norms of international law and international treaties *ratified* by the Russian parliament" are becoming an important integral part of "*Russian national law.*" If these international treaties, conventions, and agreements establish conditions other than those which have been provided by national legislation, the "*rules of international law*" apply (emphasis added). The formulations are loosely drawn, but only "ratified" treaties are deemed to be part of "national law," and the reference is to "national law" and not to the "legal system of Russia." Here the term "national law" might be read to mean "federal law," which was probably not intended, for if treaties are to have supremacy over federal laws, it would ordinarily follow that they have supremacy over inferior normative legal acts—unless the Treaty of the Federation created a barrier to this.

Danilenko gave perhaps the most detailed analysis of the draft constitutions as of 1992,[21] concentrating on the Presidential draft as it existed at

[19] See I I Il'inskii, N D Krylov, and N A Mikhaleva, "Федеративный договор и правовая система Российской Федерации" ["Treaty of the Federation and Legal System of the Russian Federation"], Конституционный вестник [*Constitutional Herald*], no. 14 (1992) 20.

[20] The article is reprinted in Rumiantsev (n. 3) III(3), 588.

[21] G M Danilenko, "Международно-правовые аспекты новой Конституции России" ["International-Legal Aspects of the New Constitution of Russia"], Конституционный вестник [*Constitutional Herald*], no. 13 (1992) 132–7; reprinted in Rumiantsev (n. 3) III(3), 724–35. The Institute of Legislation and Comparative Jurisprudence prepared conceptual provisions for a new constitution which were believed to be applicable to newly independent post-Soviet States. It was recommended that a new constitution consolidate links between the constitution and types of links with other legal acts, including "international treaties." See "Концептуальные положения новой Конституции Республики" ["Conceptual Provisions

the time. Some of the suggestions he made were later integrated into the final version of the Constitution; others were not, but they nonetheless offer insight into the mentality which informed the final version. Most of his observations are relevant to all the draft constitutions.

The drafts were unclear whether "generally-recognized principles and norms of international law" had direct effect, although insofar as they took priority over federal laws, one might assume that they did.[22] Assuming they did have direct effect, the consequences of such for Russian law were not addressed. Nothing, moreover, was said about official publication of treaties as a condition of their application—a gap ultimately addressed in the final text of the Constitution. The references to the "law of the Russian Federation" were imprecise; Danilenko did not address the question of whether being an integral part of Russian law would deprive treaties of their supremacy over Russian law; insofar as they were equal and sat side by side, the principles of the law latest in time or *lex specialis* would override the principle of supremacy. In any event, Danilenko would have confined treaty supremacy only to ratified international treaties. Although ultimately the final text of the Constitution did not impose this restriction, Russian legal doctrine and judicial practice is often of this view.

Danilenko participated a year later in the formulation of "Recommendations of the Institute of State and Law of the Russian Academy of Sciences with Regard to Reworking the Draft Constitution of the Russian Federation."[23] The Report began this section by noting:

1. The establishment of civilized relations with States of the international community is inconceivable without the constitutional consolidation of the fundamental principles of foreign policy and the status of international law, especially norms affecting human rights and freedoms, in the internal law of Russia. On this plane, the Presidential draft

of a New Constitution of the Republic"], Государство и право [*State and Law*], no. 8 (1992) 22–30; reprinted in Rumiantsev (n. 3) V, 804.

[22] These concerns also attracted the attention of the European Commission for Democracy Through Law (known as the Venice Commission), which drew attention to several inconsistencies in the drafts; these were set out in a Report of the Venice Commission dated April 28, 1992. The Russian text is translated and published in Rumiantsev (n. 3) III(3), 974.
[23] The text of the Recommendations is undated, but placed chronologically by Rumiantsev as May 1993; the Recommendations are taken from the State Archive of the Russian Federation, fund 10026, opis 1, delo 313, folios 180–219. Published in Rumiantsev (n. 3) IV(2), 725–7.

is weaker, is inferior to the draft of the Constitutional Commission and Constitution in force.

The place of international law within the system of law of the Russian Federation is not duly determined in the Presidential draft, and the priority of international-legal norms is not guaranteed, especially norms concerning human rights, over norms of internal law contradicting international obligations of the Russian Federation. Provisions concerning the principles of foreign policy of the Russian Federation are absent in the draft. The provisions of the draft concerning the use of armed force do not correspond to prevailing international law.[24]

The Institute of State and Law recommended its own version as an improvement with respect to all existing drafts: Presidential, Constitutional Commission, and Supreme Soviet:

Generally-recognized principles and norms of international law and ratified and officially-published international treaties of the RF shall be part of the law of the RF, possessing supremacy throughout the entire territory of the RF. If a ratified and officially-published treaty of the RF established other rules than a law, the rules of this international treaty shall apply.[25]

The proposal of the Institute would have resolved some issues but created others. The supremacy of treaties was confined to "ratified" treaties, and they would be merely part of the "law" of Russia, rather than the legal system.

In late June 1993 the Institute of State and Law arranged a "Round Table" devoted to the "problems of creating a new Basic Law of Russia" and discussed the drafts submitted by the Constitutional Commission and President of the Russian Federation. Danilenko was quoted as observing that both the Presidential and Parliamentary drafts lacked provisions devoted to the operation of norms of international law in Russia. As between the two versions, both were unsatisfactory, but the Parliamentary version should be taken as the basis for preparing the final version, at least with respect to several Articles.[26]

[24] Ibid, 725–6.
[25] Ibid, 727.
[26] Московская Правда [Moscow Pravda], June 24, 1993; reprinted in Rumiantsev (n. 3) IV(2), 934.

Professor Igor Ivanovich Lukashuk (1926–2007) offered a lengthy critique of the draft Constitution during a Session of the Group of Representatives of Federal Agencies of State Power for Reworking the Draft Constitution of the Russian Federation on June 25, 1993. It is worth quoting in full, noting that his remarks will have come shortly after the Round Table held at the Institute of State and Law of the Russian Academy of Sciences, where Lukashuk was a senior international lawyer. Article 15(4) of the draft Constitution, he said, was an example of "mistake after mistake":

First. "Generally-recognized principles and norms of international law and international treaties of the Russian Federation are an integral part of its legal system." The first part of this phrase "generally-recognized principles." Yes, actually in many countries they are part of the legal system of a State. But international treaties—this is completely different. Look. How can a treaty of alliance or a treaty on neutrality be part of the law of a country? This cannot be. How can an interdepartmental agreement—and this also is an international treaty of the Russian Federation—be part of the law of a country? This cannot be.

The following sentence. "If other rules have been established by an international treaty of the Russian Federation than provided by a law, the rules of the international treaty shall apply." Once more what does "international treaty of the Russian Federation" mean? This also may be an interdepartmental agreement. It means they will repeal a law? An intergovernmental treaty will repeal a law? Such a position exists only in one African country and in the draft Constitution of Ukraine; nowhere else is there anything similar?

Therefore, it would be more correct to say that generally-recognized principles and norms of international law are a part of our law, and the operation of international treaties in the law of the Russian Federation is determined by a federal law. And in a federal law all this is precisely decided.[27]

The Session of the Group of Representatives of Federal Agencies of State Power for Reworking the Draft Constitution of the Russian Federation returned to Article 15(4) on July 10, 1993. The Chairman of the Session, Aleksandr Maksimovich Iakovlev (1927–2011), reported some changes

---

[27] Filatov (n. 2) XV, 91.

to the formulation of Article 15(4), particularly the phrase that norms and principles of international law and international treaties "comprise part of the law." This provision had been criticized by representatives of the Ministry of Foreign Affairs, who preferred the formulation: "is an integral part of its legal system, principles, and norms of law."

Professor Vladimir Aleksandrovich Tumanov (1926–2011) objected, first, that if a legal system is understood as a "system of norms," international law must be placed somewhere within that system; if "legal system" is understood in its sociological meaning, it includes law, legal consciousness, and legal relations, among others. And, in his view, international law was not part of the legal system in that sense. He believed that the concept of "law" was the more appropriate term. The Chairman responded that the term "law" was not suitable because treaties would immediately become "an organic part of prevailing law, this means the impossibility of their application without special legislation."[28]

Oleg Ivanovich Tiunov (1937–2017) spoke in favor of the change:

> I believe that all the same the formulation concerning the legal system should be left in. The fact is that norms of international law in general are norms of another legal system, when we introduce these norms in the form of a treaty of the Russian Federation into the law of the State, these already are norms of another system. And therefore it would be advisable to say precisely that: "are an integral part of its legal system." From my point of view, this would be more correct.[29]

The Chairman put the amendment to a vote. There were eight votes opposed; the number in favor was not reported, but the amendment was approved by a substantial majority.

By October 22, 1993 matters had proceeded sufficiently far to submit the draft Constitution to a Session of the Working Commission for Reworking the Draft Constitution of the Russian Federation. The Working Commission returned to Article 15(4) under the Chairmanship of Sergei Aleksandrovich Filatov (b. 1936). Two questions preoccupied the Working Commission. One was a proposed amendment to insert the words "and ratified, and officially published" international treaties of the Russian

---

[28] Ibid, XVII, 9.
[29] Ibid, XVII, 10.

Federation. Viktor Leonidovich Sheinis (b. 1931) suggested the words "and entered into force" might also be added, and entry into force presupposed ratification.[30] Boris Aleksandrovich Strashun (b. 1929) suggested the amendment was unnecessary and would only complicate matters and raise new questions: "Any international treaty, even unratified, if ratification is not provided for when concluding it, all the same obliged the State, and it all the same is part of its law. In my view, it is unnecessary to touch anything here."[31] Asked his view by the Chairman, Boris Nikolaevich Topornin (1929–2005) said that the words "officially published" might be omitted, but "ratified" should remain because "not everything should be an integral part of the legal system."[32]

Boris Safarovich Ebzeev (b. 1950) responded:

The fact is that only half of the treaties concluded by the Russian Federation undergo the stage of ratification. The other treaties, the other half—this is an enormous mass—enter into force without ratification because they do not need ratification. And we must determine: do only ratified treaties comprise part of our legal system, or do any international treaties of the Russian Federation.

To this the Chairman replied: "only ratified, of course."

Ebzeev: Why? Say the Government concludes an intergovernmental agreement. That is, precisely an international treaty. Such an agreement does not need ratification.

Aleksandr Vasil'evich Maslov (b. 1963) observed that there are many interdepartmental treaties which are international treaties to the same extent. The Chairman then noted that this was a "serious question" and perhaps should await an "interpretation," perhaps from the State Duma. To this Topornin objected, noting that this question had been raised several times:

But, analyzing the entire development of international law in recent times, our specialists came to the conclusion that it was absolutely necessary to leave the word "ratified." Otherwise, as has now been said

---

[30] Ibid, XIX, 19.
[31] Ibid, XIX, 20.
[32] Ibid, XIX, 20.

precisely, either a treaty or an international act which may contain devi-
ations, may insert provisions which are not appropriate and will not be
known to others, and these will be an integral part of the legal system.
Our legal system will thereby be polluted with provisions that should not
be there. Here there must be control.[33]

Egor Mikhailovich Larionov (b. 1940), Deputy Chairman of the Supreme
Soviet of Sakha (Iakutia), pointed out that under Article 15(3) of the draft
Constitution "Any normative legal acts affecting the rights, freedoms, and
duties ... may not be applied unless they were published officially for general
information." And if, say, there were State interests or State secrecy? "Any"
treaties might be legal acts which people cannot know about—a State secret.[34]
The second question which engaged the Working Commission was the
term "generally-recognized principles." Mikhail Ivanovich Kukushkin
(1933–2017), Rector of the Urals State Legal Academy, had reservations
about the word "principles." In his view a "principle" was a basic idea, the
basic commencement of something. Where would one find "generally-
recognized principles"? And why are they generally-recognized? "I guarantee," he said, "that such 'generally-recognized principles' have not been
recognized by the States of the world." Generally-recognized norms, yes;
generally-recognized rules, yes—but not generally-recognized principles.
To this Ebzeev commented:

Those principles which have been laid down in the United Nations
Charter are generally-recognized by universal recognition. These are
Articles One and Two: the tasks and purposes of the United Nations and
principles. Article two is seven principles. We consider to be generally-
recognized those principles which were written down in 1975 in the
Final Act—nine principles. But I in this situation would wish to draw attention to Article 25 of the West German Basic Law of 1949. "Generally-
recognized norms of international law are an integral part of federal
law. They have preference over laws and generate rights and duties directly for persons residing on the territory of the Federation." In other
words, Germany in this Article does not mention international treaties.
It speaks only of generally-recognized norms of international law. As for

[33] Ibid, XIX, 19–20.
[34] Ibid, XIX, 21.

principles, I see nothing bad in this; they can be left in.[35] Topornin added that "generally-recognized" means also recognized by us: "We acceded to them, we share them, we support them."

The final word came from Maslov, of the Presidential Administration, on Article 15(4): "I want to recall that this formulation of point (4) was proposed by the Ministry of Foreign Affairs, which struggled long over it, they 'licked and polished it.'"[36]

The issue of generally-recognized principles of international law, however, did not end with the acceptance of the formulation of Article 15(4). A similar phrase was to be found in Article 17(1) of the 1993 Constitution, which provides: "The rights and freedoms of man and citizen according to generally-recognized principles and norms of international law and in accordance with the present Constitution shall be recognized and guaranteed in the Russian Federation." This formulation was finally accepted after lively debate. Initially Ebzeev suggested that the phrase "according to generally-recognized principles and norms of international law" be deleted. He observed that the 1966 human rights covenants and 1948 Declaration of Human Rights were not a legal norm or a legal act and were not generally-recognized. Given Article 15(4) and the fact that an international treaty of the Russian Federation was an integral part of the legal system and had priority force in Russia, nothing would be lost by removing the reference thereto in Article 17(1). The Chairman asked: why priority for international documents and not "ours"? Ebzeev responded that the question was not whether Russia should conform or not to these generally-recognized principles—Russia as a democratic State would, by definition, be obliged to recognize and ensure these rights to its own citizens. He challenged anyone to prove that the 1948 Declaration and 1966 human rights covenants were generally-recognized.

Topornin answered that their content was generally-recognized, but not the covenants. In Ebzeev's view, Russia was already party to the covenants,

---

[35] Ibid, XIX, 21. Tamara Georgievna Morshchakova (b. 1936) took issue with the translation of the German Basic Law. Working from the German text, she said it provided that "general rules of international law are an integral part of federal law." Ebzeev responded that "in international law neither general nor special rules exist. International law—is law, and therefore norms also exist in international law, and in this situation the translation 'norms of law' is more than adequate." Ibid, XIX, 22.

[36] Ibid, XIX, 22.

and nothing would be lost be removing the language from Article 17(1). Morshchakova responded as follows in favor of keeping the language in Article 17(1):

> The fact is that, of course, each State guarantees by its law some human rights and freedoms, but the international community always reproaches us that the rights and freedoms guaranteed by our legislation are less than those which it is accepted to guarantee in the international community. We want to be members of this community. Understand? By this phrase they will evaluate us, do we agree to guarantee rights and freedoms at the level of world standards or not? ... The standard must be international, and not ours, not our own. And we must insist on this everywhere, both in our external treaties and in our internal treaties. There must be a standard ... To be sure, this is in our law, but our may not be less. ... Our standard cannot be lower. And in this sense the minimum is given by the international level, and we may increase this as must as advantageous, if we have the spirit.[37]

President Boris Eltsin had no corrections with respect to Articles 15 and 17 of the draft Constitution.[38]

Some Implications of the Legislative History of Article 15(4) of the 1993 Russian Constitution

The constitutional legislative history of Article 15(4) invites a number of observations. The 1978 RSFSR Constitution, as amended, recognized belatedly in 1992 the priority of "generally-recognized international norms" over Russian laws with respect to human rights. This amendment was adopted while the constitutional drafting process was well underway in Russia. The formulation was implicitly criticized by participants in the working groups of the Constitutional Assembly, who sought either a less explicit reference to principles of international law or a stronger statement.

---

[37] Ibid, XIX, 24.
[38] His handwritten amendments on the draft Constitution, together with his sign-off signature and the autographs of the technical editorial group, are reproduced in ibid, XX, 473–542.

The relationship between international treaties of the Russian Federation and domestic laws and/or other normative legal acts was raised regularly during the drafting processes and was controversial. One impression is overriding: insofar as the priority of Russian treaties was to be recognized, most felt such priority should be only enjoyed by ratified international treaties. That proposal was repeatedly submitted—and rejected! The legislative history of that provision of Article 15 leads to one compelling conclusion: all international treaties of the Russian Federation—on a literal reading of the provision—enjoy priority over laws and subordinate normative legal acts. Efforts to limit the provision were rejected throughout.

Second, the legislative history discloses that the lawyers in the Ministry of Foreign Affairs of the Russian Federation were responsible for the formulation of Article 15(4); that is, the Russian jurists most familiar with international and Russian State practice. The origins of the formulation of Article 15(4) were invoked on several occasions during the constitutional assembly to resist any changes to the formulation.

Third, the drafters were well aware of the distinction between an international treaty being part of the "law" of the Russian Federation and the "legal system" of the Russian Federation. Equating principles and norms of international law—whether *jus cogens*, customary, or treaty—is to place international law in a cosmetically equal position but *de facto* subordinate position; laws later in time or *lex specialis* will supersede treaty provisions. The drafters were well aware of the issue and preserved what is, in effect, a higher legal standard.

Fourth, although the drafters, in the spirit of Soviet and post-Soviet legal doctrine, were well schooled in the distinctions between a legal principle, legal norm, and legal rule, in the end they accepted the formulation of "generally-recognized principles and norms of international law," raising questions about what "generally-recognized" meant, whether anything qualified as "generally-recognized," what was the distinction between a principle and a norm of international law, whether a difference exists between a "norm" and a "rule" (in common parlance they are often used as synonyms). Not once in the official records of the Constitutional Assembly was reference made to "customary international law," although some implied that "generally-recognized principles and norms" might amount to customary norms or rules without invoking that terminology.

There was general acceptance that, in the domain of human rights, international legal standards represented the minimum to which Russia was expected to conform. The constitutional drafting materials confirm a point widely made at the time: international standards were invoked to redress the lamentable excesses of the Soviet era, and Russian courts were given space to draw upon these as necessary. When the Russian Federation became a party to the 1950 European Convention on Human Rights and Fundamental Freedoms, Russian citizens were given direct access to the Court in Strasbourg as an additional mechanism to introduce international standards in this domain.

Outcomes of Constitution-Making

On October 10, 2003, nearly eight years after the adoption of the Federal Law "On International Treaties of the Russian Federation," the Plenum of the Supreme Court of the Russian Federation adopted Decree No. 5, "On the Application by Courts of General Jurisdiction of Generally-Recognized Principles and Norms of International Law and International Treaties of the Russian Federation."[39] The Plenum defined "generally-recognized principles" of international law by way of a general abstract definition and by way of examples.

By way of a general definition, the Plenum drew upon the language of Article 53 of the 1969 Vienna Convention on the Law of Treaties: the Plenum Decree provided as guidance to Russian courts that the "generally-recognized principles of international law" are the "basic imperative norms of international law adopted and recognized by the international community of States as a whole, deviation from which is inadmissible" (point 1). Article 53 refers to "a peremptory norm of general international law" and defines "peremptory norm" as a norm accepted and recognized by the international community of States as a whole as a norm from which no derogation is permitted. In the headnote to Article 53, the words "peremptory norm" are "explained" by the Latin phrase "*jus cogens*." The Russian language text of this Article has difficulty with this terminology. First, the word "peremptory" is translated into Russian as "imperative." For Russian jurists the concept of an "imperative" norm is quite familiar from Russian legal theory and, especially, Russian civil law. "Imperative" means a norm which the parties may not change by agreement between themselves; an example would be a period of limitations, which is established by the Civil Code and the parties may not by agreement shorten or lengthen or change in any way the legislative provision.

---

[39]   Translated in W E Butler, *Russian Public Law* (3rd edn.; 2013) 48–54.

Moreover, Article 53 of the Vienna Convention refers to "general international law," not to "generally-recognized principles of international law." And the term "derogation" implies not merely a "deviation" or "difference" between the peremptory norm and another norm but a change which detracts from, possibly violates, the peremptory norm by agreement of the parties. In short, the Russian language text of the 1969 Vienna Convention departs from the English-language version and "softens" the rigorous requirements of the English-language version. The translators experienced problems with the "*cogens*" nature of the relevant norm of international law.

These distinctions have been carried over into the 2003 Plenum Decree. They are evident in the passage translated above. The concrete examples given in the Plenum Decree are: "the principle of good-faith fulfillment of international obligations" (preamble); "the principle of universal respect for human rights and the principle of the good-faith fulfillment of international obligations" (point 1). The examples are expressed in general form and are regarded by many as an expression of *pacta sunt servanda*; the formulation, however, is broader than "pacta" and includes all obligations under international law, whether originating in *jus cogens*, customary international law, or international treaties.

The "content" of the said principles and norms of international law, the Plenum Decree says, "may be revealed, in particular, in documents of the United Nations and its specialized agencies" (point 1). This formulation is in effect a "hunting license" for Russian courts to seek evidence of the existence and meaning of generally-recognized principles and norms of international law in all kinds of United Nations documentation, including recommendatory resolutions of the General Assembly, preparatory works of the International Law Commission, and the like. The United Nations here is merely an example; all relevant materials may be consulted by Russian courts for this purpose. And Russian judges have actively taken advantage of this discretion.

The Plenum Decree provides that both "generally-accepted principles and norms of international law" and "international treaties of the Russian Federation" are, under Article 15(4) of the Russian Constitution, an integral part of the Russian legal system. This includes "international treaties in force concluded by the USSR, with respect to which the Russian Federation continues to effectuate international rights and obligations of the USSR as the State-continuer of the USSR, also are part of the legal system of the Russian Federation" (point 2).

Nonetheless, paradoxes emerge from the legislative history of Article 15(4) of the 1993 Russian Constitution. Generally-recognized principles and norms of international law are an integral part of the Russian legal system but without a place designated in the hierarchy of normative legal acts of the Russian legal system. International treaties, on the other hand, are superior to inconsistent Russian laws. In Russian doctrinal writings, that priority is or is not accorded to generally-recognized principles and norms. However, which treaties? All treaties of the Russian Federation, and Article 15(4) draws no distinctions among them, or only "ratified" international treaties—a term the Plenum Decree does not use in this connection but a result the decree achieves in a different formulation:

> 8. The rules of an international treaty of the Russian Federation in force, consent to the bindingness of which was adopted in the form of a federal law, shall have priority in application with respect to laws of the Russian Federation.
>
> The rules of an international treaty of the Russian Federation in force, consent to the bindingness of which was adopted not in the form of a federal law shall have priority in application with respect to subordinate normative acts issued by an agency of State power or empowered organization which concluded the said treaty (Article 15(4), Article 90, and Article 113, Constitution of the Russian Federation) [as amended by Decree No. 4, March 5, 2013].

The Russian Federation ratifies treaties by a federal law, so paragraph one of point 8 is an indirect reference to ratification. Thus did the Plenum of the Supreme Court by interpretation achieve what the drafters of the 1993 Constitution rejected—priority accorded over federal laws only to ratified international treaties.

Unratified treaties—those concluded by the Government of Russia (intergovernmental) or by ministries, State committees, and so on (interdepartmental) or by State corporations or agencies of local self-government, and others—have priority over the enactments of the State agency which concluded them, but no more. Contracting parties need to be fully aware of the distinctions, for under Russian doctrine (not unanimous) and judicial practice these "lower level" treaties are vulnerable to the principles of the law latest in time and/or to *lex specialis*.

6

Treaties of Subjects of
the Russian Federation

Treaties/Contracts *Sui Generis*

In Chapter 1 attention was drawn to the linguistic heritage of the Slavs and to the fact that the word договор dates back to at least the tenth century and can refer to either a contract or to a treaty. That "overlapping" of meanings has been used, the present author suggests, at various times to articulate modifications or nuances intended to compete with the stark models represented by doctrines of monism and dualism or, in more practical terms, to carve out models of nation-building or community-building that separate Muscovy-Imperial Russia-Soviet Russia-post-Soviet Russia from the rest of the world. Sometimes these models are seen as "hyper-defensive"; other times they are "aggressive" or "offensive" in character, or so they seem to the outside world. In either perception, arguably two sides of the same coin.

These are competing themes in accounts of Russian history. A country vast in dimension, under-populated if you divide nation-space per capita, no natural frontiers (even the frozen North is melting, which creates maritime vulnerability in the Arctic), conquered or attacked historically by formidable foreign interventions (Tatars, Swedes, Polish/Lithuanians, Germans, and Allied Powers in 1918–21, and others), deeply enmeshed in its borderlands on all sides and, exceptionally, other areas of the globe (Cuba, Vietnam, China, Mongolia, Syria, Afghanistan), populated by a people who love to travel but who are apprehensive about their cultural integrity and "purity," among other factors and traits. Some look back to describe Soviet nationality and internal State-building policies as a response of "genius" to a multi-ethnic conundrum, whereas others suggest that the Soviet Union in this respect sowed the seeds of its own demise by encouraging formal acknowledgements of ethnic identity (literature, poetry, music, language, costume, etc.) and ethnic awareness even within a constitutional federative framework.

One response, inchoate but visible from time to time, has been to create variants of the law of treaties/contracts that would serve, or might serve, the larger aims of nation-building—sometimes by rewriting or reconceptualizing the past and sometimes by seeking *sui generis* models for the present which, in their view, constitute exceptions or adaptations of generally accepted principles or rules.

There are several examples. The doctrinal recharacterization of "treaties" among entities which constituted pre-Muscovy or Muscovy relations as "domestic" or "non-international" relations governed not by the classical law of treaties but as "constitutional"—that is, "internal" relations governed by Muscovite or Russian law. This recharacterization would remove these treaties from the operation of the law of nations and treat them as relations *sui generis*.

The Soviet Union itself was a treaty-based federation, or confederation; Soviet doctrine over the decades, without (usually) denying the treaty origins of the Union, would frequently suggest that the 1922 Treaty of the Union was something other than a "normal" treaty and carried with it connotations of supranational State-building that ultimately transformed, or would transform, the Soviet community into a single monolithic State. The particular model of federation, however, contained both cohesive and divisive factors. At their respective apogees, the Russian Empire and the Soviet Union contained approximately 200 ethnic identities and sought ways to recognize and accommodate these without excessively forcing assimilation. "Federative in form, socialist in substance" was among the sundry formulas deployed in those days. At times used to pursue "russification" policies, and at other times used to give formal acknowledgment to the multi-ethnic realities of Russian existence, the "treaty" that bound the Soviet Union together came to be regarded in many doctrinal writings as a "treaty *sui generis*," not regulated by the law of treaties ordinarily applied in international law, but by unseen and unwritten rules peculiar to Soviet circumstances. Echoing the perceptions of the Russian past, it was a "constitutional" treaty governed by Soviet constitutional law; it contained many outward trappings of the classic international treaty, but was something otherwise in substance.

This mode of thought carried over from the 1960s into community-building in the "socialist camp" and ultimately found expression in concepts of "socialist economic integration"—which in turn engendered notions of "socialist international law." These were undertakings to segregate this group of States out from under traditional international law and conceptualize a sub-group, or even a region, of States who operated by their own rules, in this example posited to be "higher" or "more advanced" than the ordinary norms governing the relations of States. The "treaties" which contained or reflected these relations were perceived to be "treaties *sui generis*" partly because of the identity of the parties but more substantially because the treaties were directed toward "integrating" planned economies. This was an experiment that failed or did not have the opportunity to display its full potential—but from the standpoint of the law of treaties, the treaty was conceived to be the key instrument for achieving integration, a kind of extrapolation of the Soviet Union model to a domain of inter-State relations never before addressed.

For the Russian *Federation* many of the same factors operate. The treaty is among the key instruments on which the Federation rests, and underlying the treaty relations are principles of statehood, legal personality, autonomy, independence, dependence, and others which some view as constitutional questions and others as matters of international law. Movements in the direction of Eurasian integration presently underway (or not) reflect similar considerations. The treaty is the key vehicle, and one of the issues facing the architects of the Eurasian community is whether these relations are classical international-legal relations or whether there is an incipient Eurasian community law emerging that may or may not acquire attributes of supranationality. If the latter proves to be the case, one may anticipate that the treaties underpinning the Eurasian community will be recharacterized as constitutional documents.

Against this background, the "treaty" operates as a source of law, both domestic, international, and/or community, in ways that are not traditionally articulated in the classic expositions of sources of law. In the Russian context, these are roles for the treaty that deserve as much attention as the ordinary roles.

"International Treaties of Russian Federation"

There are at present eighty-five subjects of the Russian Federation—administrative-territorial units within Russia enumerated in the 1993 Constitution. They fall into several categories and have their own hierarchy, reflecting size, population, cultural tradition, history, language, and other considerations. Each has its own constitution, charter, statute, or other constitutive document and a terminology for enactments which they respectively issue. They are required to comply with normative acts issued by Federal agencies within their jurisdiction and with international treaties of the Russian Federation. On August 10, 2000 the President of the Russian Federation introduced additional measures to ensure the unity of legal space of the Russian Federation, among them the establishment of the Federal Register of Normative Legal Acts to be maintained by the Ministry of Justice. The heads of the highest executive agencies of State power in the subjects of the Federation are required to send copies of normative legal acts within a seven-day period after their adoption and the official publications in which these acts are published for inclusion in the Register so that legal expert evaluation can be undertaken to determine whether the normative legal acts are consistent with federal normative legal acts; electronic forms of the enactments are acceptable for these purposes.

The 1993 Russian Constitution relegates to the "joint jurisdiction" of the Russian Federation and the subjects of the Russian Federation: "coordination of international and foreign economic relations of subjects of the Russian Federation, and the fulfillment of international treaties of the Russian Federation" (Article 72(1)(n)). On the basis of that provision, the Russian Federation adopted on January 4, 1999 the Federal Law "On the Coordination of International and Foreign Economic Links of Subjects of the Russian Federation."[1] The treaty-making capacity of subjects of the Federation is considerable, but not unlimited. They may conclude international treaties within the limits of "powers granted to them by the Constitution of the Russian Federation, federal legislation," and the Treaty of the Federation or bilateral treaties concluded between a particular subject of the Federation and the Russian Federation itself. The parties to such international treaties may be subjects of foreign federated States, administrative-territorial formations of foreign States, or international organizations created specially for this purpose. With the consent of the Government of Russia, subjects of the Federation may create links with agencies of State power of foreign States (and not merely entities within foreign States). The subject-matter of such treaties may be trade-economic, scientific-technical, ecological, humanitarian, cultural, or "other domains."

In effect the legislation on treaties that may be concluded by subjects of the Federation mirrors the "hierarchy" of treaty-making at the federal level;

---

[1] C3 РФ (1999) no. 2, item 231, as amended July 13, 2015.

that is, a subject of the Federation may conclude a treaty itself, or its executive branch or administrative agencies may do so. At its respective level, therefore, a subject of the Federation may have "inter-subject", intergovernmental, or interdepartmental international treaties—provided that the draft treaties or agreements are agreed with the interested federal agencies of executive power.

On July 24, 2000 the Government of the Russian Federation adopted Decree No. 552 "On Confirmation of the Rules for the State Registration of Agreements on the Effectuation of International and Foreign Economic Links Concluded by Agencies of State Power of Subjects of the Russian Federation."[2] State registration is carried out by the Ministry of Justice of the Russian Federation and includes: adoption of the decision to register or refusal to register; conferral of a registration number of the agreement; the text of the agreement being registered and all annexes thereto. The materials for registration are to be submitted to the Ministry no later than ten days from the date of signature. If several subjects of the Federation are parties to the agreement, the subject first named is responsible for submitting materials for registration. In addition there are to be submitted three attested examples of the signed agreement; the draft to which consent was given or official guarantees of the Government; a document confirming consent of the Government of the Russian Federation to signature of the agreement or provision of official guarantees by the Government; official opinions of the Ministry of Economic Development, Ministry of Foreign Affairs, Ministry of Justice, and other federal agencies on the draft agreement, or if opinions are not required, the consent of the Government of Russia. Within five work days after State registration, the original text of the agreement is sent by the Ministry of Justice with the registration number conferred to the agency of State power of the subject of the Federation which submitted the agreement for State registration. These rules do not extend to agreements of subjects of the Russian Federation for foreign borrowings.

State registration may be refused if the Ministry of Justice determines that the agreement is contrary to the Constitution of the Russian Federation, generally-recognized principles and norms of international law, international treaties of the Russian Federation, federal legislation, treaties between the Russian Federation and agencies of State power of subjects of the Russian Federation on the delimitation of subjects of jurisdiction and

---

[2] СЗ РФ (2000) no. 31, item 3293, as amended to March 26, 2018.

powers, or the agreement impinges upon the legal interests of another subject of the Russian Federation. When registration is rejected, the text of the agreement is returned to the subject of the Federation which submitted it for registration, indicating the reasons for rejection. Failure to comply with the rules for submitting treaties for registration also may result in rejection of registration. Any changes in the agreement made subsequently or in annexes thereto are subject to State registration in the same procedure.

On November 29, 2000 the Government of the Russian Federation, by Decree No. 904, confirmed the Statute on the Procedure for Keeping the Federal Register of Normative Legal Acts of Subjects of the Russian Federation.[3] This enactment made no mention of international treaties or agreements of subjects of the Russian Federation. However, Decree No. 904 provided that the Ministry of Justice of the Russian Federation shall give "explanations" with regard to the application of the said Statute.

By an Order of the Ministry of Justice of the Russian Federation of August 20, 2013, No. 144, as amended, the Ministry confirmed "Explanations" of what acts should be included in the federal register. These included: "agreements concerning the effectuation of international and foreign economic links concluded by an agency of State power of a subject of the Russian Federation," "changes made in agreements, and also all annexes thereto subsequently adopted," "legal acts of subjects of the Russian Federation concerning the expression of consent to the bindingness of the agreement" (point 13). Treaties would fall under these categories, unless they contain information constituting a "State secret," and also other acts relegated to limited access categories (with notations "For Official Use," "Not for press," "Not subject to publication") (point 14).[4]

These requirements of registration were recorded in the 1999 Federal Law in an addition introduced on July 13, 2015, as follows:[5]

Article 5. State Registration of Agreements on Effectuation of International and Foreign Economic Ties

State registration of agreements on the effectuation of international and foreign economic ties concluded by agencies of State power of a subject of the Russian Federation shall be in the procedure established by the Government of the Russian Federation and is an obligatory

---

[3] СЗ РФ (2000) no. 49, item 4826, as amended March 26, 2018.
[4] The text as amended appears on Consultant Plus.
[5] See n. 1.

condition of the entry of agreements into force for a subject of the Russian Federation.

Treaties concluded by subjects of the Russian Federation do not enjoy priority under Article 15(4) of the 1993 Russian Constitution and are not an integral part of the Russian legal system. Article 12(3) of the 1999 Federal Law provides:

3. The operation of agreements on the effectuation of international and foreign economic links concluded by agencies of executive power of subjects of the Russian Federation and containing provisions which are contrary to the Constitution of the Russian Federation, federal laws, generally-recognized principles and norms of international law and international treaties of the Russian Federation may, in accordance with Article 85(2) of the Constitution of the Russian Federation, be suspended until resolution of this question by a respective court.

Many subjects of the Russian Federation have taken advantage of the provisions in the Treaty of the Federation and the 1993 Russian Constitution to establish a legislative framework for entering into international treaties. These treaties are quite distinct from treaties concluded among subjects of the Federation or between a subject of the Federation and the Russian Federation—at least for legislative purposes. So far as can be determined, no one has undertaken an exhaustive study of the relevant legislation relating to international treaties of subjects of the Federation. A partial survey suggests considerable difference in approach.

Tiumen Region. The Tiumen Regional Duma adopted the "Law on International Agreements of Tiumen Region and Treaties of the Tiumen Region with Subjects of the Russian Federation" on December 26, 1995, as amended to October 13, 2009. Here the terminology "agreements and treaties" is used, and both are an "integral part of its legal system" (Article 2). The priority clause provides that agreements on the effectuation of international and foreign economic links may not contain provisions contrary to the 1993 Constitution of the Russian Federation, generally-recognized principles and norms of international law, international treaties of the Russian Federation, federal legislation, treaties between agencies of State power of Tiumen Region and those agencies of other subjects of the Federation, or provisions impinging the legal interest of another subject of the Russian Federation. On the other hand, references to normative legal acts of Tiumen Region as justification for the failure to fulfill an agreement or treaty are "inadmissible" (Article 17) and, following the 1969 Vienna Convention on the Law of Treaties, the agencies of State power and agencies of local self-government of Tiumen Region are obliged to refrain from actions which would deprive an agreement, before the entry thereof into force, of its object and purposes (Article 17).

Tiumen provides for the direct effect of agreements and treaties which contain concrete rights and duties addressed to agencies, organizations, and persons (presumably natural persons) not requiring the issuance of special acts—in other words, self-executing agreements and treaties—provided they have been officially published (Article 20). If special acts or amendments to existing legislation are required, the Law simply provides that these should be adopted. Agreements and treaties may be suspended or terminated: (a) pursuant to the provisions of the agreement or treaty; (b) by consent of the parties; (c) in the event the parties conclude another agreement or treaty between the same parties on the same question (an odd formulation, reminiscent of *res judicata* clauses); (d) in consequence of a material violation by the other parties; (e) or "in other instances provided by legislation in force."

The Tiumen Law extends both to international treaties and treaties between subjects of the Russian Federation, conflating the two with very little to differentiate them.

Volgograd Region. Volgograd Region adopted a Law "On International Links and Foreign Economic Activity of Volgograd Region" on October 31, 2002.[6] The text followed, with some creative departures, the 1999 Federal Law. The term "agreements" is preferred to "treaties," but, following the pattern of the 1969 Vienna Convention on the Law of Treaties, applies to all agreements "irrespective of their type and name." Nonetheless, reference is made to "international treaties of the Russian Federation" and "international agreements of Volgograd Region" (Article 7). The Volgograd Law is explicit that (Article 11):

> Agreements on the effectuation of international ties and foreign economic activity concluded by agencies of State power of Volgograd Region, irrespective of form, name, and content, are not international treaties of the Russian Federation.

---

[6] Available on Consultant Plus, as amended June 11, 2008, No. 1703-ОД; October 4, 2013, No. 113-ОД; and June 27, 2014, No. 110-ОД.

In the event an agreement is violated, the Volgograd Law provides that the "retaliatory measures shall be taken by the Russian Federation for international violations or unfriendly actions of a foreign State" (Article 12).

No claim to sovereignty is made: the Volgograd Region is an "autonomous participant of international and foreign economic relations," whose power to conclude agreements flows from Article 73 of the 1993 Russian Constitution (Article 3). If any agreements concern questions within the jurisdiction of agencies of local self-government in Volgograd Region, local government is given the opportunity to review the draft and make proposals. No mention is made of ratification, but the Regional Duma "confirms" international agreements.

Apparently oral agreements are prohibited, for the Volgograd Law provides that "international agreements of Volgograd Region are concluded in written form" in the Russian language and native language of the foreign partner, both texts being equally authentic. Secret agreements or parts thereof are prohibited (Article 8). Accession to international agreements of other subjects of the Federation is permitted provided that the Ministry of Foreign Affairs of the Russian Federation so agrees (Article 9).

The grounds for termination or suspension of the operation of international agreements differ from those in the 1969 Vienna Convention on the Law of Treaties and include: (a) competent international agencies adopting a decision to introduce sanctions with respect to a State to whose territory the operation of the Volgograd Region agreement extends; (b) guarantees of the safety of citizens of the Russian Federation are absent as a result of the aggravation of the political situation or military actions; (c) an international agreement of the Volgograd Region is contrary to legislation of the Russian Federation or to the economic or political interests of the Russian Federation; (d) there are other grounds recommended by the Ministry of Foreign Affairs of the Russian Federation.

Sverdlovsk Region. The Sverdlovsk Region on October 28, 2005 adopted a Law "On International and Foreign Economic Links of Sverdlovsk Region and Participation of Sverdlovsk Region and Agencies of State Power of Sverdlovsk Region in International Information Exchange," as amended to September 26, 2017 eleven times.[7] There is no definition of "international

---

[7] Available on Consultant Plus. The 2005 Law replaced the Regional Law of July 16, 1998, No. 25-O3, "On International and Inter-Regional Treaties (or Agreements) of Sverdlovsk Region" and two other laws, combining in total three prior laws into one, which explains the reference to international information exchange.

information exchange," but it is clearly something different from international and foreign economic links. The Legislative Assembly of Sverdlovsk Region confirms agreements on international and foreign economic links upon the proposal of the Governor of the Region. The Law speaks of "dissolution" of an agreement, rather than termination or denunciation, and requires that dissolution be confirmed by the adoption of a respective Law to this effect.

In Sverdlovsk, international agreements of the Region are considered to be "legal acts" regulated by federal and regional legislation, which follows from the Law of Sverdlovsk Region "On Legal Acts in the Sverdlovsk Region" of June 14, 2005.[8] The legal status of international agreements of the Region, however, is not expressly addressed and can be determined at best only by examining several enactments and drawing appropriate inferences. The 2010 Statute on the Sverdlovsk Region distinguishes between "legislation of Sverdlovsk Region" and "international agreements of the Sverdlovsk Region"; the last are ranked equally in the Statute with "generally-recognized principles and norms of international law and international treaties of the Russian Federation" and said to be an integral part of the legal system of Sverdlovsk Region (Articles 6, 12, and 13). Nothing more is said in the Statute about international agreements, and they go unmentioned in the statutory provisions determining the hierarchy of norms of law of Sverdlovsk Region (Article 61).

In the Sverdlovsk Law on Legal Acts, Article 9 enumerates in hierarchical order the "system of legal acts of Sverdlovsk Region." First place is accorded to normative and non-normative legal acts of the Russian Federation and second place to "treaties and agreements of the Russian Federation and treaties and agreements of State agencies of the Russian Federation." Fourth place is occupied by "treaties and agreements of Sverdlovsk Region or State agencies of the said Region"; and sixth place to treaties and agreements of municipal formations located in Sverdlovsk Region. But when it comes to the "correlation of the legal force of normative legal acts of Sverdlovsk Region," treaties and agreements are not mentioned (Article 18, Law on Legal Acts). It has been suggested that the treaties and agreements of Sverdlovsk Region logically should occupy the place within the hierarchy of normative legal acts as the law confirming it. Under this approach, the international treaties and agreements would be exposed to the rules of the

---

[8] Available on Consultant Plus.

"law latest in time" and *"lex specialis"*—and this would represent a departure from Article 15(4) of the 1993 Russian Federation Constitution.[9]

St Petersburg. The City of St Petersburg is a subject of the Russian Federation, together with Moscow and Sevastopol—one of three cities in Russia on which this status is conferred. On June 18, 2008 St Petersburg adopted the Law "On Agreements concerning the Effectuation of International Cooperation and International and Foreign Economic Links," as amended December 11, 2015.[10] Here too the term "agreements" is preferred to "treaties," but the Law applies to "agreements irrespective of their name (treaty, protocol, memorandum, exchange of letters, or other name)" stipulated by the parties. Agreements are concluded on questions relegated to the subject-matter of jurisdiction of St Petersburg determined by the Statute on the City and must not be contrary to other agreements of the City or to the Constitution or federal legislation of the Russian Federation. The precise procedures to be followed when concluding agreements are laid down by the Reglament of the Legislative Assembly of St Petersburg or the Government of St Petersburg. Any agreement of St Petersburg is subject to "confirmation" by a Law of St Petersburg.

Irkutsk Region. On December 9, 2009 the Irkutsk Region adopted the "Law on Treaties and Agreements Concluded in the Name of Irkutsk Region."[11] The scope of this Law was more sharply delineated than the others discussed above. First, the Law extends to: (a) treaties between the Irkutsk Region and other subjects of the Russian Federation, irrespective of the name thereof; and (b) agreements of Irkutsk Region on international and foreign economic ties, irrespective of their name. But the Law does not extend to: (a) treaties between Irkutsk Region and the Russian Federation delimiting jurisdiction and powers; (b) agreements between federal and Irkutsk agencies of executive power transferring powers from one to the other; (c) agreements to change the boundaries of Irkutsk

---

[9] See O V Kocheva, "Заключение международных соглашений Свердловской области: пробелы и коллизии в законодательном регулировании и пути их устранения" ["Conclusion of International Agreements of Sverdlovsk Region: Gaps and Conflicts in Legislative Regulation and Ways of Eliminating Them"], Русский юридический журнал [*Russian Legal Journal*], no. 3 (2010) 61–6.

[10] Available on Consultant Plus. The Law replaced the Law of St Petersburg of December 13, 2000, No 693-79, "On Agreements concerning the Effectuation of International and Foreign Economic Links of St. Petersburg."

[11] Available of Consultant Plus. The Law replaced a Law identically titled Law of Irkutsk Region of April 6, 2000, No 23-ОЗ, " 'On Treaties and Agreements Concluded in the Name of Irkutsk Region," as amended July 5, 2002.

Region; (d) treaties or agreements concluded in the name of the Legislative Assembly of Irkutsk Region, Governor, Government, other agencies of State power or other State agencies of the Region within the framework of the exercise of their powers—the last being a curious exception of potentially unlimited range (Article 2).

The treaties and agreements to which the Irkutsk Law extends are "part of the system of legal acts of the Region" (Article 3(1)) and must correspond to the Statute on Irkutsk Region (the regional equivalent of a constitution). But this is an opaque formulation. It does not follow Article 15(4) of the 1993 Russian Federation Constitution and make treaties an "integral" part of the "legal system"; it merely declares them to be a "part" of the "system of legal acts"—not even "normative" legal acts. The regional "constitutionality" of a treaty or agreement may be tested before the Charter Court of Irkutsk Region; if found to be "unconstitutional," the treaty or agreement is not subject to application and terminates. If some provisions of the treaty or agreement are determined to be "unconstitutional," these are not to be applied or the agreement is subject to being changed by the parties. Apart from the Statute on Irkutsk Region, however, if a duly confirmed treaty or agreement is contrary to a law of the Region, the provisions of the treaty or agreement prevail unless provided otherwise by federal normative legal acts. Irkutsk, therefore, gives a treaty or agreement priority over all of its laws except its Statute. Treaties or agreements not confirmed by a Law of the Irkutsk Region do not enjoy priority over other laws of the Region.

In addition to conforming to the Russian Federation Constitution and international treaties of the Russian Federation, treaties and agreements of Irkutsk Region do not enjoy priority over federal laws, other federal normative acts, or the Statute of the Region, nor should they be "contrary to the State interests of the Russian Federation or impinge the rights and legal interests of the Region and other subjects of the Russian Federation" (Article 6(2)). Rather unusual is the provision that "treaties and agreements concluded in the name of the Region give rise to rights and duties only for the parties (or participants) of treaties and agreements, unless established otherwise by federal laws and other federal normative legal acts" (Article 6(3)).

Attention is given to the language of treaties. Those which are "interregional" are to be in the Russian language and, by agreement of the parties, in the State language of the other subject of the Federation if the State language is not Russian (Article 9). If the treaty is concluded with a foreign party, the treaty may be in Russian and the language of the foreign party, or in a third language. Texts of treaties drawn up in two or more languages are equally authentic unless provided otherwise by the treaty or agreement.

"Confirmation" of treaties is required by a separate Law of Irkutsk, irrespective of whether the treaties are with other subjects of the Russian Federation or, if with foreign parties, confirmation is required by agreement of the parties or by Russian federal or Irkutsk legislation.

"Constitutional Treaties of Russian Federation"

The Treaty of the Federation delimits the subjects of jurisdiction and powers between federal agencies of State power and the agencies of power of the (now) eighty-five subjects of the Federation. These treaties are expressly referred to in Section Two, Concluding and Transitional Provisions, of the 1993 Russian Constitution.[12]

Russian doctrine takes the view that these treaties of the Federation were not "international treaties of the Russian Federation" in the meaning of the 1995 Law on Treaties. Nonetheless, some subjects of the Federation consider that they have international legal personality and are members of the Russian Federation on a treaty-basis (Chechnya, Tatarstan, among others). For the moment these are latent issues of Russian federalism.

Russian legal doctrine is reticent as to whether these treaties of the Russian Federation or international treaties of the Russian Federation should be or are placed in the hierarchy of sources of law. Depending on their subject-matter, they may be a source of rules in particular branches of law. There is a compelling argument that treaties between subjects of the Federation may override inconsistent provisions of federal laws, but given that the Federal Assembly is not, as a rule, involved in their conclusion or termination, there are conceptual problems with this view.

---

[12] The texts are translated in W E Butler, *Russian Public Law* (3rd edn.; 2013) 686–99. The Russian Federation quietly concluded a substantial series of bilateral treaties with individual subjects of the Federation. At the peak of such treaty-making, it is believed that more than a thousand such treaties were concluded. Beginning in November 2001, large numbers of these treaties were terminated by mutual agreement or permitted to lapse.

Treaties between Subjects of Federation and Russian Federation

The category "subjects of the Russian Federation" is a constitutional law category. The 1993 Russian Constitution does not define the term, but rather enumerates the administrative-territorial entities which are "subjects of the Federation." The subjects of the Federation are enumerated in alphabetical order and category.

The 1993 Russian Constitution (Article 65) distinguishes among six categories of subjects of the Federation: (a) republics; (b) territories; (c) regions; (d) cities of federal significance; (e) autonomous regions; and (f) autonomous national areas. With various mergers and additions since 1993 (Crimea and the City of Sevastopol in 2014), the total number of subjects of the Federation is eighty-five. The three Treaties of the Federation, each concluded on March 31, 1992, group these eighty-five subjects of the Federation into three: (a) republics; (b) territories, regions, and cities of federal significance; and (c) autonomous region and autonomous national areas. The various mergers and additions seem to have resulted in no formal accessions or withdrawals from the Treaties of the Federation.

Although one associates the Russian Federation with the nationality principle, the great majority of the subjects of the Federation are configured purely on territorial considerations, and the remaining subjects are far from homogeneous nationality entities. Each has its own constitution, charter, law, or other constitutive document. Although their names are embodied in the Russian Constitution, each retains the right to change its name, such changes to date being incorporated without amendment of the Constitution by edict of the President of the Russian Federation.[13]

The highest category of subjects of the Federation—republics within the Russian Federation—have many attributes of sovereign States, even though they have surrendered their right of unilateral secession. The hierarchy amongst the others, except for the sequence of enumeration in the Constitution, is obscure. The Constitution speaks of subjects of the Federation changing their status (Article 66(5)), but why they should do so if each has equal rights is unclear. In matters of shared jurisdiction, however,

---

[13] See, for example, Edicts of the President of the Russian Federation of January 9, 1996, February 10, 1996, June 9, 2001, and July 25, 2003. СЗ РФ (1996) no. 3, item 152; no. 7, item 676; (2001) no. 24, item 2421; (2003) no. 30, item 3051.

they are identical, as too are they equal in representation in the Soviet of the Federation. The subjects of the Federation went through a period from 1993 to 2001 when they quietly concluded treaties clarifying the sharing of jurisdiction with the Federation. In some cases the powers of the subject of the Federation were enlarged. No longer could it be said that each enjoyed necessarily the same powers as other subjects of the Federation.[14] On March 12, 1996 the President confirmed by edict, as amended, the Statute on the Procedure for Work Relating to Delimitation of the Subjects of Jurisdiction and Powers Between Federal Agencies of State Power and Agencies of State Power of the Subjects of the Russian Federation and on the Mutual Transfer of the Effectuation of Part of Their Powers by Federal Agencies of Executive Power and Agencies of Executive Power of the Subject of the Federation.[15] A Commission attached to the President of the Russian Federation works with the draft treaties and agreements. The principles guiding the Commission include: the principles of delimitation of the subjects of jurisdiction and powers are established by federal laws; a treaty may not establish or change the constitutional status of a subject of the Federation; the treaty may not allow an exception or redistribution of subjects of jurisdiction of the Russian Federation or subjects of joint jurisdiction established in accordance with Articles 71 and 72 of the 1993 Russian Constitution, and powers may not be transferred to a subject of the Federation which relate to guaranteeing the foundations of the constitutional system, the equality of rights and freedoms of citizens, or which would otherwise violate the territorial integrity of Russia or the supremacy of the Constitution and federal laws throughout the Russian Federation. The edict of March 12, 1996 was replaced by the Federal Law of October 6, 2003 "On General Principles of the Organization of Local Self-Government in the Russian Federation" and the edict of the President of the Russian Federation of November 27, 2003 "On Measures for the Development of Federal Relations and Local Self-Government in the Russian Federation."

---

[14] This process ceased in the late Eltsin years. From June 1998 few, if any, treaties or agreements were concluded between the center and the subjects of the Federation and no existing treaties renewed or extended, although agreements were concluded in November 2001 between Far Eastern subjects of the Federation and the Russian Ministry of Justice on bringing regional legislation into conformity with federal laws. See J Kahn, *Federalism, Democratization and the Rule of Law in Russia* (2002) 237. Commencing in November 2001 treaties began to be concluded between the federal government and subjects of the Federation which terminated the earlier treaties on the grounds that they had served their purpose. See, for example, СЗ РФ (2002) no. 12, 3277-80.

[15] СЗ РФ (1996) no. 12, item 1058; no. 49, item 5534.

Subjects of the Russian Federation have their own legal systems emanating from their own constitutive documents, laws, and subordinate legal acts. While each therefore has its own constitutional law, it must form part of an integral and non-contradictory whole with the legal system of the Russian Federation.

Of the eighty-five subjects of the Federation, only certain republics seem to have entertained aspirations of being, or as being recognized as, full-fledged subjects of international law; that is, regarded their treaty relations with the Russian Federation as regulated by the public international law of treaties and not by Russian municipal law. How active these claims are is perhaps immaterial; in the views of proponents of this position, the claims are latent and not renounced or withdrawn. Most republics claiming international-legal status are "frontier" republics physically adjacent to other States: Chechnya being an example. A republic which historically has pressed this claim and is not contiguous to a foreign States on any of its borders—completely enclosed by the Russian Federation—is the Republic Tatarstan.

Tatarstan. The Republic Tatarstan is the direct descendant of one of the most powerful Empires ever to exist on this planet. In modern history what is regarded as the first State in the region was formed in the ninth and tenth centuries as the Khanate of the Volga Bulgars, who converted to Islam in the tenth century. This Khanate was overrun by the Mongols, who completed their conquest in 1236 and incorporated the Khanate into the Golden Horde; by about the 1420s the Khanate of Kazan liberated itself from the Golden Horde but continued to raid Muscovy. For centuries the princes of Muscovy paid tribute to the Tatars. In 1552 the fortunes of Muscovy reversed, and the Khanate of Kazan was absorbed as an integral part into what became in due course the Russian Empire.

During the late nineteenth and earlier twentieth centuries a latent Tatar national consciousness revived in various forms, including movements supporting Pan-Islamism. When the Russian Empire collapsed in 1917, Tatarstan formed its own parliament, Government, State council, and military council as a functionally independent entity. Tatars fought on both sides of the those contesting for power after the Russian revolutions; an Idel-Ural State had a brief existence, followed by the entity which existed throughout the Soviet period: the Tatar Autonomous Soviet Socialist Republic.

The Tatar authorities pursued Tatarstan statehood vigorously from 1990 onward. On August 30, 1990 Tatarstan declared State sovereignty in the form of the Declaration on State Sovereignty of the Tatarstan Soviet Socialist Republic, renamed the Republic Tatarstan two years later.[16] Tatarstan's Declaration on State Sovereignty was the first such to be enacted by an entity within the RSFSR. On October 24, 1990 the Tatar Soviet Socialist Republic declared its independence from the Russian Soviet Federated Socialist Republic through the Decree of the Supreme Soviet of the Tatar Soviet Socialist Republic on the Act of State Independence. The Preamble to the Constitution of Tatarstan was amended on April 18, 1991 to remove provisions stipulating that Tatarstan was part of the Russian Federation and that federal laws took precedence over Tatarstan legislation.

Relations with the Russian Federation were addressed through bilateral international treaties. Tatarstan refused to sign the relevant Treaty of the Federation that the Russian Federation concluded on March 31, 1992 with all the other subjects of the Federation but two: Tatarstan and Chechnya.

Notwithstanding an adverse ruling of the Russian Constitutional Court, a referendum was held in Tatarstan which confirmed that Tatarstan was a sovereign State and a subject of international law. In keeping with the positive result of the referendum, the Constitution of Tatarstan was adopted in November 1992 that incorporated the Declaration of Sovereignty and asserted that Tatarstan was associated with Russia on the basis of a Treaty concerning a mutual delimitation of powers. More than a year of further negotiations was required to finalize the text of such a Treaty, eventually achieved on February 15, 1994.[17] The extent to which Tatarstan is a subject of international law and has separate citizenship was left open (in October 1997 Tatarstan rejected the use of Russian internal passports on the ground that there was no space for the entry of "nationality"). In 2002 further arrangements were reached between Russia and Tatarstan which brought the Constitution of Tatarstan into conformity with the 1993 Constitution of the Russian Federation; these were supplemented by an agreement in 2007. The 2002 Agreement, concluded for a period of fifteen years, lapsed on July 24, 2017.

---

[16] See B L Khamidullin, "Татарстан" ["Tatarstan"], in Большая Российская энциклопедия [*Great Russian Encyclopedia*] (Moscow, 2016) XXXI, 689–91.

[17] See the Treaty of the Russian Federation and Republic Tatarstan "On Delimiting the Subjects of Jurisdiction and Mutual Delegation of Powers between Agencies of State Power of the Russian Federation and Agencies of State Power of the Republic Tatarstan," trans. in W E Butler, *Russian Legal Texts: The Foundations of a Rule-of-Law State and a Market Economy* (1998) 73–9.

In the view of Tatarstan, the Republic Tatarstan is an independent sovereign State which is a subject of the Russian Federation pursuant to international treaties concluded between itself and the Russian Federation. In the view of the Russian Federation, the Republic Tatarstan is one of twenty or so "republics within the Russian Federation" which have accepted integration into the Russian Federation in that form. Tatarstan is therefore a full-fledged subject of the Russian Federation that has surrendered a significant portion of its sovereign statehood in the process of becoming a constituent entity of the Russian Federation.

The implications of treaties between the Russian Federation and Tatarstan being governed by international law and not by Russian law are several. First, the treaty would be subject to the 1969 Vienna Convention on the Law of Treaties and secondarily to Russian law. The treaty would qualify for priority under Article 15(4) of the Russian Constitution. Tatarstan as a sovereign republic would enjoy a stature analogous to that of a union republic of the former Soviet Union. And Tatarstan would enjoy more autonomy in managing its own affairs than other republics within the Russian Federation.

Treaties between Subjects of Russian Federation

Subjects of the Federation have concluded treaties with one another on a variety of matters. Russian legal doctrine regards these arrangements as "constitutional treaties" and not subject to the international law of treaties. Whether two subjects of the Federation could stipulate in a treaty between themselves that the applicable law of the document was public international law would not seem to be regulated by Russian legislation.

Treaties between Subjects of Federation and Foreign States or Entities of Foreign States

The subjects of the Russian Federation are, in principle, at liberty to enter into treaties with foreign States or with subdivisions (regions, cities, and so on) thereof, provided that such treaties are entered into with the authorization of the Ministry of Foreign Affairs of the Russian Federation and, once concluded, duly registered. Sverdlovsk Region, for example, has entered into a number of such treaties.[18] Assuming that the particular subject of the Russian Federation possesses and has acted pursuant to its legal capacity when entering into such treaties, these would seem to be "international treaties of the Russian Federation" for which the Russian Federation bears State responsibility.

This observation is reinforced by the fact that some countries have concluded treaties with the Russian Federation that actually removed any agreements concluded with subjects of the Russian Federation from the category of international treaties. Under the Agreement between the Government of the Russian Federation and the Government of Canada on the Principles and Foundations of Cooperation between Subjects of the Russian Federation and Provinces and Territories of Canada of December 18, 2000, "arrangements concluded between subjects of the Russian Federation and provinces and territories of Canada shall not be international treaties."[19]

---

[18] Between 2005 and 2010 Sverdlovsk Region concluded a trade agreement with Azerbaidzhan in 2006; on economic cooperation with Hungary in 2006; with Kyrgyzia in 2006 on trade, scientific-technical, and humanitarian cooperation; with a federal unit in Austria on economic cooperation in 2007; and with Armenia in 2008 on trade, scientific-technical, and humanitarian cooperation. See Kocheva (n. 9).

[19] Бюллетень международных договоров [*Bulletin of International Treaties*], no. 6 (2001) 579–84. Russia has analogous treaties with China and Vietnam.

7

International Treaties in Russian Judicial and Arbitral Practice

Although the true role of Soviet and post-Soviet Russian courts in interpreting and applying international treaties is a topic hardly explored, it is clear that Soviet courts dealt more frequently with treaties than the scanty published judicial practice of that period suggests. This would especially appear to be the case from the late 1950s onward, when the Soviet Union concluded a number of bilateral treaties with other socialist countries relating to legal assistance in family, criminal, and civil cases. That body of treaties may also have contributed to the emergence in the early 1960s of priority being accorded to Soviet treaties insofar as they contained rules providing otherwise than Soviet legislation.

Whatever the volume of cases involving treaties that were considered by Soviet courts prior to 1991, the inclusion of Article 15(4) in the 1993 Russian Constitution transformed the situation. A further transformation occurred when the Russian Federation acceded to the 1950 European Convention for the Protection of Human Rights and Fundamental Freedoms and began to participate in the deliberations of the European Court of Human Rights in Strasbourg.

Article 15(4) was sufficient to make international treaties an integral part of the Russian legal system, which meant they were to be applied by Russian courts and arbitral tribunals—the latter whenever Russian law was the applicable law of a transaction. Active steps were taken to train Russian judges in the rudiments of public international law and draw their attention to the sources of international law which might be relevant to cases being considered. It is possible that Russian judges were instructed or encouraged to cite relevant international documents whenever this appeared to be appropriate. Computer data banks would make it possible to determine how often Russian judicial decisions made reference to international treaties or other international acts; such data is available in the field of Russian international commercial arbitration.[1]

---

[1] See, for example, A N Zhiltsov and A I Muranov (comps), *Practice of the International Commercial Arbitration Court at the Chamber of Commerce and Industry of the Russian Federation: 2004–2016*, ed. P D Savkin (2017).

Guiding Documents of Plenum of Supreme Court of Russian Federation

Judicial "activism," if that term is appropriate in this context with respect to international law and, in particular, treaties, is manifest at several levels on the Russian judicial system, sometimes in ways unknown to or impossible within foreign legal systems. An example is decrees of the Plenum of the Supreme Court of the Russian Federation. These are issued from time to time by the Supreme Court in selected areas of the administration of justice and are commonly based on reviews of lower court practice but not, as a rule, generated by a single case. They have no equivalent in Anglo-American judicial practice and are an inheritance of the Soviet legal tradition with certain antecedents by analogy in prerevolutionary Russian practice. Several dealing expressly with international law, most notably Decree No. 5 of October 10, 2003, have been referred to repeatedly in the present work. In addition to those, however, other decrees touch upon issues of treaty law and serve as instructions to lower courts. These decrees collectively represent generalized judicial practice.

Russian doctrinal characterizations of guiding explanations and decrees of the Plenum of the Supreme Court differ significantly as to whether they have normative effect and may amount to a form of law-making, or merely "restate" the law against the background of judicial decisions in individual cases. A good example of "judicial lawmaking" is the Decree of the Plenum of the Supreme Court of October 10, 2003 which accords supremacy over federal laws only to "ratified" international treaties of the Russian Federation even though the 1993 Constitution of the Russian Federation does not so provide and the legislative history of the Constitution indicates that such a provision was rejected by the drafters. Other such decrees have reinforced the position on ratification and/or drawn the attention of lower courts to individual treaties whose provisions should be taken into account when considering cases. With respect to the law of the sea, for example, the Plenum of the Supreme Court reminded lower courts that when applying the Code of the Russian Federation on Administrative Violations:

International treaties of the Russian Federation by virtue of Article 15(4) of the Constitution of the Russian Federation are an integral part of its legal system If other rules have been established by an international treaty of the Russian Federation than provided by legislation on administrative violations, and also on fishing and the preservation of aquatic bioresources, the rules of the international treaty shall apply.[2]

The Supreme Court confined this principle to ratified treaties, observing that this rule should be applied by taking into account the Plenum Decree of October 10, 2003, No. 5. The 2010 Plenum Decree draws the attention to a number of international treaties ratified by the Russian Federation which determine spatially where certain administrative penalties may be applied, including internal sea waters, the territorial sea, continental shelf, exclusive economic zone, and high seas. The Supreme Court noted that when applying federal laws and/or the 1982 Convention on the Law of the Sea or the 1958 Geneva Convention on the High Seas, a different legal regime may have been established by international treaties of the Russian Federation.[3]

---

[2] Decree of the Plenum of the Supreme Court of the Russian Federation, November 23, 2010, No. 27, "On the Practice of the Consideration of Cases Concerning Administrative Violations Connected with a Violation of Rules and Requirements Regulating Fishing," as amended October 31, 2017. Available on Consultant Plus.

[3] From the content of the Treaty between the Russian Federation and Ukraine on Cooperation in the Use of the Sea of Azov and the Kerchensk Strait of December 24, 2003, interpreted in aggregate with other international treaties of the Russian Federation, it follows that the Sea of Azov and Kerchensk Strait are internal sea waters of the Russian Federation and Ukraine and living resources of the said waters are in the joint use of these States (as amended October 31, 2017).

From the provisions of the Agreement between the Russian Federation and Republic Kazakhstan on Delimitation of the Seabed of the Northern Part of the Caspian Sea for the Purposes of the Effectuation of Sovereign Rights to Subsoil Use of July 6, 1998, Agreement between the Russian Federation and Azerbaidzhan Republic on Delimitation of Adjoining Plots of the Seabed of the Caspian Sea of September 23, 2002, Agreement between the Russian Federation, Azerbaidzhan Republic, and Republic Kazakhstan concerning the Point of Juncture of Lines of Delimitation of Adjacent Plots of the Seabed of the Caspian Sea of May 14, 2003, Declaration of the Azerbaidzhan Republic, Islamic Republic of Iran, Republic Kazakhstan, Russian Federation, and Turkmenistan of October 16, 2007, and Treaty on the Fundamental Principles of Relations and Principles of Cooperation between the Russian Federation and Islamic Republic of Iran of March 12, 2002, it follows that with respect to the Caspian Sea the provisions of the Convention on the Law of the Sea providing, in particular, the right of the coastal State to internal waters, territorial sea, continental shelf, and exclusive economic zone do not operate.

The Russian Federation as the State-continuer of the USSR realizes its rights and duties under the Treaty on Trade and Navigation between the USSR and Iran of March 25, 1940, from which it follows that each of the Contracting Parties retains for vessels of its flag the right to catch fish in waters washing its shores up to limits of ten nautical miles.

As one Russian jurist observed:

> One should realise that in Russia and other post-Soviet countries the explanations of supreme courts assume the role which in other legal systems is left for precedents … they enjoy a privileged position in the Russian legal system, since they guide the court practice, on one hand, and are outside the ambit of judicial review, on the other.[4]

In its decree of June 27, 2017, the Plenum of the Supreme Court of the Russian Federation determined what arbitrazh courts should do in the event an international treaty of the Russian Federation established other rules for a court proceeding than those provided by legislation of Russia on court proceedings in arbitrazh courts.[5] The position of primacy of the international treaty was affirmed, citing the Code of Arbitrazh Procedure of the Russian Federation (Article 3(3) and Article 13(4)). However, in matters of time and space, the Plenum directed that arbitrazh courts be guided by the 1969 Vienna Convention on the Law of Treaties:

> In applying the rules for a court proceeding established by norms of international treaties, an arbitrazh court shall determine the operation of these rules in time and space in accordance with Article 3(2) of the Vienna Convention on the Law of Treaties of 23 May 1969 (hereinafter: Vienna Convention).
>
> If several international treaties of the Russian Federation have been concluded with a foreign State in regard to the rules of a court proceeding with respect to cases concerning economic disputes arising from relations complicated by a foreign element, the arbitrazh court shall establish the international treaty subject to application, being guided by norms of the Vienna Convention, the Federal Law of 15 July 1995, No. 101-ФЗ, "On International Treaties of the Russian Federation," and norms of the international treaty itself, the question concerning whose application is being decided by the court.

---

[4] A Vereshchagin, *Judicial Law-Making in Post-Soviet Russia* (2007) 110.
[5] Decree of the Plenum of the Supreme Court of the Russian Federation of June 27, 2017, No. 23, "On the Consideration by Arbitrazh Courts of Bases relating to Economic Disputes Arising from Relations Complicated by a Foreign Element." Available on Consultant Plus.

A special international treaty is subject to priority application irrespective of the group of its participants and time of adoption unless established otherwise by norms of international treaties.[6]

In the same decree the Plenum of the Supreme Court of the Russian Federation offered another example:

Arbitrazh courts should take into account that bilateral and multilateral international treaties of the Russian Federation may contain other rules determining the competence of arbitrazh courts in relation to cases with the participation of foreign persons than the rules provided in the Code of Arbitrazh Procedure of the Russian Federation. In this event when determining the competence of the court, norms of the international treaty determining the status concerning subject-matter jurisdiction are subject to priority application by virtue of Article 3(3) and Article 13(4) of the Code of Arbitrazh Procedure of the Russian Federation.

For example, Article 4 of the Agreement on the Procedure for the Settlement of Disputes Connected with the Effectuation of Economic Activity of 20 March 1992 (hereinafter—1992 Agreement), a special international treaty regulating the cooperation of States in the domain of the settlement of disputes connected with the effectuation of economic activity, provided grounds for the competence of arbitrazh courts of the Russian Federation relating to disputes named in Article 1 of the 1992 Agreement.

Unless provided otherwise by the rules on exclusive competence, when there is a rogatory agreement and international treaty established the rules for determining competence, the provisions of the rogatory agreement shall apply.

Thus, a suit relating to a suit which arose on the occasion of carriages effectuated in accordance with the Convention on the Contract for the International Carriage of Goods by Road Geneva, 19 May 1956) (hereinafter—1956 Geneva Convention) may be filed at the competent court of the countries-participants of the 1956 Geneva Convention specified in the rogatory agreement of the parties. In the absence of such an agreement, the competent court is determined at the discretion of the plaintiff in accordance with the 1956 Geneva Convention (Article 31(1)).[7]

---

[6] Ibid, point 2.

[7] Ibid, point 17. In a different consideration of the 1956 Geneva Convention with the same outcome, see the Information Letter of the Presidium of the Supreme Arbitrazh Court of

European Court of Human Rights

Russian accession to the 1950 European Convention for the Protection of Human Rights and Fundamental Freedoms fundamentally altered the discussion of precedent in Russian legal circles.[8] The Convention became binding upon Russia from May 5, 1998.

Russian international and constitutional legal doctrine has been preoccupied with the issue of the extent to which, if at all, the jurisprudence and judicial practice of the European Court of Human Rights (hereinafter: ECtHR) may be binding upon the Russian Federation and may be a source of law in Russia. The Federal Law on the ratification of the 1950 European Convention provided that the Russian Federation, in accordance with Article 46 of the Convention, "recognizes *ipso facto* and without special agreement as binding" with regard to questions of interpretation and application of the Convention and Protocols thereto in instances of a supposed violation by the Russian Federation of the provisions of these treaty acts when the supposed violation occurred after their entry into force with respect to the Russian Federation.[9]

Russian legal doctrine accepts that by virtue of this language the Russian Federation is bound to comply with judgments and decisions of the ECtHR concerning cases in which Russia is a party. This follows as a treaty obligation under the 1950 European Convention, and by virtue of Article 15(4) of the 1993 Russian Constitution the provisions of the said Convention are an integral part of the Russian legal system.

Residual issues remain. When acceding to the 1950 European Convention, did Russia also become bound by the jurisprudence, judgments, and decisions of the ECtHR which preceded Russian accession, and is Russia bound by the judgments and decisions of the ECtHR in cases that do not concern Russia as a party? Irrespective of whether the answer to the preceding questions is affirmative or negative, do judgments and decisions

---

the Russian Federation of January 18, 2001, No. 58, "Survey of Practice of the Settlement by Arbitrazh Courts of Disputes Connected with the Defense of Foreign Investors." Available on Consultant Plus.

[8] The Convention was ratified by Russia with changes made in the Convention made by Protocols 3 (May 6, 1963), 5 (January 20, 1966), and 8 (March 19, 1985) and additions contained in Protocol No. 2 (May 6, 1963) and Protocols thereto Nos. 1 (March 20, 1952), 4 (September 16, 1963), 7 (November 22, 1984), 9 (November 6, 1990), 10 (March 25, 1992), and 11 (May 11, 1994).
[9] СЗ РФ (1998) no. 14, item 1514.

of the ECtHR constitute a form of judicial precedent that is binding upon Russia and, indeed, part of the Russian legal system?

The Supreme Court of the Russian Federation instructed the courts of general jurisdiction that "the application by courts of the ... Convention must be effectuated by taking into account the practice of the European Court of Human Rights in avoidance of any violation of the Convention for the Protection of Human Rights and Fundamental Freedoms."[10] No limitation was placed upon what "practice" of the ECtHR should be considered. Some Russian jurists doubt that such "practice" has the value of judicial precedent:

> ... one of the necessary indicia, properties, of a judicial precedent as a source of law is that such precedent (or decision of a court) should contain a legal norm, that is, generally binding rule of behavior ensured by the compulsory power of the State (if we speak of national legal norms). Can one assert that decisions and/or judgments of the ECtHR contain a legal norm? To this question it is necessary to give a negative answer.[11]

Zimnenko takes the view that the ECtHR does not create law, but merely applies the norms contained in the 1950 European Convention; to do otherwise would be contrary to the treaty empowering the ECtHR: "[D]ecisions and judgments of the ECtHR are the result of law-application and not law-creative activity ... and therefore these judicial acts may not contain any legal norms. There is no substantiation for speaking about the existence of a law of precedent of the ECtHR."[12] It would be admissible, though, to speak of "precedents of interpretation" by the ECtHR, which form "legal positions" to assist the ECtHR thereafter to more effectively and efficiently consider a case. A "legal position" developed by the ECtHR is characterized as a "special form of subsequent practice of the States-parties connected with the application" of the 1950 European Convention and judgments of the ECtHR are "a form of the existence of legal positions," but these are binding upon Russia only insofar as Russia is a party to the case concerned. As regards other cases not involving Russia, State agencies of the Russian

---

[10] Point 10 (n. 5).
[11] B L Zimnenko, *International Law and the Russian Legal System*, ed. and trans. W E Butler (2007) 257.
[12] Ibid, 258.

Federation may be guided in their activities by these decisions and the legal positions consolidated in them, but they are not bound by them.[13]

Other Russian jurists take a different view: Russian legislation and judicial practice both under the 1950 European Convention and the 1993 Russian Constitution may not diverge from the provisions and standards of the Convention nor "may Russian laws diverge from the case law created by the principal official interpreter of the European Convention—the European Court of Human Rights."[14]

The foregoing positions have been altered by a Decree of the Constitutional Court of the Russia Federation of July 14, 2015, which took the position that judgments and decisions of the European Court of Human Rights might not be enforced in Russia if those judgments and decisions were contrary to provisions of the 1993 Russian Constitution. In relevant part the decree provided:

[I]n a situation when the very content of the decree of the European Court of Human Rights, including with respect to prescriptions applicable to a defendant State based on the provisions of the Convention of the Protection of Human Rights and Fundamental Freedoms interpreted by the European Court of Human Rights within the framework of a concrete case, is unlawful—from a constitutional legal point of view—the principles and norms of the Constitution of the Russian Federation, Russia may by way of exception depart from the fulfillment of obligations placed on it when such deviation is the sole possible means of avoiding a violation of the fundamental principles and norms of the Constitution of the Russian Federation.[15]

The Constitutional Court turned for support to the 1969 Vienna Convention on the Law of Treaties:

The fundamental principle of international law consolidated in Article 26 of *pacta sunt servanda* (each treaty is force is binding for its participants

---

[13] Ibid, 260–8.

[14] See P A Laptev and G A Gadzhiev, "Предисловие" ["Preface"], in Iu Iu Berestnev (ed.), Европейские правовые стандарты в постановлениях Конституционного Суда Российской Федерации [*European Legal Standards in Decrees of the Constitutional Court of the Russian Federation*] (2003) 7.

[15] Point 2 (n. 5). The full text of the decree is translated in W E Butler, *Russia & The Republics: Legal Materials* (loose-leaf service; 2006).

and should be fulfilled by them in good faith), the Vienna Convention established also a general rule for the interpretation of treaties, providing that a treaty should be interpreted in good faith in accordance with its ordinary meaning to be given to the terms of the treaty in their context and in the light of its object and purpose (Article 31[1]).

Thus, an international treaty is for its participants binding in the sense which may be elucidated with the assistance of the said rules of interpretation. From this point of view, the European Court of Human Rights, interpreting in the process of consideration a case of an provision of the Convention of the Protection of Human Rights and Fundamental Freedoms attaches to it a concept other than ordinary meaning or effectuates an interpretation contrary to the purposes of the Convention, the State with respect to which the decree was rendered in the particular case has the right to refuse the execution thereof as going beyond the limits of the obligations voluntarily assumed by this State when ratifying the Convention. Accordingly, the decree of the European Court of Human Rights may not be considered binding if as a result of the interpretation of a concrete provision of the Convention of the Protection of Human Rights and Fundamental Freedoms on which the particular decree is based was effectuated in violation of the general rule of interpretation of treaties, the sense of this provision departs from the imperative norms of general international law (*jus cogens*), among which undoubtedly is the principle of sovereign equality and respect for rights inherent to sovereignty and also the principle of non-interference in the internal affairs of States.

Moreover, as follows from Article 46(1) of the Vienna Convention, a State has the right to block the operation with respect to it of individual provisions of an international treaty, referring to the circumstance that consent to the particular treaty being binding on it was expressed in violation of a particular provision of its internal law concerning the competence to conclude treaties if the particular violation was manifest and concerned a norm of its internal law of especially important significance. In the Russian Federation among such norms in priority are relegated the provisions of Chapter 1 and 2 of the Constitution of the Russian Federation, a change of which is not permitted by means of constitutional amendments, and may be effectuated, as established in Article 135 thereof, solely by means of the adoption of a new Constitution of the Russian Federation.[16]

---

[16] Point 3 (n. 5).

The Constitutional Court did not see the issue as one in which the 1950 European Convention was inconsistent as such with the 1993 Russian Constitution, but rather an interpretation of that Convention which was inconsistent with the Constitution:

> Insofar, however, as the expression by the Russian Federation of consent to the bindingness of an international treaty on it in violation of a particular provision of the Constitution of the Russian Federation may be identified only after the adoption of a decision by an empowered inter-State agency based on the construction of a concrete norm of the particular international treaty in the sense leading to its non-agreement with a respective provision of the Constitution of the Russian Federation, we refer in such instances not to the validity or invalidity of the international treaty for Russia as a whole, but merely to the impossibility of complying with the obligation to apply its norms in a construction imparted thereto by the empowered inter-State agency within the framework of the consideration of a concrete case.
>
> In the context of the cited provisions of the Vienna Convention on the Law of Treaties, this means that the decision of an empowered inter-State agency, including a decree of the European Court of Human Rights, may not be executed by the Russian Federation in the part of measures of an individual or common character imposed on it if the interpretation of a norm of the international treaty on which this decision is based violates respective provisions of the Constitution of the Russian Federation.[17]

The Constitutional Court of the Russian Federation therefore decreed that:

> a court of general jurisdiction or arbitrazh court when reviewing cases in the procedure established by procedure legislation in connection with the adoption of a decree by the European Court of Human Rights in which a violation is stated in the Russian Federation of human rights and freedoms when applying a law or individual provisions thereof, leading to the conclusion that the possibility of the application of a respective law may be decided only after confirmation of its conformity to the Constitution of the Russian Federation requests the Constitutional Court

---

[17] Ibid.

of the Russian Federation for a verification of the constitutionality of this law; in any event the court of general jurisdiction or arbitrazh court effectuating a proceeding with regard to a review of a judicial act which has entered into legal force upon the application of a person whose appeal was accepted by the European Court of Human Rights, the decree stating the violation of the Convention of the Protection of Human Rights and Fundamental Freedoms by provisions of legislation of the Russian Federation applicable to the case of this person shall be obliged to suspend the proceedings and request the Constitutional Court of the Russian Federation for a verification of the conformity thereof to the Constitution of the Russian Federation.[18]

The position taken by the Constitutional Court has been commented upon in public statements by the Chairman of that Court, V D Zorkin:

The participation of Russia in international agreements and conventions means merely that Russia voluntarily assumes the obligations enumerated in these international documents. And retains the sovereign right of final decision in accordance with the Constitution of the Russian Federation in the event of controversial moments or legal conflicts.[19]

The Decree of the Constitutional Court of July 14, 2015 is likely to be treated as precedential in proceedings before that Court. In the perception of many Russian jurists, the 2015 Decree is a reflection of a "sharp political and juridical turn away from European cooperation and fulfillment" of ECtHR judgments and a movement "back towards the previous method of 'erecting walls' of sovereignty and prioritizing the opinion of just one State body on the implementation of Russian international obligations."[20] Several judgments of the ECtHR, especially from 2013 onward, have been

---

[18] Ibid, point 1, para. 3, Resolutive Part.

[19] Remarks made in May 2015 at an International Legal Forum in St. Petersburg. Quoted in Ведомости [Gazette], February 1, 2018, 9. In May 2017 in a lecture at the VII Petersburg International Legal Forum Zorkin declared: "The defense of human rights should not undermine the moral pillars of society and destroy its religious identity. Ensuring the rights of citizens should not create a threat to State sovereignty. Finally, the defense of the dignity of a person should not lead to a rejection of those moral universals on which mankind sometime formed and which still enabled it to save itself from self-destruction." Ibid.

[20] Marochkin, *The Operation of International Law in the Russian Legal System: A Changing Approach* (2019) 293; reviewed: *Journal of Comparative Law*, XIV, no. 1 (2019) 360–7 (W E Butler).

perceived by Russian policy-makers as a challenge to fundamental Russian values or express provisions of the 1993 Russian Constitution: the constitutional prohibition in Russia against persons serving punishment in the form of deprivation of freedom being allowed to vote; judgments concerning the rights of gays and others under Russian law, for example. Marochkin suggests that those who favor national sovereignty over binding international adjudication succeeded in establishing the "prevalence of the 'party of power' over the 'rule of law' principle."[21] In his view, the relationship between international and domestic law is central to the rule of law. In its original understanding Article 15(4) of the 1993 Constitution represented the "importation" of international law to protect human rights and legal order and help prevent a return to the Soviet past.

That there has been a reorientation and readjustment of Russian foreign policy conceptions away from an Atlantic and European concentration toward a Eurasian and Asian orientation there is no disagreement.[22] This is perceived by some Russian jurists as a more "balanced approach" to the tensions between human rights under Russian constitutional law and judgments of the ECtHR, that the "existing model of correlation between national and international law has to be changed, corrected, and adjusted."[23] Any such change or readjustment would necessarily engage Article 15(4) of the 1993 Constitution, described as the "quintessence" of Russia's post-Soviet "self-identity and positioning in the world."[24] Quintessence symbolically and substantively:

In the historical situation that existed at that time [1993] and until 2014, [Article 15(4)] was viewed as a "one-way street," as an instrument for changing the national legal system to include legal standards, solutions, and mechanisms that were lacking, were not sufficiently effective, or needed further adjustment; as a "green light" for legitimizing internal

---

[21] Marochkin (n. 20) 282.

[22] See W E Butler, "Foreign Policy Discourses as Part of Understanding Russia and International Law," in S Morris (ed.), *Russian Discourses on International Law: Sociological and Philosophical Phenomenon* (2019) 177–96.

[23] M Entin, E Entina, and E Osokina, "A Balanced Approach to the Protection of National Law and Order and the European Court of Human Rights," *Journal of Comparative Law*, XIV, no. 1 (2019) 275.

[24] Ibid, 277. "The formal recognition of generally-recognized principles and norms of international law, that is, customary rules of international law, to be an integral part of the Russian legal system is among the most momentous changes of the twentieth century in the development of Russian Law." W E Butler, *The Law of Treaties in Russia and the Commonwealth of Independent States: Text and Commentary* (2002) 36.

legal and institutional reforms proposed by international organizations and prepared by international teams of specialists; as a say to optimize being the recipient of foreign legal standards, a status assumed or temporarily preferred by the Russian Federation; and finally, as one of the strongest signals indicating that Moscow was open to broad international cooperation, that it did not seek a position of dominance or exclusiveness, that it pursued and would pursue legal integration with the West and strive for the common understanding of the values and needs of society.[25]

Treaties, Judicial Practice, and Hierarchy of Sources of Law

Although the 1950 European Convention was not specifically mentioned in the discussion of Article 15(4) of the Russian Constitution during the Constitutional Assembly, it has been suggested that "Russia did not specify the place of international law in its legal system, thus reserving the right to address this issue flexibly" and "intentionally entered almost no reservations that could obfuscate or limit the supremacy of European law, as construed and applied by the ECtHR over national law or complicate or restrict the incorporation" of the 1950 European Convention law into Russian law.[26]

This observation raises a different aspect of an issue that, latent or explicit, has plagued Russian legal theory and international legal doctrine for decades: where precisely are generally-recognized principles and norms of international law and international treaties of the Russian Federation placed in the hierarchy of sources of Russian law? In Russian doctrine a wide variety of views has been expressed. One of the early Soviet jurists to address the subject was Igor Pavlovich Blishchenko (1930–2000), whose pioneering work suggested that in the event of a conflict between international law and municipal legal norms, they should be considered to be of equal force; his monograph[27] was published prior to the 1961 Fundamental Principles of the USSR and Union Republics on Civil Legislation, which

---

[25] Entin (n. 23) 277. This re-evaluation of the position of the Russian Federation is reflected also, with respect to international treaties, in the amendments to the Constitution of the Russian Federation of March 14, 2020. See the Conclusions, later in this volume.

[26] Ibid, 278.

[27] I P Blishchenko, Международное и внутригосударственное право [*International and Municipal Law*] (1960) 200.

accorded priority to the treaty in that event. Valentina Iakovleva Suvorova considers the primacy of international-legal norms to be absolute and would place such norms at the highest level in the hierarchy of norms of law within a State—above the Constitution,[28] a view shared by B I Osminin.[29] Some Russian jurists invoked the principle of *lex specialis*, suggesting that international law and municipal law operate in symbiosis: when inter-State relations are to be regulated, international law has priority over municipal on the principle of the more specialized law governs; if municipal legal relations are to be regulated, municipal law is applied on the same principle, that the *lex specialis* governs.[30]

Many post-Soviet republics have adopted laws on normative legal acts, a full survey of which is beyond the scope of the present study.[31] These laws are noteworthy for avoiding the issue, but the failure to do so leaves an incomplete hierarchy and a vast chasm in legal theory. The Russian Federation has refrained from such legislation, but draft laws on the subject are revealing.

At least three draft laws of the Russian Federation have been submitted to regulate the preparation, adoption, and status of normative legal acts. None has been passed. Each of them betrays difficulty with accommodating the place of international treaties either within or outside the hierarchy of sources of Russian law or the hierarchy of Russian normative legal acts. In a draft deposited in the Archive of the State Duma of the Russian Federation on April 13, 1999 and again on April 17, 2003, "On Normative Legal Acts of the Russian Federation," Article 5 provided that "The procedure for the preparation, submission, consideration, adoption (or issuance), entry into force, and official publication of laws and *other normative acts comprising legislation of the Russian Federation* shall be determined … by the Federal Law 'On International Treaties of the Russian Federation … ' " (emphasis added). This formulation characterizes treaties as an "other normative act"

---

[28] V Ia Suvorova, Реализация норм международного права [*Realization of Norms of International Law*] (Ekaterinburg, 1992) 15.

[29] B I Osminin, Заключение и имплементация международных договоров и внутригосударственное право [*Conclusion and Implementation of International Treaties and Municipal Law*] (2010).

[30] R A Müllerson, Соотношение международного и национального права [*Correlation of International and National Law*] (1982).

[31] Kazakhstan, for example, adopted the "Law on Legal Acts" of April 6, 2016, as amended January 21, 2019. Article 6(2) provides: "International treaties ratified by the Republic Kazakhstan shall have priority over its laws and shall be applied directly, except for instances when it follows from the international treaty that the publication of a law is required for the application thereof."

comprising legislation of the Russian Federation. Article 6, paragraph 3, of the same draft repeated the constitutional formulation that an international treaty of the Russian Federation establishing other rules than provided by a law will apply. These are the only mentions of treaties in this draft. The hierarchy of normative legal acts (Article 10) makes no mention of treaties.

What is called an "initiative draft law" (hereinafter: 2013 draft law) prepared by the Institute of Legislation and Comparative Jurisprudence attached to the Government of the Russian Federation enumerated twelve types of normative legal acts, beginning with the Constitution of Russia down to municipal normative legal acts, but international treaties are not mentioned (Article 13), nor are treaties mentioned in the draft article devoted to the hierarchy of normative legal acts (Article 16). However, "international legal acts"—a defined term in the 2013 draft—are said (Article 17) to "consolidate generally-recognized principles and norms of international law and official treaty relations of the Russian Federation with other States and are an integral part of its legal system." The provision entitled "International Treaties of the Russian Federation in the Legal System of the Russian Federation" (Article 18) essentially repeated the language of Article 15(4) of the Constitution and reiterates that "international treaties ... consent to the bindingness of which was adopted in the form of a federal law have priority in application with respect to laws of the Russian Federation." This formulation avoids the question of position in the hierarchy of normative legal acts or sources of law and simply provides that treaties have priority in application without requiring that such application should occur only when the treaty contains a rule differing from a rule in a federal law. If a treaty was not ratified, it has priority, according to this draft, in application with respect to subordinate normative legal acts adopted by the agency of State power which concluded the international treaty on behalf of the Russian Federation (Article 18(5)).

In a draft Federal Law "On Normative Legal Acts in the Russian Federation" (hereinafter: 2014 draft) prepared by the Ministry of Justice of the Russian Federation but not submitted to the State Duma,[32] treaties are not mentioned either as normative legal acts or as being part of the hierarchy of normative legal acts. Chapter 3 of the 2014 draft is entitled: "Use of Norms of International Law in the System of Normative Legal Acts in the Russian Federation," which is quite a different perception of the role of

---

[32] Available on Consultant Plus.

treaties in the Russian legal system. This chapter merely sets out the situations in which Russian normative legal acts need to be adopted by virtue of the conclusion of an international treaty of the Russian Federation and does not address the role, status, or place of treaties in the Russian legal system.

The drafters of laws on normative legal acts have thus been confounded by the issue of the role and place of treaties in the legal system of the Russian Federation. The 2013 draft discussed above actually would have strengthened the place of treaties without ascribing any clarification of their stature in the Russian legal system. The legacy of dualism remains strong. Treaties are part of the legal system, but no one wants to go beyond that position to spell out in greater detail precisely where in the legal system they reside. Here the role of Russian legal theory is suspect: the failure of Russian jurists to develop an all-encompassing general theory of law and State of the Russian Federation means that those who draft Russian legislation or the legislator himself is left without moorings to prepare appropriate legislative formulations. Legal theory informs Russian thinking about the hierarchy of sources of law in general and the hierarchy of some of those sources in particular—the normative legal acts. Russian legal theory has not yet accepted that binding international treaties which the Russian Federation concludes as binding on the State, as a rule participates in the formulation of those treaty provisions, and ratifies, confirms, adopts, accepts, or acceded to in the form of a federal law, edict, decree, regulation, or other normative act create domestic or municipal rules of behavior and that these norms of behavior need to be accommodated as part of the normative framework of social relations within society.

Other International Courts

Although the ECtHR was the first to raise for the Russian Federation the role of judicial precedent and/or interpretative judicial practice within the Russian legal system but from an outside source, that issue has arisen with respect to the Court of the Eurasian Economic Union (EAEU). Initially a Customs Union operating in what was called Common Economic Space, on May 29, 2014 Eurasian integration achieved a new level pursuant to the Treaty on the EAEU. This institution is a supranational organization, to which its members (Republic Armenia, Republic Belarus, Republic Kazakhstan, Kyrgyz Republic, and the Russian Federation) transferred competence to establish and interpret binding legal norms (common policy) in certain areas of economic relations. The judicial role in this process is played by the EAEU Court, an organ responsible for judicial review and interpretation of the law of the EAEU. This organ has been operative since January 1, 2015,[33] providing judgments and advisory opinions on various issues of integration.

The role of the Court as the chief interpretive body of EAEU law is set out in the Statute of the Court of the EAEU (Appendix No. 2, Treaty on the EAEU): "the purpose of the Court shall be to ensure in accordance with the provisions of the present Statute the uniform application of the Treaty by member States and organs of the Union, international treaties within the framework of the Union, international treaties of the Union with a third party, and decisions of organs of the Union." Because the Court ensures the uniform application of law, one function of the Court is to supervise compliance with legal norms of the Union in order to verify uniformity of enforcement; that is, perform a form of judicial review.[34]

According to Chapter IV of the Court Statute, the Court considers disputes arising in connection with the realization of the treaty, whether in decisions of national authorities, or in the form of a request from Union organs, international officials, or the authorities of Member States. Legal disputes are resolved by the Court through the adoption of binding decisions or recommendatory advisory opinions. Thus, the EAEU Court exercises judicial control over application of law of the EAEU. This control function was transferred by Member States to the Court of the EAEU as a supranational body. The EAEU Court rules on the validity or invalidity of Union law, the legality or illegality of an action or failure to act of organs of the Union and officials of Member States. The Court may suspend a decision of the Eurasian Economic Commission if it does not conform to the treaty or to international treaties concluded within the framework of the treaty (Articles 112 and 113, Statute of the Court).

Thus, the decision of the Court of the EAEU is a form of "negative" lawmaking. In addition, as a result of the recognition of the norm as invalid ("not in accordance with the Treaty"—the wording of Articles 104 and 106, Statute) within the Union regulatory and legal systems, there may be a

---

[33] From January 1, 2012 to December 31, 2014 the Court of the Eurasian Economic Community, a predecessor of the EAEU Court, operated with competence comparable to the present EAEU Court.

[34] S V Nikitin, Судебный контроль за нормативными правовыми актами в гражданском и арбитражном процессе [*Judicial Control over Normative Legal Acts in Civil and Arbitrazh Procedure*] (2010).

gap in legal regulation which can be filled only by the relevant organ of the Union. However, the existence of such a gap is impossible by reason of the basic purposes of the Union, according to which the Court is obliged to ensure uniform law enforcement on an ongoing basis in order to create conditions for the stable development of the economies of the Member States in the interests of raising the standard of living of their population (Article 4, Treaty). The judicial decision, which contains a rule for the future behavior of actors in international relations, is called a "legal position," and in the view of many lawyers constitutes a form of law-making.

In practice the Supreme Court of the Russian Federation has instructed lower Russian courts:

> When applying respective norms of the law of the Union adopted in the sphere of customs regulation, courts also should take into account the acts of the Court of the Eurasian Economic Union rendered in accordance with point 39 of the Statute of the Court with regard to the results of the consideration of disputes connected with the realization of the provisions of the Treaty, other international treaties within the framework of the Union, and/or decisions of organs of the Union.[35]

As a result of this decree, Russian courts have been referring to the case law of the Eurasian Economic Community (EurAsEC) and EAEU courts. Consequently, despite different doctrinal opinions, a uniform approach has been formed in practice—the legal positions of the EAEU court entail legal consequences *erga omnes*, which effectively distinguishes these courts from international courts whose decisions are binding only for the parties to the dispute before the court.[36] Nonetheless, the Constitutional Court of the Russian Federation noted that:

> merely confirming the conformity of disputes normative provisions to international treaties concluded by States-Participants of the Customs Union and not touching upon the question of their constitutionality, these legal positions in and of themselves cannot serve as grounds for derogating from the requirements contained in Article 17(1) of the

---

[35] Point 3, para, 2, Decree of the Plenum of the Supreme Court of the Russian Federation of May 12, 2016, No 18, "On Certain Questions of the Application by Courts of Customs Legislation." Available on Consultant Plus.

[36] See T N Neshataeva and P P Myslivskiy, "Court of the Eurasian Economic Union: The Beginning," *Russian Law Journal*, no. 2 (2019) 134–54.

Constitution of the Russian Federation recognizing and guaranteeing rights and freedom of man and citizen not only according to generally-recognized principles and norms of international law, but also in accordance with the Constitution of the Russian Federation, the more so taking into account the direct reference of the Preamble of the Treaty of the Eurasian Economic Union to the need for unconditional compliance with by all of its parties of the principle of the constitutional rights and freedoms of man and citizen.[37]

This assumes, of course, that the acts of the EAEU are not applied retroactively to the prejudice of individual human rights.

The case law of the Court is viewed by Russian jurists as a key element of the supranational integration process within the EAEU. In their perception, the Court of the EAEU faces the quintessential set of choices: will the law of the EAEU operate only in relations between States as traditional international law, or will it prove to be capable of directly influencing the legal status of private persons, endowing them with rights and duties? The initial response of the EAEU Court was affirmative in a decision of February 21, 2017 in Case No. CE-1-1/1-16-BK regarding the application of the Russian Federation against the Republic Belarus: the Court held that a norm of the Treaty of the EAEU or of an international treaty within the framework of the Union will possess "direct application" if the norm is of an imperative character and does not contain exceptions or *renvoi* provisions.[38] This position means that within an integration Union the norm automatically becomes part of the national "legal order" and should be applied on the territory of Member States on the same basis.

The next step in the judicial world of the Court of the EAEU was an Advisory Opinion of April 4, 2017, the Case on Vertical Agreements, in which the Court consolidated the position that norms of law of the Eurasian Union have direct effect in the field of competition and should be directly applied by Member States of the Eurasian Union because those norms

---

[37]   Point 2.2, para. 6, Ruling of the Constitutional Court of the Russian Federation, March 3, 2015, No. 417-O, "Re: Query of the Arbitrazh Court of the Central District on Verification of the Constitutionality of Point 4 of the Procedure for the Application of Relief from Payment of Customs Duties When Bringing in Individual Categories of Goods to the Unified Customs Territory of the Customs Union." Available on Consultant Plus.

[38]   This position does not address the meaning of the word "imperative": whether it is being used in the mistaken translation meaning of *jus cogens* from the 1969 Vienna Convention on the Law of Treaties or in the Russian private-law sense that the parties may not by agreement depart from the rule.

were embodied in an international treaty. This view is regarded widely in Russian doctrine as opening the door to private individuals and State anti-monopoly agencies, together with national courts, applying the norms of the treaty even in the absence of implementing national legislation—which on this view is unnecessary.

What constituted the criteria of "direct effect" was addressed in the Advisory Opinion of the EAEU Court of December 7, 2018, the "Case concerning Professional Sportsmen," Advisory Opinion No. CE-2-2/5-18-BK, upon the application of the Eurasian Economic Commission. The EAEU Court determined that the grounds for deeming norms to have direct effect and direct application was that they were sufficiently precise and clear and did not require implementation in national legislation.[39] The EAEU Treaty does not give private individuals the right of direct access to the Court of the EAEU (unlike, for example, the ECtHR), either by direct application or by way of appeal. Under the Advisory Opinions of the Court of the EAEU, private individuals may apply to national courts in order to seek direct application of the EAEU Treaty to their situation. The development of EAEU law between 2017 and 2018 is that in the Vertical Agreements case the EAEU Court relied on treaty priority, whereas in the 2018 Professional Sportsmen case, the Court of the EAEU turned directly to the features of EAEU norms themselves as embodied in or on the basis of international treaties.[40]

The Court of the EAEU in one sense is more challenging for the Russian legal system. Unlike the ECtHR, which is not part of a supranational community, the Court of the EAEU is explicitly that. The Constitutional Court of the Russian Federation has so far confined the supremacy of the 1993 Russian Constitution vis-à-vis EAEU Court decisions, advisory opinions, and recommendations only to the human rights provisions of the Constitution, which are in effect non-amendable. The rest of the provisions remain open; on the other hand, the EAEU is based merely on a treaty—and just as the former Soviet Union itself, subject to the international law of treaties. If the intention is to develop a "supranational law of the Eurasian Economic Union"—which is advocated by some Russian jurists and believed to be in gestation—a different question will arise as to

[39] Available on Consultant Plus.
[40] See K Entin and E D'iachenko, "Обзор практики Суда Евразийского экономического союза в 2018 году" ["Survey of the Practice of the Eurasian Economic Union in 2018"], Международное правосудие [*International Justice*], no. 1 (2019) 6.

the relationship between the 1993 Russian Constitution, the international law of treaties, and the law of the EAEU.

International Arbitral Tribunals

Two permanently operating arbitration institutions specializing in international commercial and maritime arbitration exist in the Russian Federation: the International Commercial Arbitration Court (MKAC) and the Maritime Arbitration Commission (MAK), both attached to the Chamber of Commerce and Industry of the Russian Federation. MKAC is the legal successor to the Foreign Trade Arbitration Commission, founded in 1932, and attached to the USSR Chamber of Commerce and Industry. Its Statute, as amended, comprises Annex 1 to the 1993 Law on International Commercial Arbitration. In recent years MKAC has been considering from 250 to 350 cases per year, the great majority involving parties from other post-Soviet republics.

MAK is the legal successor to the Maritime Arbitration Commission founded in 1930; it too is attached to the Chamber of Commerce and Industry of the Russian Federation and its Statute comprises Annex 2 to the aforesaid 1993 Law.

Both MKAC and MAK are often called upon to apply international treaties during an arbitration either because the parties to the arbitration so stipulated in their arbitration clauses and/or because Russian law was the applicable law to the dispute or to the contract. In 2016 MKAC arbitrators applied the following international treaties in the cases considered:[41]

  1956 Geneva Convention on the Contract for the International Carriage of Goods by Road: one case;

  1958 New York Convention on the Recognition and Enforcement of Foreign Arbitral Awards: one case;

  1961 European Convention on International Commercial Arbitration: one case;

  1975 Geneva Customs Convention on the International Carriage of Goods under cover of TIR Carnets: one case;

---

[41] The data is drawn from Zhiltsov and Muranov (n. 1) 99–100.

1980 Vienna Convention on Contracts for the International Sale of Goods: sixty-seven cases;

1990 General Conditions for the Delivery of Goods from the USSR to the Chinese People's Republic and from the Chinese People's Republic to the USSR; four cases;

1993 Kyiv Convention on Mutual Legal Assistance with Regard to Civil, Family, and Criminal Cases: six cases;

2016 UNIDROIT Principles of International Commercial Contracts: one case.

Thus, in 2016 some eighty-two cases involved the application of treaties to international commercial disputes between the parties which were submitted for resolution to MKAC.

These arbitral awards do not formally have the value of precedent, but it is the practice of MKAC to publish extensive reports of arbitral practice and make these available to all interested individuals. For the purpose of analysing the law of treaties in the Russian Federation, they are as relevant as judicial practice.

8

Generally-Recognized Principles and Norms of International Law

If one were guided by notions of hierarchy of sources of international law, a good case could be made for considering generally-recognized principles and norms of international law as an integral part of the Russian legal system earlier in the present work rather than last. Most international lawyers would "rank" them higher than mere treaties because they are more fundamental, more universal, perhaps more venerable at least in origin, and, in Article 15(4) of the 1993 Russian Constitution they are enumerated ahead of international treaties of the Russian Federation. However, they become important in Russian law and State practice precisely because they are provided for in Article 15(4) and thus are a comparatively recent addition to the repertoire of rules which Russian institutions, officials, and courts must apply, as a rule in priority over Russian normative legal acts. Chronologically, therefore, they appear in the Russian legal system long after treaties.

During the Soviet period it was widely but not universally accepted in doctrinal writings that the reference in Article 38(1) of the Statute of the International Court of Justice to "general principles of law" had in view "the historical origin of a certain category of principles recognized as norms of international law. Therefore 'general principles of law' can only be principles of international law."[1]

Although the drafting history of Article 15(4) of the 1993 Constitution (see Chapter 5) discloses that the phrase "generally-recognized principles and norms of international law"[2] was included from 1992 onward, the formulation has generated widespread doctrinal debates about precisely what the phrase means and what are the sources of such principles and norms.

---

[1] G I Tunkin, "Co-Existence and International Law," in W E Butler and V G Tunkin (eds.), *The Tunkin Diary and Lectures* (2012) 155.

[2] In fact, the phrase was used in the 1977 Constitution of the USSR (Article 29). See W E Butler, *The Soviet Legal System* (1978) 9.

Some have argued that generally recognized principles and norms origi-nate in customary rules and international treaties. Zimnenko accepts this position: the phrase means "the provisions fixed ... in international custom recognized by all or the majority of States of the world community."[3] The phrase has international currency, for example in the 1970 Declaration on the Principles of International Law Concerning Friendly Relations and Cooperation Between States in Accordance with the United Nations Charter and the 1975 Final Act on Security and Cooperation in Europe. The Russian draftsmen did not invent the formulation, but incorporated it from inter-national documents which the Soviet Union had supported previously and from the 1977–78 generation of USSR and union republic constitutions.

Revolutionary in the 1993 Russian Constitution was the incorporation of these principles and norms in the legal system of the Russian Federation. What had occasioned only passing comment between 1977 and the early 1990s became a burning issue after 1993 and continues to be such. First, distinctions are drawn between "principles" and "norms." They are not the same, at least in the majority view, although they may overlap. "Principles" are considered to be "higher" than norms, perhaps more general in na-ture, but binding nonetheless. Norms may be narrower in scope, more specific in nature, more detailed in application. Under this approach, examples of "principles" might be *pacta sunt servanda*, sovereign equality, respect for sovereign rights, equality of subjects of law and legal systems, non-discrimination, *lex fori*, and so on. Others would confine "generally-recognized" principles and norms to norms *jus cogens*, often mistakenly translated as "imperative norms." Yet others believe that obligations arising from generally-recognized norms are of a universal character (*erga omnes*).

There is consensus that an exhaustive list of "generally-recognized prin-ciples and norms" does not exist in doctrine, State practice, or in Russian legislation. Some Russian jurists strongly urge the creation of such a List. Russian doctrinal writings, in the absence of authoritative guidance, are populated with examples that purportedly fall into these catego-ries. Zimnenko distinguished "principles" from "norms" as follows: "any generally-recognized principle is a generally-recognized norm of inter-national law, but not every generally-recognized norm is a generally-recognized principle of international law."[4] The closest official definition of

---

[3] B L Zimnenko, *International Law and the Russian Legal System*, trans W E Butler (2007) 171.
[4] Ibid, 176.

a "generally-recognized norm" of international law is found in the Decree of the Plenum of the Supreme Court of the Russian Federation, No. 5, of October 10, 2003 (point 1):

> By generally-recognized principles of international law should be understood the basic imperative norms of international law adopted and recognized by the international community of States as a whole, deviation from which is inadmissible.
>
> To generally-recognized principles of international law, in particular, are relegated the principle of universal respect for human rights and the principle of good-faith fulfillment of international obligations.
>
> The content of the said principles and norms of international law may be revealed, in particular, in documents of the United Nations and its specialized agencies.[5]

Characteristics of "Generally-Recognized Principles"

Doctrinal criteria (there are no other criteria) for determining what is or is not a "generally-recognized" principle vary from one jurist to another. Some would reduce such principles to "basic principles" and stress their "fundamental" nature, those which constitute the "carcass" of international law. For example, principles that consolidate and defend the foundations of the system of international relations, or determine the foundations of the interaction of States, or act as the foundation of the international legal order, and the like. Some have stressed the overlap between principles and norms, observing that certain principles are called norms and others are not—without a clear rationale for either category.

Sometimes a distinction is drawn between "general" and "generally-recognized" principles; on this basis "general" principles are less specific than "non-general" principles. Under this approach some principles may be more general and less specific than others, and some principles may simultaneously be "generally-recognized" norms. Zimnenko complained with reason that a legal norm cannot be of a general character irrespective of whether it is considered to be or to contain a principle; a legal norm

---

[5] Trans. in W E Butler, *Russian Public Law* (3d edn.; 2013) 48. The formulation closely resembles Article 33 of the 1969 Vienna Convention on the Law of Treaties and was based on it.

must always be specific; if it is indefinite or imprecise, then it should not be regarded as a legal norm, and principles and norms of international law should be no exception.[6]

Even this précis of an interminable abstract discussion is regarded by some Russian jurists as bringing into doubt the practical utility of Article 15(4) of the 1993 Constitution in this respect: first, the classification of principles and norms is too vague; second, the ambiguity should operate against the possibility of actual application of generally-recognized principles and norms within the legal system (by analogy, if municipal legal norms were so characterized, they could not be applied); third, "generally-recognized principles" are regarded by many as "imperative" norms, by which most understand norms *jus cogens*. This leaves the issue of whether the terms *"jus cogens"* and "imperative" are accurate reflections of one another. The Russian text of the 1969 Vienna Convention on the Law of Treaties translates the English/Latin *jus cogens* as "imperative"; in the present author's view, the word "imperative" does not satisfactorily convey the "cogens" element of the rule and is the more confusing because Russian legislation and doctrine distinguish between "imperative" and "dispositive" norms of law. Inevitably a confusion between the use of the terms by the two legal systems (international law and Russian law) exists. Russian international lawyers associate the imperativeness of "generally-recognized principles" with their universality, with their fundamental character, and with their containing obligations *erga omnes*. This has led some to the ultimate conclusion that all generally-recognized principles should be deemed to be imperative, that is, *jus cogens*.[7] If principles lack the quality of imperativeness, States might change their substance at will through the conclusion of treaties or they may enact municipal legislation contrary to imperative principles—or so it is argued.

On the other hand, if a generally-recognized principle of international law is not imperative, the principle loses its "social essence" or "social purpose" of being part of the "carcass" of international legal relations. Here some Russian international lawyers introduce the civil-law concepts of "imperative" and "dispositive" into international law and suggest that

---

[6] Zimnenko (n. 3) 185.
[7] And yet the distinction between imperative and dispositive persists in Russian international legal doctrine. Zimnenko writes that "the dispositiveness of certain norms of international law has become an obstacle to the achievement of certain common purposes." He suggests the need has arisen to curb the freedom of States to enter into "particular treaties." Ibid, 187.

States may conclude treaties contrary to dispositive generally-recognized principles and norms or adopt national legislation which may change or enrich them.

General Characteristics of a Norm

A norm of law (usually embodied in a "normative" legal act) contains a rule of behavior of general application. There is a truly vast literature, mostly in the Russian theory of State and law, addressed to defining a "norm." Key questions include whether a norm of international law and a norm of Russian law possess the same "quality" or the former, when becoming part of the Russian legal system, are in some manner transformed into something else. International-legal norms bind States, to be sure, leaving the issue of how and when may they bind actors within municipal legal systems. In the international system as presently constructed, the responsibility for implementation and enforcement of generally-recognized norms and principles lies with individual States and their municipal legal systems, although there is some jurisprudence to the effect that a violation of international law by a State may lead to natural persons have a right to compensation, including for moral harm.

A "generally-recognized norm" is universal in operation, or nearly so (many Russian jurists accepting the position that "universal" does not necessarily mean "unanimity"). The position is widely shared in Russian doctrine that the Russian Federation is bound by all "generally-recognized norms" of international law to which in the person of State agencies an active objection has not been made (this view contemplates passive acceptance of such a norm, as distinct from having to prove that Russia has positively accepted the particular norm).

Doctrinal writings are replete with examples of generally-recognized principles and norms of international law, at least in the opinion of the respective authors; among them: good faith fulfillment of international obligations, universal respect for human rights; sovereign equality of States, non-use or threat of the use of force, territorial integrity of States, peaceful settlement of international disputes; non-interference in internal affairs of States; self-determination of peoples; principle of cooperation— many of which become generally-recognized "branch" principles or norms in human rights law, law of the sea, diplomatic and consular law, environmental protection, and so on. Some jurists according distinguish between "basic" and "branch" generally-recognized principles—the practical consequences of which distinction are obscure.

Application of Generally-Recognized Principles and Norms

International treaties have the virtue of usually being in written form, and their text may incorporate generally-recognized principles and norms of international law. In this case the principles and norms have received written expression and confirmation which contributes to their precision, clarity, and certainty. But they exist independently of the treaty, few of which enjoy universality of acceptance and ratification.

Marochkin has observed that when Russian courts do make reference to generally-recognized principles and rules, they do so either by citing the entire formulation of Article 15(4) of the Constitution and/or by citing principles and rules that have been embodied in a treaty to which the Russian Federation is a party. All of the weaknesses of generally-recognized principles and norms come into play when they are not embodied in a treaty. If the Russian court relies solely on "non-treaty" norms (for example, the 1948 Universal Declaration of Human Rights), requirements of specificity may be imposed/expected that are impossible to satisfy. Russian jurists have repeatedly called for the compilation of a full list of generally-recognized principles and norms, but none has been forthcoming and Russian doctrine has confined itself, for entirely understandable reasons, to examples rather than an exhaustive enumeration.

The Supreme Court of the Russian Federation set out in 2008 a List of generally-recognized principles and norms which were contained in international treaties to which the Russian Federation was a party—but this amounted to a List of treaties more than a list of principles and norms and, in a sense, weakened rather than strengthened the status of generally-recognized principles and norms. Reference has been made in occasional individual court rulings to such principles and norms as non-discrimination in education, equality before the law and court, the adversariality of a judicial proceeding, the right to a fair trial, and so on—all principles and norms likewise recorded in the 1993 Constitution. Overall, however, Marochkin observes that the general characteristics of the principles and norms lead to "randomness and approximation and poor argumentation" in their application within the Russian judicial system.[8]

At one extreme, reference is made to "generally-recognized principles and norms" without any judicial explication as to why and how they are "generally-recognized"; that is, assumption without any argumentation or explanation. At the other, reference is made to recommendatory or "soft law" materials which are alleged to contain norms of law and constitute evidence of being "generally-recognized." With respect to regional treaties such as the 1950 European Convention on Human Rights and Fundamental Freedoms, the court needs to extrapolate from the regional nature of the Convention to demonstrate that its provisions are "generally-recognized."

Most often the courts make exceedingly general references to "international acts," or to "norms of international law," or to "generally-recognized principles and norms" without any indication whether they are in force for or apply to the Russian Federation and without specification as to precisely which principles and norms are being discussed.

---

[8] See S Yu Marochkin, *The Operation of International Law in the Russian Legal System: A Changing Approach* (2019) 247.

Conclusions

The purpose of the present study was to consider when and how Russian legal practice and doctrine began to examine the impact of and relationship between public international law and the municipal law of Russia in its pre-Muscovy, Imperial, Soviet, and post-Soviet periods.

Treaties are the extant legal foundation of the societies formed by the Slavic population inhabiting the modern territories of Belarus, Russia, and Ukraine; no earlier or other documents survive. These materials document the presence of the Slavic and neighboring populations, including Varangian, on these territories, something of their relations *inter se* and with their near and far neighbors, and some knowledge of the institutions of the law of nations of their time. For the most part, State practices seem to have been consistent with those of western Europe. Kievan Rus, Muscovy, and then Imperial Russia also acted as a conduit for the transmission of Byzantine and European practices eastward and southward in their relations with Tartary, Mongolia, China, Persia, India, Japan, and elsewhere, and as a recipient and conduit of eastern practices, widely speaking, in Europe. The Ambassadorial Department of Muscovy became in the course of time a treasure-house of knowledge about patterns of diplomacy, including the international-legal component.

So far as can be determined, the conclusion and confirmation (later, ratification) of treaties remained the prerogative of the ruler of the time. There is fragmentary evidence that treaties were considered to enjoy supremacy over inconsistent municipal law in Russian practice, but a formal hierarchy of sources of law was in its infancy and doctrinal writings did not address the matter at all or confined themselves to municipal legal materials. The adoption of the 1906 Basic Law in the Russian Empire and provision therein that the Emperor enjoyed exclusive authority over foreign relations, including treaty-making, was a formal recognition of the pre-existing view rather than an innovation in Russian constitutional law.

The short-lived Russian Provisional Government (February to October 1917, old style) and the successor Soviet and other governments on the territory of the former Russian Empire accepted the position that the ratification and/or confirmation of treaties should be the responsibility of the highest parliamentary body and/or the collective or individual Head of State. No view was taken as to the relationship between treaties and municipal normative legal acts. A *de facto* dualism emerged under which the Soviet State was bound under international law to comply with its international legal obligations, and municipal normative legal acts operated autonomously within the national legal order.

The Russian Soviet authorities found themselves instantaneously confronting issues of the law of treaties: to expose the perfidious actions of the predecessor Imperial Russian Government in concluding cabalistic treaties to divide the spoils of World War I; to seek peace terms at any cost from the belligerent enemies of Russia; to cultivate relations with colonies or newly independent States and restructure Russian foreign relations. State practice preceded revolutionary doctrines so far as the law of treaties was concerned, and in principle treaties, properly concluded, were in the interests of the Bolshevik leadership as a means of diplomatic self-defense, securing recognition of the revolutionary State and government, establishing trade, economic, transport, frontier, and other relations, and proselytizing ideological views, principles, or maxims. The initial reaction was to emulate prior Imperial Russian practice by placing treaty ratification in the hands of what were perceived as the highest agencies of State power—those best positioned to act as the collective Head of State.

Doctrinal views on treaties followed later. During the 1920s, Soviet international lawyers endorsed treaty-making in principle, criticized the lack of legislative and administrative infrastructure to determine the internal procedures for drafting and considering treaties, savaged treaties of the past which were considered to be "imperialist," or "predatory," or "unequal," and ultimately contributed to the preparation of Soviet legislation that by the mid-1920s would address these issues.

Much of this procedural treaty legislation dating from the mid-1920s remained in place for more than five decades. What Soviet international legal doctrine did originate, however, was a strongly dualist approach to treaties—an approach which dominated to the end of the Soviet Union. The decision reflected in Soviet civil and other legislation from 1961 to give priority to treaties over laws which contained different rules was not a compromise with dualism, and the reasons for introducing that principle remain obscure. The purpose may have been to reduce potential complications in foreign relations that might arise from a conflict between a Soviet treaty and Soviet law at a time when the Soviet Union was determined to expand international cooperation with foreign States. The possibility of creating a treaty "exception" to an inward-looking Soviet domestic legal system may have seem an attractive alternative at the time. Consular conventions, for example, contained exceptions to rules of Soviet criminal procedure which the parties found to be desirable. Legal assistance conventions required Soviet courts to administer international treaty provisions in treaties concluded with, principally, other socialist legal systems.

The 1978 USSR law on treaties gave municipal legal recognition to much of the 1969 Vienna Convention on the Law of Treaties and laid down internal procedures for the proposal, drafting, coordination, agreeing, approval, and ultimate ratification, authorization, adoption, or accession to treaties. It also introduced to Soviet law the distinctions between inter-State, intergovernmental, and interdepartmental treaties—distinctions preserved in all post-Soviet jurisdictions.

The introduction of Article 15(4) into the 1993 Russian Constitution represented a major step in increasing the influence of public international law into the Russian legal system. The very concept of the "legal system" of the Russian Federation is understood in Russian legal doctrine as the aggregate of all legal phenomena—both domestic and concomitant legal phenomena, including international—in Russia. This is an immensely powerful legal concept. Generally-recognized principles and norms of international law and international treaties of the Russian Federation are therefore, in aggregate, an integral part of the legal system. Whether these expressions of international law become norms of domestic law is debated: some see these integral international legal norms as "incorporated" into the legal system; others see a different level of dualism—these international legal norms are an integral part of the legal system but not norms of Russian domestic law. They retain their "international-ness" and are not transformed into domestic law.

Thus, the legal system of the Russian Federation contains two different kinds of law—international law and domestic law. What is the internal correlation between them? Two distinctions are drawn with respect to international-legal norms: those having direct effect and not requiring domestic legislation in order to implement them; and those not having direct effect precisely because they do require implementing legislation. Although international law requires States acting in good faith to implement international legal obligations, in practice often that implementation never happens or occurs with great delay.

Although not without controversy, the better position seems to be that generally-recognized principles and norms of international law enjoy priority over norms of Russian law which provide otherwise. International treaties of the Russian Federation having direct effect take priority over domestic legislation because either they do not differ from domestic legislation or there is no domestic legislation relating to the legal relations which these treaties regulate. However, if international treaties of the Russian Federation contain rules other than those provided by Russian law, they take priority over Russian law because (a) Article 15(4) so provides; and (b) rather more controversially, because they have been ratified—a view which precludes priority being accorded to non-ratified treaties, principally intergovernmental and interdepartmental.

The requirement of ratification is not contained in Article 15(4) of the 1993 Russian Constitution and was explicitly rejected during the Constitutional Assembly which drafted the 1993 Russian Constitution. The majority of drafts submitted to the Constitutional Assembly contained the requirement of ratification for priority—and that requirement was excluded from the final version of the Constitution approved by national referendum in December 1993. Aggressive judicial law-making confirmed the requirement of ratification in a decree of the Plenum of the Supreme Court of the Russian Federation of October 10, 2003.

Why should Russia accord priority only to ratified international treaties of the Russian Federation with respect to different rules contained in municipal law? Why not all treaties—inter-State, intergovernmental, and interdepartmental. The view is not contested in Russian international doctrine that the Russian Federation bears State responsibility for all treaties concluded at all levels. It is acknowledged that the terms of art commonly used in Russian treaties—concluded "in the name of the Russian Federation," "in the name of the Government of the Russian Federation," or "in the name of [a department] of the Russian Federation"—are for convenience only and do not deprive the State of responsibility for fulfillment of treaty obligations. The answer appears to lie in the legal mentality that is mesmerized by the hierarchy of normative legal acts. These are classifications of the science of law as reflected in doctrinal writings and legislation. Russian jurists are disturbed by the possibility that a ministry might conclude a treaty that could override a rule or norm of law enacted by the Federal Assembly or a norm contained in an edict of the President or decree of the Government.

In fact, the Russian legal system contains a virtually foolproof answer to the issue of hierarchy. The answer lies in the internal procedures set out in remarkable detail for treaty-making at all levels of the State. Those detailed procedures ultimately provide for coordination and agreeing of drafts, opportunities to comment or oppose, rational discussion of all relevant policies, interests, and preferences, such that no treaty at any level fails to pass through the bureaucratic process. All levels of the Russian State are involved in every treaty, irrespective of which of the three classifications it may fall into.

The present system is an uneasy and illogical scheme in which considerations of the hierarchy of domestic legal enactments and of State institutions interfere with principles of State responsibility for treaties and do not take into account the presence of generally-recognized principles and norms of international law.

Judicial practice probably was underestimated or not taken into account when Article 15(4) was drafted. There were brief mentions of these during the Constitutional Assembly, in passing, but their implications were not pursued. Russia rightly entrenched human rights in Chapter 2 of the 1993 Constitution, replicating provisions principally from the 1948 Universal Declaration of Human Rights, the 1950 European Convention, and the 1966 United Nations human rights covenants. When Russia acceded to the 1950 European Convention and, after much debate, accepted the jurisprudence of the European Court of Human Rights (ECtHR) as generally binding and not merely the outcome of cases in which the Russian Federation was a party, a new ingredient was injected into the interface between international law and municipal law. These human rights elements also became part of the legal system of the Russian Federation, and from a direction and by a process not familiar to the Russian or the Soviet legal traditions. The Constitutional Court of the Russian Federation has invoked the Russian Constitution as an impediment against the implementation of human rights judgments and decisions from the ECtHR which the Court considers to be contrary to the Russian Constitution and now found express constitutional support for this position. At literally the same juncture in history, Russia has initiated processes of Eurasian economic integration which depend upon the Court of the Eurasian Economic Union (EAEU) performing a supranational role and issuing decisions, advisory opinions, and recommendations that will override domestic legal rules of Member States, excluding in Russia, at least, human rights provisions.

The EAEU is likewise a treaty-based organization with supranational aspirations and relies upon international treaties within the framework of the EAEU to achieve the purposes intended by the parties/members. The interface between Russian approaches to international law and the legal system of the Russian legal system will, in all likelihood, continue to mature.

On March 14, 2020 a Federal Constitutional Law was adopted to substantially amend the 1993 Constitution of the Russian Federation.[1] In aggregate these amendments increased the word count of the Constitution by nearly half. The law of treaties is affected in three major respects:

(1) Article 67 has been added to the Constitution, providing in point 1 that:

The Russian Federation shall be the legal successor of the USSR on its territory, and also the legal successor (or legal continuer) of the USSR with respect to membership in international organizations, organs thereof, participation in international treaties, and also with respect to obligations and assets of the USSR provided for by international treaties beyond the limits of the territory of the Russian Federation.

This formulation, for the first time in Russian law, seems to conflate the concepts of "legal continuer" and "legal successor," which have been widely regarded as distinct concepts—the notion of "legal continuer" being the antithesis of "legal succession." On one reading, they are viewed as synonyms; on another, as separate realms differing in their domestic and international consequences.

(2) Article 79 was amended to read:

The Russian Federation may participate in inter-State associations and transfer to them part of its powers in accordance with international treaties of the Russian Federation if this does not entail a limitation of the rights and freedoms of man and citizen and is not contrary to the foundations of the constitutional system of the Russian Federation. Decisions of inter-State agencies adopted on the basis of provisions of international treaties of the Russian Federation in a construction thereof contrary to the Constitution of the Russian Federation shall not be subject to execution in the Russian Federation.

This revised version of Article 79 represents an attempt to balance two potentially divergent directions in Russian foreign and international-legal

---

[1] СЗ РФ (2020), no. 11, item 1416.

policies. On one hand, the Russian Federation has sought to limit the impact of the judgments of the European Court of Human Rights which are contrary to perceived Russian values, including, for example, those deemed to challenge the family, religious convictions, or electoral rights. On the other hand, Russia is actively pursuing Eurasian economic union—an enterprise which is resulting in self-limitations of sovereignty agreed in international treaties and possibly the formation of supranational institutions.

(3)   These new directions in legal policy are reflected in the revised role of the Constitutional Court of the Russian Federation, expressed in the addition of the following subpoint to Article 125 of the Constitution:

5. The Constitutional Court of the Russian Federation shall: …
(b) in the procedure established by a federal constitutional law, settle the question concerning the possibility of the execution of decisions of inter-State agencies adopted on the basis of provisions of international treaties of the Russian Federation in a construing thereof which is contrary to the Constitution of the Russian Federation, and also the possibility of the execution of the decision of a foreign or international (or inter-State) court or foreign or international arbitration court imposing duties on the Russian Federation if this decision is contrary to the fundamental principles of public policy of the Russian Federation;

Although Article 15(4) of the Constitution remains intact, the clear intentions of the changes of March 2020 to the Constitution are to limit the primacy of international treaties in the legal system of the Russian Federation by according a greater measure of priority to constitutional law vis-à-vis international law.

Further Reading

For those who may wish to continue to read further on the subject, the following works will be helpful. For general background on Russian law, see:

Butler, W E, *Russian Law* (3rd edn.; Oxford, Oxford University Press, 2009).

Butler, W E, *Russian Law and Legal Institutions* (2nd edn.; London, Wildy Simmonds & Hill, 2018).

On the law of treaties, in addition to materials cited in the footnotes, see:

Butler, W E, *The Russian Law of Treaties* (London, Simmonds & Hill Publishing Ltd, 1997).

Butler, W E, *The Law of Treaties in Russia and the Commonwealth of Independent States: Text and Commentary* (Cambridge, Cambridge University Press, 2002).

Butler, W E, *Russian Foreign Relations and Investment Law* (Oxford, Oxford University Press, 2006).

Butler, W E, "Russian Federation," in David Sloss (ed.), *The Role of Domestic Courts in Treaty Enforcement: A Comparative Study* (Cambridge, Cambridge University Press, 2009) 410–47.

Marochkin, S Yu, *The Operation of International Law in the Russian Legal System: A Changing Approach* (Leiden/Boston, Brill | Nijhoff, 2019).

Triska, Jan F and Slusser, Robert M, *The Theory, Law, and Policy of Soviet Treaties* (Stanford, California, Stanford University Press, 1962).

Zimnenko, B L, *International Law and the Russian Legal System*, trans. W E Butler (Utrecht, Eleven International Publishing, 2007).

Index